Treating Adult Children of Alcoholics

A Behavioral Approach

DOUGLAS H. RUBEN, PH.D

Academic Press
San Diego London Boston New York Sydney Tokyo Toronto

This book is printed on acid-free paper.

Academic Press
A Harcourt Science and Technology Company
525 B Street, Suite 1900, San Diego, California 92101-4495
http://www.academicpress.com

Academic Press
Harcourt Place, 32 Jamestown Road, London NW1 7BY, UK
http://www.academicpress.com

Library of Congress Cataloging Card Number: 00-107105

International Standard Book Number: 0-12-601130-3

PRINTED IN THE UNITED STATES OF AMERICA
01 02 03 04 05 06 MM 9 8 7 6 5 4 3 2 1

In memory of an exemplary ACOA,
who beat the odds against her recovery,
who rose above fears and failures,
who reached the quintessence in
career and loving relationships,
and knew she was a model,
inspiring generations of
followers.

She was also my friend. You will be missed, Alyce Faye Sewell.

CONTENTS

PART II

Treatment Methodology for Adult Children of Alcoholics

FOREWORD

There is an obvious reason why mental health practitioners are fascinated with Adult Children of Alcoholics (ACOAs). Trained clinicians are compassionate; they are naturally and emotionally sensitive to traumatically troubled patients—patients who struggle to rebuild their lives. Abused and neglected patients suffering a plethora of psychopathololgy since childhood agonize in pain. Their elevated anxiety for cures compel caring practitioners to act swiftly and efficiently. They seek treatment for debilitating symptoms before those symptoms cause irreversible emotional damage.

Treating chronically pathologic patients also is highly rewarding for clinicians. Reducing symptom severity is invigorating and typically, adds to therapist credibility. Pleasure from observing pre-treatment to post-treatment changes derives from knowing one has reached a higher caliber of competency in solving challenging cases. Therapists feel reinforced by hearing laudable remarks from the healed patient.

Illness severity in Adult Children of Alcoholics may be the reason why so many clinicians are drawn to treat this unusual population. Professional fascination sparks almost an occult attraction to ACOAs, witnessed by the prolific market of self-help books, audiotapes, seminars, and even magazines dedicated to recovering ACOAs. Topics range from understanding categories of ACOAs (scapegoat, mediator, etc.) to accelerated self-interventions for overcoming dysfunctional behaviors. Remedies abound for changing personality defects, employing either watered-down versions of cognitive–behavior therapy, or adaptations of Eastern philosophy. The infinite litany of methodologies—some tested, others extremely theoretical—provide genuine hope for cerebrally astute readers who believe the methods they read are empirically sound.

For example, an article appeared in Changes magazine several years ago attesting to the validity of Shamanic therapy in reducing intrafamily discord. Healing ceremonies for "soul retrieval" supposedly empowered recipients to channel their inner spiritual resources to recover from devastating wounds. This ancient remedy, using "journeying," safely transitioned a distressed person through passages of pain to relaxed karma, gaining ethereal experiences along the enlightening path until reaching renewal of soul and, consequently more rational, functional coping skills. Altered states of consciousness accompanied this cleansing process through a meditative phase and back to reality. The whole process boasted miraculous results in escaping depression and binding loose ends of family trauma.

Empirically minded clinicians find meditation a tenable modality for anxiety reduction and relief of depression. Certainly, meditation, relaxation, doubles for ACOAs as moments of emotional "decompression." They can take refuge in de-escalating tension and achieving sensory equilibrium. Scientific logic, in other words, lends credibility to employing meditation in any cognitive-altering technique.

So, why do we have to spoil the science by calling the method "soul retrieval?" "Meditation" is perfectly acceptable without reifying its positive effects with supernatural-like descriptions. Calling the procedure "Shamanism" dilutes the empirical purity and conjures a mysterious belief that magical healing powers occur through unknown properties, a spiritual quick-fix that surpasses traditional therapy. Testimonials of soul-retrieval survivors assure that the journeying is completely harmless and transformed them from chronic worriers to a celebrated believer. Shamanistic promises are persuasive and extremely enticing to the vulnerable.

That's why they are effective—not because they are scientific. Sadly, no personified spiritual journey, no matter how galactic the travel, will erase childhood dysfunctions of ACOAs because *the structure of ACOA behavior is too intricately rooted in both individual history and current life*. Another name for "structure" is *contingencies*. Contingencies represent one or many functional relationships between the patient's behavior and countless consequences amassed over the patient's lifespan. In childhood, for example, simple contingencies are formed in reflexive reactions to sensory stimuli, such as the Babinski response, in which an infant's toes fanning out or big toe flexing when the foot is gently stroked from heel to toe, or, the Palmar Grasp, where babies grasp objects when a rod or adult fingers press against the infant's palms.

Biological reflex (respondent) contingencies may remain or vanish but are simple to understand. As neonates grow and encounter verbal and nonverbal experiences, reflexes comprise a minuscule fraction of their total contingencies. Children equally respond to speech and tonal patterns, facial and gestural reactions, and develop visual sequence learning, whereby they act one way or another way depending on adult behaviors. A child observing his parent rush upstairs yelling loudly responds differently than an infant who sees a parent gently smile and walk slowly. These event sequences constitute the overall picture or "field" within which infants are rapid learners. Infants learn and change behaviors discriminately to minimize adversity and maximize gratification.

The logical reasoning is quite simple. Human beings avoid pain and seek satisfaction. To this extent, a female child terrified by parents who explosively shout vulgarities and lash out at her for no apparent reason learns to remain quiet, passive, and shy. Inhibitory responses may progress from being bashful and withdrawn in childhood to being isolative and docile in adolescence. That same shy child in adulthood may be unassertive, passive–dependent, anxious, and avoid any semblance of conflict, leading to her marrying a viciously controlling and domineering spouse who dictates her every move and obviates the need for decision making. Insulated and protected from adversity, she becomes an emotional hostage to her complacency and history of interpersonal deficits. In other words, contingencies of aversive conditioning originate in childhood and evolve unchanged throughout life. The child passes from young to old, suffering episodes of anxiety and depression without a clue of what went wrong.

Now consider the obverse. A male infant affectionately nurtured and adored learns at the outset to speak freely, be creative, and autonomously explore new horizons. He asks questions, disagrees and even mildly debates with adult authorities. Stimulated curiosity feeds his passion for seeking personal challenges and information. In teenage years, his reinforced experiences build confidence to assume leadership roles and he embarks on courageous undertakings either in school or in extracurricular activities. Positive thinking and self-assurance carry into adulthood because he knows that success is attainable. He treats failure as normal and builds upon failure with growth opportunities. He marries an intellectually and emotionally compatible partner with whom communication is spontaneous and common place. As a parent, his lessons of self-achievement trickle down to his offspring, who carry the message to new generations.

Is this too idealistic? Do happy-go-lucky, achievement-oriented people really exist? They sure do. It all depends on the contingencies. John B. Watson's controversial claim in 1930 that anybody can be shaped by proper or improper conditioning is still true today. ACOAs are not genetic mutations engineered by a cruel conspiracy of alcoholic parents determined to ruin the lives of their offspring. Instead, ACOAs, develop and cease maladaptive behaviors by activities reinforced or punished along a learning system. A young child—boy or girl, rich or poor, smart or dumb—

who suffers adversity and deprivation predictably forms a defective personality symptomatic of ACOAs. Place that same child in reinforcing environments enriched with opportunities and symptoms of ACOA never appear. The difference is that simple.

Life may hold surprises, but behavior is not one of them. ACOA behavior does not operate in a vacuum. It grows with a predictable trajectory easily traceable by examining its "field" or system of movement. Consequently, viewing ACOA behaviors from a system or field learning perspective accomplishes two goals. First, it preserves the integrity of studying a phenomenon in scientific terms. Analyses derive from established principles of conditioning already tested in applied and experimental settings. Opinions that emerge are not reified concepts or abstract, supernatural beliefs without foundation. Instead, they are theories, carefully synthesized from assessing variables found in research and logical extensions of known behavioral etiology. The ACOA syndrome, in other words, undergoes systematic operationalism.

A second purpose of a learning perspective in this book is to erase the very powerful sentiment traditionally attached to the ACOA syndrome. Like Shamanism, yoga, and homeopathic remedies, rapid solutions that promise swift recovery from emotional problems are delusional and damaging. They exaggerate the result potential by pompously glorifying self-healing and pretending the methods are fresh and unique. Sadly, personified methods are really recycled versions of behavioral interventions published and widely used since the early 1960s. The mentality of impulse–purchase cures superimposed on gullible buyers will not advance the research of ACOA or benefit thousands of painful and lonely victims. Misbeliefs about change may do the opposite; progress may revert to ancient superstitions viewing mental illness as an evil and irrevocable blemish on a personality.

This book does not offer hyperbolic promises of recovery. It is for college students and practitioners dedicated to treating ACOA survivors with dignity. Etiology and methodology throughout the book attempt to offer concrete guidelines, describing why patients behave the way they do. Patient motivation always is strong when seemingly inextricable problems present clear explanations and solutions. Part I on assessment of ACOAs conceptually lays out fundamental tenets underlying the systems paradigm. "Personality types," defined behaviorally, simplify the integrative contingencies and response patterns longitudinally developed over the ACOA's lifetime. Chapter 5 is particularly valuable for clinicians since it addresses non-ACOA spouse reaction in marriages and problems expected in conjoint therapy.

Part II on treatment methodology translates many current cognitive–behavioral techniques into ACOA-reversal procedures. Strategies literally supply skill prerequisites for ACOAs that were absent during their childhood. Like vitamin supplements, implemented skills remove the void in coping repertoires and build stronger, more enduring behaviors. Chapter 9, reminds therapists there are familial side-effects of patient recovery. A healthy patient does not mean the family wants the patient healthy or is receptive to being changed by the patient.

Readers are welcome to refine and advance ACOA interventions as their own experience creatively dictates. Students, especially, will have the acumen to look at procedural flaws of the ACOA behavioral approach, and declare what this author declared when reading similar books during his own graduate study: *That's nice, but I can do better.*

So, go for it.

PART I

Assessment of Adult Children of Alcoholics

CHAPTER 1

What is an Adult Child of an Alcoholic (ACOA)?

The millennium marks a period of incredible scientific breakthroughs in the field of psychology—from Wundtian and Gestalt labs, the dynamics of psychoanalysis, to the neurobiological basis for memory. Innovations matured psychology from its infancy to middle adulthood. Conceptually, every orientation in psychology underwent metamorphic revolutions. Particularly in behaviorism, innovative investigations in experimental research opened pathways to multiple branches of applied sciences. Behavioral paradigms evolved from pre-Watsonian and Skinnerian models to interdisciplinary and politically correct models such as cognitive–behavior modification, behavioral medicine and social learning theory (Plaud & Eifert, 1998; Schlinger & Poling, 1998). Advanced thinking sparked a torrent of remarkably creative and aspiring analyses to describe the workings of human and infrahuman behavior (Fishman, 1999; Follette, 1998; Lipke, 1999; O'Donahue & Kitchener, 1999; Uttal, 1998).

This explosion of scientific analyses contributed valuable knowledge in a variety of ways. It debunked many reified concepts or myths plaguing behavioral phenomena—for example, that child misbehavior is not genetic or that origins of violence are not racially or ethnically predetermined. Mental mysteries embodying the human condition were unraveled as explorations covered uncharted topics in behavioral sciences. Many examples figure prominently in clinical areas. Guilt, for example, previously a religious topic, received a behavioral reinterpretation through examination of its unusual compound contingencies (e.g., Ruben, 1993a). Domestic violence, previously a sociologic problem, underwent a thorough behavioral autopsy that shattered myths about gender differences and punctuated the reciprocity of partner abuse (Barbour, Eckhardt, Davison & Kassinove, 1998; Cherek & Dougherty, 1997; Jacobson & Gottman, 1998; Yuksel, Kora, Benzci-Ozkan, Karali, Gok & Tunali, 1999).

Similarly, reformulations of behavioral analysis inspired visionary perspectives in child abuse and neglect (Peterson, Gable, Doyle & Ewigman, 1997; Vogeltanz & Drabman, 1995), HIV-related anxiety and coping (Heffner, Lejuez & Freeman, 1999; Sikkema & Kelly, 1996), self-awareness (Dymond & Barnes, 1997), sexual offenses (Marshall, Fernandez, Hudson & Ward, 1998; Nezu, Nezu & Dudek, 1998), over-medication among the elderly (Mansdorf, Calapai, Caselli & Burstein, 1999; Ruben, 1984b, 1990) and youth violence (Macciomei & Ruben, 1999; Ollendick, 1996).

Expanding behavioral analysis to interdisciplinary problems (cf. Morris, 1997, Kunkel, 1997; Ruben 1984a) produced another advantage. It signaled that behavioral psychology was not an hypothesis anchored in abstract thinking, offering techniques of "behavior modification." Rather, proponents were clever engineers of science who formulated laboratory-tested methods and derived universal principles and laws governing how human behavior responds to its environment (Chorpita, 1997; Eifert, Forsyth, Zvolensky, & Lejuez, 1999; Mechner, Hyten, Field & Madden, 1997).

This book explores still another mysterious domain of human behavior. For decades, addiction researchers loyal to the disease model, and sociologists loyal to family-systems thinking, trampled through the morass of problems in children raised by chemically dependent parents. Polydrug-using mothers, fathers, grandparents, uncles, aunts, or whoever provided principal care for the child, displayed polymorbidity that showed up later in the offspring. Intergenerational transfers of behavior provided obvious cues that behaviors observed among parents might influence the child's development; in turn, early exposure nearly guaranteed drinking and drug-using patterns when the child became an adult. Detailed longitudinal studies further hypothesized that adult offspring of addicted parents not only drank but also exhibited *peculiar* and *habitual* patterns unmatched in nonaddiction family populations (Chassin, Pitts, DeLucia & Todd, 1999; Hans, 1999; Hunt, 1997; Jennison & Johnson, 1998).

Family addiction researchers amassed several reasons for the genesis of these behavior patterns, later disseminated in both scholarly and lay press (see Ackerman, 1983). Certainty that prenatal and postnatal exposure to alcohol, either biologically or socioculturally, increased risk of pathology helped to explain causes of childhood disorders such as Attentional Deficit and Hyperactivity Disorders (ADHD) and related cognitive pathology (Ruben, 1993a; McGrath, Watson, & Chassin, 1999; Molina, Pelham & Lang, 1997), antisocial behavior (Kuperman, Schlosser, Lidral & Reich, 1999; Nurco, Blatchley, Hanlon & O'Grady, 1999), inhibition and shyness (Hill, Lowers, Locke, Snidman, & Kagan, 1999), and violence (Malpique, Barrias, Morais, Salgado, Pinto da Costa, Rodriques, 1998).

Since second-generation offspring manifested unique pathologies in childhood lasting into adulthood, researchers conceived the generic term Adult Children of Alcoholics (ACOA) to cover adults suffering post-family effects of alcoholism.

But, really, what is an Adult Child of an Alcoholic? And are the behavioral phenomena displayed in adult survivors entirely due to parents who drink or use drugs? That is a quandary. What if parental drinking or drug abuse never occurred? Might the same childhood and adult behavioral anomalies result? Questions like these pose unusual complications for sociologic and traditional psychological researchers because their investigative approaches may lack measurable acuity to arrive at specific conclusions.

Research methods employing longitudinal or field study suffer three shortcomings. First, research is holistic. It combines many subtle variables into aggregate variables and projects a hypothetical path of these variables. "Alcoholism," for example, is a bundled conceptual term encompassing a myriad of emotional, cognitive, behavioral, and sociocultural contingencies—all predicted to move in the same direction. In other words, progressive stages of alcoholism include vague and abstract changes in personality expected to worsen.

Second, the focus of research is on the effects of unilateral, not bilateral, parental drinking or violence on offspring and assumes a descending influence from parents' behavior to children's behavior. The unilateral trajectory grossly overlooks interactions unique to the offspring's life that defuse or aggravate acquired traits. Foster children removed from their biological addicted family and placed in functional households, for example, may be spared from maladaptive symptoms. Rehabilitative settings like some foster homes or treatment centers may reverse disabling problems and supply a corrective pathway for healthy childhood.

Third, research is exclusionary. It focuses primarily on organic explanations such as inheritability, or on family transmission theories that postulate one dysfunctional system automatically will penetrate future dysfunctional family systems. Interfamily transmission, however, does not operate on auto-pilot. Nor do unmistakable predispostions to alcohol or drug tolerance pass from parent to child due to neurobiology. In both cases, family practices negatively or positively influence successive generations. Inheritable diabetes offers a comparison. Proclivity for juvenile or late-onset diabetes depends on the physical health of the carrier and particularly his or her weight; overweight, underexercised, out-of-shape carriers risk rapid appearance of diabetes over their healthy, slenderized, and fitness-conscious counterparts.

Awareness of such research pitfalls opens our discussion of the ACOA. Readers may already be familiar with definitions of ACOA. If so, they may wish to skip ahead to the tenets of learning theory. However, for health service providers confused by its many connotations, the next section promises a user-friendly introduction to the basic ACOA syndrome, presenting current beliefs and widely disseminated concepts about victimized children of addicted families. The repeated theme underlying the theories is that alcohol and drug abuse are the prime culprits for childhood disorders, and that child victims automatically become defective adults.

A clearer understanding of ACOAs sets the stage for shifting the paradigm. The second section may be a review for many behaviorally trained readers. In any case, terminology or conceptual descriptions may be different from what behaviorally competent readers are used to. The review includes principles of learning generated from two models. The first set of constructs come from radical and methodological behaviorism that typically appear in introductory courses on applied or experimental behavioral analysis. The second set of principles derives from behavioral analysis following a `integrative-field" or contextual approach; expanded units of analysis broaden coverage from single contingencies to multiple contingencies. This background in the language and philosophy of behavioral and field (ecobehavioral) analysis will facilitate the reading of the remaining chapters.

Defining the term "ACOA"

The term "Adult Children of Alcoholics" carries a double meaning: an adult who is trapped in the fears and reactions of a child, and the child who was forced to be an adult without going through the natural stages that result in a healthy adult. ACOAs most often come from homes where rules are subject to the whim of the person in the room at the time. ACOAs may have been ordered to do one thing by a father, forbidden to do the same thing by a mother, told to do it differently by a grandparent, and ridiculed for doing it (or not doing it) by an uncle or friend of the family. As a result, ACOAs grow up hearing they can never do anything right; that they are somehow defective (Baker & Stephenson, 1995; Filstead, McElfresh & Anderson, 1981).

In a healthy home, parents are loving authority figures who make their likes and dislikes understood, freely express their needs, and permit open disagreement and imperfection without threatening to remove underlying trust and love. A healthy parent can make a mistake and it is not traumatic for the children. Rather, mistakes signal the freedom and honesty of a healthy family. Healthy children learn that their parents are vulnerable and not perfect, and the children learn that they are not expected to be perfect but to do the best they can.

By contrast, in dysfunctional ACOA homes the parents are authorities whose words and actions cannot be questioned. In the face of blatantly wrong information or actions, the ACOA learns that his or her own wants, needs and safety are less important than supporting the family system. Independence, which is allowed in healthy families, is a threat to the authority of dysfunctional parents. ACOAs become used to comments such as "Who do you think you are?," "You'll never amount to anything," and "What makes you so great?"

ACOAs learn not to exceed their parents' level of competence. They learn that it is dangerous to be a better student, to make more money, to have a saner family; or to win recognition. The dysfunctional parent takes such successes as threats of subordination and may harshly reprimand achieving children for excelling and upstaging their parents. Later in adulthood, ACOAs may not be aware of the self-sabotage they apply to their own lives and wonder at their inability to achieve success.

As children, ACOAs learn to behave in whatever way allows them to survive. Behavior can range from defying authority to suppressing their own needs and attending to the needs of other people; caretaking others' needs simply is a continuation of how they responded to their parents in childhood (Crespi, 1995; Shemwell, Dickey & Timothy, 1995). Children living within a dysfunctional family carry their perceptions of family rules with them as they grow into their teens and adulthood, and the warped foundation may continue to function well enough to permit the illusion of a functional family.

Scientific Etiologies of ACOAs

In this section we briefly examine several research-based or "scientific" etiologies of Adult Children of Alcoholics (Ackerman, 1983, 1987; Johnson & Leff, 1999). While many explanatory systems already exist (Friel & Friel, 1988; Kritsberg, 1985; Russell, Henderson & Blume, 1984), these systems give generalized categories in which symptoms are clustered and presumed correlated. Literature is replete with examples of taxonomies that define ACOAs in terms of personality types. As children, victim types include the *family hero,* the *rescuer,* the *mascot,* the *adjuster,* the *doormat,* the *scapegoat,* the *bully,* the *lost hope,* and many others (Black, 1982; Deutsch, 1982; Wegscheider-Cruse, 1986; Woititz, 1985).

Adult personality classifications are also grouped by behavior. By adulthood, pathologic symptoms from childhood evolve into sophisticated and pervasive traits highly enmeshed in a survivor's life (Bellieveau & Stoppard, 1995). Chang & Krantz (1996), for example, explained how defects in family lifestyle directly deteriorated coping skills of offspring. Similarly, when early dysfunctions persist into adulthood, the resulting chronicity incapacitates emotions, thoughts and behaviors. Progressively degenerative effects cause what might be called *response erosion,* meaning, responses either are extinguished or extremely fragile. Two predictable side-effects arising from response erosion include *excesses* and *deficits.* While these are reviewed elsewhere (Kazdin, Kraemer, Kessler, Kupfer & Offord, 1997; Segrin & Menees, 1996), common deficits and excesses reported in decomposed personalities may also appear in ACOAs. A summary of these adult symptoms appears below:

ACOA Personality is One of Two Major Types: *Passive* and *Aggressive* Dichotomy of behavior is predictable. ACOAs raised under a random, untrusting, and frequently punitive environment adapt by responding in one of two major ways. First, rebellion toward that environment appears in the form of challenging the abusing adults. Expressed anger is outwardly aggressive, violent, or oppositional in terms of severe tantrums, noncompliance, running away, lying, stealing, and hyperactivity. In adolescence, when verbal skills are more complex, refusals and defiance intensify as the child completely distrusts his parents and assumes total control over personal goals and gratification. In adulthood this controlling behavior appears manipulating and domineering. Ironically, partners attracted to controlling ACOAs typically are inept or behaviorally deficient caretakers. Controlling ACOAs have low tolerance for disruptions in rigidly planned schedules. They also resist changes. Hostility over disruptions, however, is not to evoke conflict, which ACOAs strive to avoid.

At the other extreme is the gentle, docile, repressive, isolative, and passively withdrawn ACOA. In childhood, this person withdrew from familial antagonism or turned into a mediator, trying to arbitrate peace among disputing parties. Placating aggressive or domestically violent parents denied the ACOA his own personal pleasures and opportunities for peer growth; thwarted opportunities robbed the ACOA of a childhood and instilled fear of being autonomous in the outside world. Kept within family boundaries, the frightened child developed hypersensitivity to parental approval and was unconditionally submissive. Approval was the only source of love, affirmation, and proof of the child's worthiness. ACOAs seek approval by pleasing, caretaking or by overburdening themselves with responsibility in order to avert confrontation.

The irony in both personality patterns is that conflict is absolutely anathema. Conflict threatens the fragile balance between feeling safe and feeling abandoned; that is, victimized children shift from self-hatred to distrust and malevolence toward their addictive parents. Above all, they fear criticism for any reason. Aggressively controlling ACOAs anticipate and dismantle conflict by abrasively scaring their predators. Rude remarks, hostile provocations, using predators as brunt of jokes, and even "egging on" predators until they explode function to delay or escape from confrontation. Clinicians may disagree, claiming the aggressor is naturally belligerent and volatile. Diagnostically, AXIS I codes may identify the ACOA as having "intermittent explosive disorder" (312.34) or "impulse control disorder (312.30), when actually the outbursts arise from fear and avoidance behavior.

Passively controlling ACOAs seek the same goal—to defuse rising hostility. Thus their behaviors operationally are identical. However, efforts at defusal involve satisfying the legitimate or illegitimate demands of predators in anticipation of conflict. ACOAs may surrender unwillingly to peculiar demands imposed upon them by predators, hoping the outcome will instantly restore peace. How long this peace lasts is irrelevant.

ACOAs Have Trouble Expressing Feelings ACOAs suppress their feelings internally and refuse to share anything personal or vulnerable. Disclosure would risk exposure of faults, of looking incompetent, of being disapproved, or causing anger in others.

Consequently self-expression is very selective, labored and edited, and words expressed are replayed in thought over and over to test in advance whether they may upset the listener.

ACOAs Cannot Seem to Relax ACOAs appear highly active, constantly busy, and unable to slow down their pace for fear of feeling unproductive, wasteful, and lazy. Even sitting is accompanied by fidgeting, irritability, working on projects, and racing thoughts. Slow, calming or vegetative actions evoke sudden panic and shame. Panic arises from the expectation that authority figures (parents, significant others) may make punishing remarks about the ACOAs for "doing nothing." Anticipatory fears compel obsessive, "busy-beaver" behavior, even if the ACOA lives alone Reactions of guilt or shame spring from wanting to relax but believing it is awful and immoral to relax.

These anticipatory fears evolved from lack of opportunities to relax or play independently because addictive parents ordered the child to be responsible for other siblings and remain constantly "on call" to help other people.

ACOAs Are Loyal (Codependent) Beyond Reason ACOAs become dependent personalities who are terrified of abandonment and would do anything to hold onto a relationship. Loyalty also means self-appointed commitment to any cause, group, or friendships, no matter how problematic or dysfunctional the situation becomes. Metaphorically speaking, ACOAs *must* stay aboard the Titanic even if every passenger abandons ship. This martyrdom reassures ACOAs of being perceived as comparably superior to other people and deserving of approval.

ACOAs Are Overly Responsible A corollary to *loyalty beyond reason* is taking on far more responsibilities than the adult can handle. ACOAs have an inflated perception of responsibility, focused entirely on the welfare of another person. Deflection from selfish thoughts and conceited actions to concerns of others safely spares ACOAs from drawing too much attention to their faults and virtues. Helping others, also called *caretaking* or *enabling*, involves total preoccupation with organizing, solving, or directing lives of emotionally underprivileged people. In this respect, ACOAs forfeit personal needs, ranging from small sacrifices to complete self-neglect. Targets for enablers are generally weak people suffering some emotional or physical disability, or who exhibit underdeveloped social skills. Enablers "instinctively" welcome the natural challenge to rehabilitate or "rescue" derelicts, alcoholics, indigents, and other social misfits.

ACOAs Fear Losing Control Loss of control translates into panic over looking vulnerable, which poses serious threats to inadequacies that remain private. Lack of leadership—or denied opportunities to direct, coordinate or organize people or things—instills a fear of abandonment. That other people do not need them or regard their services as unimportant conveys that the ACOA is incapable, incompetent, and has shortcomings. Inferring this rejection, ACOAs believe they failed a partner's or friend's expectations. Rather than be dismayed, ACOAs may immediately rebound with double the amount of energy and commitment to please the person at all costs.

ACOAs Have Difficulties with Relationships There are two types of relationship failures. The first is with social interactions, while the second type involves interpersonal and intimate partners. Building social peer groups is difficult because the composition of people must be passive, weak, or amenable to AOCAs' idiosyncrasies. For ACOAs who are shy, reserved, and passive, attraction gravitates toward an assertive leader who commands authority and compliance from members. For ACOAs who are aggressive, perfectionistic, and workaholics, peer groups must be passively receptive to autocracy and offer continuous praise. In intimacy, aggressive ACOAs match with passive partners, and passive ACOAs attract domineering, aggressive partners. While folklore may hold that opposite partners attract one another and build solid foundations, opposite partners frequently evoke severe conflict and high statistics of domestic violence (Dutton, 1998; O'Leary, 1993)

ACOAs Fear Conflict Aggressive or passive ACOAs are equally afraid of conflict. Conflict refers to any disagreement, criticism, or opinion marshaled against the adult for inappropriate behavior. Conflict resembles situations of inescapable and unavoidable parental punishment causing shame, self-criticism, and desperate need for approval. Hatred of conflict becomes so fierce that ACOAs will say or do anything to avert confrontation, even if escaping ultimately means paying the price of another confrontation.

ACOAs Are Overly Self-Critical Self-criticism develops from replaying what ACOA therapists call "mental tapes." Tapes are essentially obsessive thoughts (rule-governed behaviors) in the form of religious, moral, or powerfully persuasive beliefs on what behavior should be, ought to be, and must be. Such "musterbations" (Ellis & Grieger, 1977) take two forms. One form is constant negative assaults on imperfections or mistakes believed to be preventable or controllable, using the same words, phrases or intonations recalled from the adult's verbally assaultive parents. Replays of parental verbal abuse shift from the occasion in question to generalized attacks regarding the adult's integrity ("You're so stupid") or unrealistic perception of life ("Who do you think you are anyway; you won't amount to anything").

A second form of self-criticism includes internal recitations of anger toward another person for *causing this mistake or making the ACOA look stupid* (see Ruben, 1992a). Projected hatred toward another person (usually an innocent bystander or good friend) disguises the adult's own unconfronted faults and protects the adult from feeling vulnerable.

ACOAs Are Addicted to Excitement, Alcoholics, Domestic Abusers, or Compulsive People ACOAs either become alcoholic, marry alcoholics, or both; or they find another compulsive personality such as a workaholic or overeater to fulfill their own compulsive needs. Attraction to excitement largely occurs in the passive adult dissatisfied with the monotony of boring daily routines, desperate for escapism but incapable of achieving this objective without becoming a caretaker for an energetic, but impulsively uncontrollable person.

More aggressive ACOAs at first resist excitable, impulsive people. They drift toward reserved, docile, or emotionally disabled persons who repress their abuses until the relationship (friendship or intimacy) develops fully. Both extroverted and introverted ACOAs, however, share a reason for addiction to excitement. Whether their parents were polydrug abusers or nonsubstance abusers, the verbal and physical abuse stifled natural childhood impulsivity, playfulness, and creativity. Consequently, having this fun in adulthood becomes possible around profoundly impulsive adults.

TENETS OF LEARNING THEORY

This section addresses the learning theory paradigm supporting research on the ACOA syndrome. Learning theory borrows from the canons of quantitative science to formulate behavior as a measurable entity, capable of being reduced, manipulated, replicated, and studied as a universal rather than exclusive phenomenon of human organisms.

After a review of basic principles of learning used in personality theory, fundamental concepts are defined under "Structure of Learning Theory." Using this structure, we describe the principles of operant and respondant conditioning and explore two different variations of response typology integrating a multicausal analysis. Finally, expanded behavioral units are described within a field or ecobehavioral system. This background is helpful in converting complex human behavior into simpler patterns for application in field research and clinical investigation.

Basic Principles

Taken in its strictest form, the behavioral approach requires that all concepts and propositions be anchored precisely to measurable properties in the empirical world. Empirically unanchored speculation is anathema to behaviorists; hypothetical constructs, which abound in intrapsychic and phenomenological theories, are rarely found in behavioral theories, although exceptions to this cardinal rule have been frequent (e.g., Morris, 1988; Reese & Parrot, 1986; Ullmann & Krasner, 1975; Zimmerman, 1996).

Behaviorism originated with the view that subject introspection was "unscientific" and that it should be replaced by the use of objectively observable behavior. Further, all environmental influences upon behavior were likewise to be defined objectively. If unobservable processes were thought to exist within the individual, they were to be defined strictly in terms of observables that indicate their existence.

More recent theories of behavioral pathology have included concepts generated from experimental learning research (e.g., Davey & Cullen, 1988; Malloy & Levis, 1988; Maser & Seligman, 1977). They are not simple translations of psychoanalytic concepts into behavioral terminology, as were earlier theories of behavioral pathology. Instead, they are based on the ostensible "empirical laws" of learning. Behavioral researchers, in other words, employ concepts of science, since their heritage lies with the objective studies of systematic learning and not with the dubious methods of clinical speculation (O'Donahue & Kitchener, 1998; Ruben & Ruben, 1985a; Schlinger & Poling, 1998; Staats, 1996).

That learning concepts are helpful in understanding pathology that cannot be denied. But behavioral theorists take a stronger position. They state that pathological behavior is learned behavior that develops according to the same laws as those governing the development of normal behavior (Hawkins & Forsyth, 1997; Staats, 1994). Disturbed behavior differs from normal behavior only in magnitude, frequency, and social adaptiveness. Were these behavior patterns more adaptive, or less frequent and extreme, they would possess no other distinguishing features.

Three general positions act as the bedrock to understanding a learning theory approach to personality: associationism, hedonism, and environmentalism.

Associationism Associationism is a broad doctrine evolving at the beginning of the twentieth century that stresses the laws of combination. Theories of associationism essentially stated that knowledge was transformed from simpler ideas into more complex ideas through connection with one another. Early research of Ebbinghous and Thorndike experimentally showed a unique learning curve from repeated contact of two stimuli, two responses, and between stimuli and responses (Thorndike, 1969). Even Pavlov's seminal studies on response conditioning verified the essential principle of repetitive or sequential stimulus-response contact.

Hedonism Hedonism explains the motivation underlying a behavioral system. It permeates the theories of Hull, Skinner, and many of today's leading behaviorists. Hedonism conjectures that human behavior arises out of a need to gain pleasure and avoid pain. Pleasure-seeking responses—seen in reinforcement studies, pain-reducing responses, and avoidance research—largely verify the fundamental "fight or flight" patterns generated (e.g., Honig, 1966; Reiss, 1987).

Environmentalism Environmentalism is the third position that gives behavioral psychology a clear identity. It denotes that behavior is largely influenced by factors outside the individual—that is, within the environment. A pure environmental position excludes all internal causes such as emotions and thoughts. Pioneering works of J.B. Watson (e.g., Watson, 1924) advocated a "methodological behaviorism," which sought translation of all organismic processes as externally based. By the late 1960s, and with the advent of integrative cognitive-behavioral psychologies, a renaissance in behaviorism led to a less strict approach called "radical behaviorism" (Biglan, Glasgow & Singer, 1990; Skinner, 1974).

Thoughts, emotions, states of deprivation (hunger, thirst, etc.), even past history, all contributed to the totality of response acquisition and maintenance. Skinner's posture in later years (Skinner, 1989) refined his beliefs that organismic functioning depends on many factors reacting with the environment. His nemesis, J. R. Kantor (1959, 1980; Pronko, 1980) asserted this belief twenty years before Skinner, calling for a reanalysis of the science of behavior in which all events were not just reactive, but interactive.

Structure of Learning Theory

Essentially, modern learning theorists define the structure of personality as a composite of the following critical variables: stimuli, responses, history of behavior or "repertoire," media of contact, deprivational states, and propensity for behavior, also known as interbehavioral potentials.

Stimuli refer to current or impending events evoking action in a person. External or internal stimuli, also known as *cues,* can prompt any variety of behavior. Stimuli occurring before behavior arises are known as *antecedents.* When they follow behavior and either increase or decrease the likelihood of that behavior occurring again, they are called *consequences* (e.g., Matson & DiLorenzo, 1984). *Responses* are sequential, concurrent, or single acts of behavior arising within a context. *History of behavior or behavior repertoire* means what it suggests—that a human organism develops a cumulative past of interactions with the environment that is predictive of current and future behavior (Rutter, 1980).

The repertoire is one of the few reified concepts in behavioral psychology, largely tolerated because it suggests learning is measurable and contained "in the personality." The personality is analogous to players on a football field. Each player represents a learnable behavior; players on defense or players on offense go on or off the field as team possession of the football changes. Likewise, learnable behaviors enter or exit the stimlus field based on changing interactions.

Media of contact refer to the intervening factors between stimuli and human organism that account for responses. Light and dark affect visual responses, hot and cold affect thermal responses, sour and sweet affect gustatory responses, and the list of sensory receptors goes on. Each mediating factor in the environment either enables or disables responses. Media of contact ingeniously provide the "missing link" in many multivariate contingency analyses.

Take, for example, repeated mistakes in copying notes from a chalkboard by a 21-year-old male college student whose academic history was exemplary. Operational analysis ruled out historical variables such as poor study skills or associative aversive properties about the classroom. Strong notetaking skills actually befuddled clinicians, who were searching for salient external stimlus-response cues. Closer inspection of variable details showed it was not a repertoire impairment but a visual impairment causing the skill disruption. The student had undergone surgery in the left eye on a cataract that reduced visual acuity in short- or long-distance reading when the ambiance was dark. Increasing illumination (i.e., media of contact for photoreception) immediately restored visual clarity and permitted the student to copy correct information from the board. As this example of *behavioral ophthalmology* shows, new variables not only are important additions to the traditional "S–R model," but frequently these variables help explain why the S–R model works.

Deprivational states pertain to the absence or presence of some need or drive motivating a person. Thirst, hunger, anxiety (fear), anger—all induce a propensity for responses without which the individual may not respond despite the antecedents and consequences in effect. In recent years, operational definitions of deprivation have become sharper and more predictive of human response. Deprivation now comes under the rubric of an *establishing operation* (Michael, 1982, 1993a, 1993b; Sundberg, 1993). Establishing operations, simply put, increase the probability of a certain response over its normal response rate under nondeprivational circumstances. ACOAs respond vigilantly to establishing operations (EOs). A female ACOA fearful that her physically abusive partner may be assaultive if she is late for dinner may drive faster and more recklessly on the days her partner comes home for dinner. On the days the partner works late, driving speed is slower and safety more observed. The establishing operation in this case is fear of being rejected and physically injured.

Finally, *interbehavioral potentials* involve a prognostic concept that helps to predict the trajectory of behavior, given the individual's past history (repertoire) and current patterns (Ruben, 1983b). These potentials are also calculated in part based on the placement or variation of stimuli (antecedents and consequences), states of deprivation, and media of contact.

Principles of Conditioning

This basic structure sets the stage for principles of operant and respondent conditioning. Operant and respondent conditioning are two scientific systems engineered to construct, alter, and maintain organismic behavior through a series of systematic manipulations. This section reviews these basic principles as examples of how experimental science can advance our understanding of common responses in everyday life, and particularly in reference to the ACOA syndrome.

Stimulus cues Cues make it possible to see the world in a natural way. All actions have a starting point, and with human behavior the starting point involves objects or things preceding behavior. There are two ways these events precede behavior. First is through respondent conditioning. The second is through operant conditioning. However, bear in mind that separating each type of conditioning is only an academic task. Most human interaction involves both operant and respondent learning (e.g., Rehfeldt & Hayes, 1998; Rescorla, 1988).

Respondent Conditioning Respondent conditioning follows very simple principles of association. It deals primarily with the sympathetic and parasympathetic nervous system. Historically, Pavlov started by conditioning the salivary response. Meat powder (unlearned stimulus) presented to a dog produces salivation (unlearned responses). If a bell (neutral stimulus) rings prior to presenting meat powder (unlearned stimulus), pairings between the bell and meat powder change the properties of the bell. Now the bell alone can produce salivation.

Many events trigger direct reflexes in people, such as onion odors causing tearduct reflexes or puffs of air across the face causing an eye-blink reflex. Biologically, the sensory systems react involuntarily to stimuli as a normal process of daily living. For example, when onion odors are paired with seeing an onion, crying might occur even before the person slices the onion; just looking at the onion might trigger crying.

This harmless process of natural conditioning involves biology and learning on simple and complex levels. Order from simple to complex involves; (a) conditioned emotional responses, (b) simultaneous conditioning, and (c) higher order conditioning.

Conditioned Emotional Responses Respondent conditioning explains how early fears are learned. Continuous pairings of an unlearned or unconditioned fear (stimulus) and a neutral stimulus can suppress a behavior. Usually the unlearned fear occurs first, warning of the onset of another fearful stimulus. This creates instant anxiety and the need for avoidance and escape. Yelling and screaming, for example, are loud sounds to an infant's ear. This is an unlearned fear. But then something happens. Yelling pairs with many neutral stimuli preceding the yelling. The infant hears footsteps or the voice of a parent coming in the bedroom before yelling happens. Such "neutral stimuli" used to mean nothing. Now they warn the infant that yelling is about to occur.

Simultaneous Conditioning This is when two stimuli, unlearned and neutral, occur at exactly the same time. These simultaneous pairings usually produce more abrupt, stronger, and longer lasting conditioning effects.

Higher Order Conditioning Conditioning on simple levels occurs between an unlearned and neutral stimulus. This is the first level of conditioning. A higher order of conditioning starts with the neutral stimulus that is now a "learned" stimulus—an event that triggers behavior in a person, where before it did not. This learned event pairs with even more situations. The link is endless. For example, first yelling scared the infant. Then hearing footsteps of the parent (before yelling) scared the infant. Now, smelling the father's aftershave or mother's perfume (before hearing the footsteps) scares the infant. New links are called "second levels of conditioning."

Conditioning on second and higher levels generates weaker and weaker fears. Pairings get lost between old and new stimuli. Think again of all the stimuli the infant experiences in fear: yelling, footsteps, visually tracking the parents, smelling the parents. These represent only a few of the infinitely many pairings. They are hard to keep track of and each stimulus does not trigger as much fear as the first unlearned stimulus did.

Operant Conditioning A second learning mechanism is like stopping at a traffic light. The red light cues a person to apply the brakes and stop the car. Cues all around us trigger behavior. People learn that certain behaviors produce certain outcomes. Consider fear again. A toddler hears his parents' footsteps, which signal a choice of behavior. One choice is not moving and being punished (yelled at); a second choice is escaping the situation entirely to terminate punishment. Choices are split-second and based on a history of trying both options. If staying and waiting for the parent to enter the room is not scary, the toddler takes the first choice. If waiting for parent to enter the room is highly fearful and escaping the room delays, interrupts, or permanently eliminates yelling, the toddler takes the second choice. It's that simple.

Does it always happen that way? Do human beings always choose the path of least resistance and escape punishment? Yes. Exceptions to this rule are rare (Boe & Church, 1968; Emmendorfer & Crosbie, 1999; Ulrich, Wolfe & Dulaney, 1972; Weiner, 1969).

Cues understood in this straightforward way make it easier to trace roots of people's behavior. Even complex cues are easy to trace. Cues take on many properties, from texture to shape. Properties define the cue and can be relevant or irrelevant. Relevant properties are obvious features that most people consider when picturing the cue. Dogs, for instance, have four legs, fur, a tail, and bark. Cars have four wheels, a chassis, hood, trunk, passengers, and are for transportation.

So, why is it that people who see cars think of dogs, or people who see dogs think of cars? Why is it that a car reminds a person of good and bad memories of other cars? Peculiar conditioning of this sort occurs because of external and internal cues. An external or internal stimulus may control behavior directly because of very relevant properties of that stimulus; properties previously associated with the stimulus trigger reactions, such as an alarm clock arousing a sleeper. Sounds, sights, smells, and tastes conveniently familiar to behavers appear to belong to stimuli. Onset of familiar cues "instinctively" evokes a repertoire of conditioned behaviors that are logically explainable to the naive observer.

The trouble is that units of conditoning are never purely elementary. Complexly integrated contingencies blur the origins of stimulus-to-response connection, confusing both behavers and observers of behavior. Parents of oppositionally defiant children, for example, may insist their children's tantrums really are inherited from their fathers'. Domestic abusing fathers might seem to transmit genetic codes of behavior from one generation to the next. Perhaps no other salient antecedents for Johnny's bad behavior seem present. But environmental cues do exist; thus, concluding that Johnny's behavior is genetic is superficial. The reason cues seem to "disappear" is due to an unusual form of higher order conditioning, in which both relevant and irrelevant stimulus properties may functionally exert control over behavior. Stimulus properties may share: (a) the same things (generic extension); (b) similar things (metaphorical extension); or (c) different things (metonymical extension) (Hayes & Chase, 1991; Skinner, 1957; Sundberg & Partington, 1983).

Same Things Cues that have all the relevant properties so that one cue looks exactly like another cue, are called same things (generic extension). Fear of hearing the same loud noise each time, despite when or where one hears it, is due to the noise having all of the relevant properties for fear.

Similar Things Cues that have some but not all of the relevant properties and still produce fear are called similar things (metaphorical extension). Loud noises vary by intensity, duration, and quality. But they may still invoke fear exactly as if the noises were identical. A Vietnam Vet who is mowing the lawn and hears the engine sputter then backfire might feel fear. It is not fear of a lawnmower. Fear comes from the sounds being similar to artillery firing in wartime.

Different Things Cues that have none of the relevant properties but still produce fear are called "different things" (metonymical extension). People react to irrelevant properties of the cue, as well as to relevant properties of competing cues.

Irrelevant means properties are hidden, vague, or not the typical things people react to in that cue. For example, nothing about a shower curtain should produce anxiety. But some shower curtains that are hooked above showers in small motels may remind people of the scene from *Psycho*—the shower curtain in the Bates Motel. Now they are afraid. Likewise, people who think they see ghosts may be looking at irrelevant or different things. Ghosts that appear in the house they lived in may not be ghosts at all, but rather objects that remind the perceiver of the deceased person. If, say, the deceased person used to stand by the Christmas tree on Christmas Eve, seeing that tree and its shadows may trigger strong memories. Shadows of the tree thrown upon the wall may look like the person being thought of. The silhouette may resemble somebody standing there (Ruben, 1987).

Types of Consequences Outcomes or consequences apply to both respondent and operant conditioning. Respondent outcomes are the conversion from a neutral to a learned stimulus. Operant outcomes are a little more complex. As people behave, the world responds in four different ways: with positive reinforcement, negative reinforcement, positive punishment, and negative punishment.

Positive and Negative Reinforcement To say outcomes are "reinforcers" means they can increase a particular behavior (Bolles, 1972). Positive reinforcers are events or objects given to a person after some behavior that increases the likelihood of their behaving that way again in the future. Examples of positive reinforcers surround all of us. A smiling child receives affection from her parent. This increases the future probability of that child smiling again at the parent. Money, food, material goods, status—all are powerful rewards exchanged on a daily basis.

However, reinforcers that are desirable and effective under one situation might be ineffective under different situations. For example, under deprivation (hunger, thirst, etc.), urges for reinforcers strongly motivate behavior. But remove deprivation, and motivation disappears; this is due to the presence or absence of the establishing operation. People do not want the reinforcer anymore. So, events surrounding the behaver determines the effectiveness of the reinforcers.

This is uniquely so for negative reinforcement. A negative reinforcer removes something after the person responds. This encourages future responses of the same type. Negative reinforcers also enter into daily routines. Take a panic attack. Escaping a panic attack by rushing out of the mall removes the fear and increases the future probability of escaping again under like situations. Events clearly signal negative reinforcement if they achieve the following:

1. Delay the fearful person, place, or thing, until later.
2. Remove the fearful person, place, or thing.
3. Produce behavior that delays or eliminates the fearful person, place, or thing.

Positive and Negative Punishment "Punishment" conceptually is a misleading term, conjuring ideas ranging from cruelty and corporal discipline to traumatic physical and sexual assault. None of these is correct. Punishment, instead, means the opposite of reinforcement; it decreases behavior. Two types of punishment are positive punishment and negative punishment (Crosbie, 1998; Matson & DiLorenzo, 1984). Positive punishment occurs after a person responds, and it decreases the thing he is doing both at the moment and in the future. Yelled at for talking loudly, a frightened child learns quickly not to repeat loud talking in the future and risk being yelled at again.

Negative punishment delays or removes things after a person behaves. If the person who fears panic attacks refuses to go to the mall, panic is avoided. But, so are all the normal behaviors causing anxiety: traveling by car, entering public places, and talking to strangers. Not going to the mall, in other words, causes more problems than bargained for. It also decreases routine social behaviors to the point of the person refusing to go anywhere where there is high risk of anxiety.

Positive and negative reinforcement, positive and negative punishment may seem hard to understand, at first, but there are simple formulas to determine them:

1. If behavior increases, it means the behavior is reinforced.
2. If behavior decreases, it is means the behavior is punished.
3. If behavior increases because of things received or given, it means there was positive reinforcement.
4. If behavior increases because of things removed, it means there was negative reinforcement.
5. If behavior decreases because of things received or given, it means there was positive punishment.
6. If behavior decreases because of things removed, it means there was negative punishment.

Response Types

Responses involve what people do and how they behave after cues occur. In both cases, responses vary by their topography and function. Topography refers to the shape, form, or movement of behavior in space and time. An example is anxiety. Topography asks: (a) how many times does the behavior occur (frequency); (b) how long does each behavior last (duration); (c) how intense is the anxiety (magnitude/intensity)? Function of behavior describes how the behavior impacts the environment: (a) what events caused the anxiety (cues); (b) what effect did the anxiety have on others around the person (outcomes); and (c) is the anxiety a recurrent or one-time problem?

Using "topography" is like reading a map. Reactions further divide into two types of patterns: simultaneous (concurrent) response patterns, and sequential response patterns (Delprato, 1986; Delprato & McGlynn, 1988; Ray & Delprato, 1989)

Simultaneous (Concurrent) Response Patterns Responding never occurs in isolation. It occurs instead in connection with other responses. Behavior is like a constellation of stars all strung together, so that changes in one behavior have specific or broad effects upon linked behaviors. One constellation is called simultaneous or "concurrent" response patterns (Lyon, 1982), involving two or more behaviors that occur simultaneously. Anxiety, for example, consists of many simultaneous behaviors. These include respiratory elevation, increased glandular secretion, increased muscular contractions, and private, self-defeating thoughts.

Sequential Response Patterns A response sequence is a series of linked behaviors like a row of dominos. Knocking one will tumble the rest in the chain. This means that removal of one response in the sequence will directly affect the remaining behaviors. Fear follows sequential response patterns. For example, a rapid heart beat, sweaty palms, and dizziness nearly always increase action, either by avoiding or escaping the situation (Reiss, 1987). Or, fear can immobilize the person, in which case, sequential response patterns would be more private. The person might watch people closely, or think a lot.

Ecobehavioral or Field-Integrated Approach

Sobell, Sobell, and Nirenberg (1982) identify the main purpose here: "Each client enters treatment with a different set of past experiences, abilities, strengths, and dysfunctions. These factors should be carefully considered and incorporated into the treatment plan when appropriate" (p. 1141). Slightly altering their view, this author contends these factors should be carefully considered and incorporated into the treatment plan *all the time*. Radical change for ACOAs seems ambitious after half their lives have been spent in a dysfunctional setting. If treatment planning follows a systems approach, with difficult variables separately targeted, behaviors stand a better chance of being modified.

What are these variables? Three major interrelated factors in ACOA include: (a) biochemical effects, (b) behavioral effects, and (c) social effects. Traditionally, criteria for behavioral treatment outcome include the clear correlation between elimination of biochemical and behavioral effects and improvement of social effects. However, as discussed earlier, treatment success also implies the concurrence of learned adjustment in sequential or collateral behaviors. This is because learned adjustment in one response does not automatically affect other response patterns. Human interaction is likened to a domino effect, where similar responses covary from only one stimulus manipulation. Although covariation exists, each behavior is a function of individual "fields."

Field Concept Along the continuum of a scientific ecology are the basic principles of modern behaviorism to solve family problems. This approach is gaining widespread recognition in clinical circles and involves the expansion of the unicausal behavioral model (Kunkel, 1996; Midgley & Morris, 1988; Reese & Parrott, 1986; Ruben & Delprato, 1987; Smith & Smith, 1996). Enlarging the unit of analysis from single stimulus-response (S→R) to complex stimulus–response connections echoes the sentiments of many behaviorists (Biglan, Glasgow & Singer, 1990; Morris, 1988) who support a contextualist approach. It replaces the artificial distinction between behavior and stimulus. Principles of field theory, for example, replace purely Skinnerian concepts to help describe human behavior naturalistically, where stimulus and response constitute the overall transaction of events. Human behavior, in other words, is part of a process in a field of connected, interdependent things and events.

Field thinking is unusual for a learning theory. It rejects heredity, environment, mind, cognition, stimuli, reinforcers, independent variables, and so on as exclusive controlling forces in behavior. In fact, behavior itself must be totally redefined as an event. Such events not only involve actions of an active organism but also the stimulating objects, media of contract between organism and environment, functional stimulus and response attributes, and attending setting factors. All of these events constitute the *psychological field.* Antecedents and consequences are among many interactive parts of the whole. Reinforcement, punishment, conditions of deprivation, pharmacologic interactions, and response properties more closely resemble kinetic energy in machinery. There are no singular units of action per se but rather the synthesis of many larger aggregates of action (Thompson & Lubinski, 1986).

Field thinking puts the problem of ACOA syndrome into proper perspective. If the ACOA syndrome is like a geometric organization, with the total composed of interrelated parts, then structurally significant patterns defining the ACOA might be: (a) susceptibility to alcohol or drugs, (b) past history of random punishment and deprivation, and (c) maladaptive reactions to irrelevant stimluus properties (also called superstitious behavior). Structural definitions of the parts of a system pinpoint the relative or absolute locus of parts in space and time. In the ecobehavioral approach, this space and time represent a field of analysis.

For example, consider both the behavioral and ecobehavioral view of sobriety. Behavior analysts may view refusals to drink beer in a bar as the result of competing antecedents, conditions of deprivation (Michael, 1982), or reinforcement and punishment consequences. The client, for example, may travel a different route home (antecedents), arrange to have his spouse expect him at home by a particular hour (deprivation), and consequently avoid and escape intoxication, spouse criticism, and even the risk of arrest for drunk driving (an increase in abstinence, or negative reinforcement).

By contrast, ecobehavioral or *interbehavioral* analysts do not commit to certain causal links in action (Hayes, Adams & Dixon, 1996). A systems perspective examines antecedents and consequences as one among many interactive parts of the whole. Reinforcement, punishment, antecedents, conditions of deprivation, pharmacologic interactions, and response properties more closely resemble kinetic energy in machinery. There are no singular units of action per se but rather the synthesis of many larger aggregates of action (Todd & Morris, 1995). The refusal to drink beer is an aggregate response perpetuated by a series of orderly, continuous fields, from which learned experiences accumulated.

In short, field analysis paints an empirically broader picture of interactive variables. With ACOA symptoms, expanded field variables provide concrete evidence of why childhood patterns emerge as caretaking, aggression, and anxiety, among other predictive prototypes (Brown, 1988). Disabling responses by adults no longer are mysterious, equivocal, or ascribed to reified concepts such as "Type A personalities," "Alcoholics," or "dysfunctional families."

The chapters ahead reveal logical behavioral units explicitly causing deficits and excesses in children raised in addiction households. By this scientific approach to understanding ACOA, an at-risk clinical population is given the fast track for assessment and treatment cures.

CHAPTER 2

Operational Analysis of the ACOA Syndrome

In this chapter, the process of "operational analysis" undergoes careful scrutiny to reduce ACOA patterns from general to specific. Scientifically, reductionistic thinking has many advantages. Phenomena that previously were unclear or reified as genetically inheritable are transformed into measurable, concrete and confrontable terms. This allows us to examine why ACOAs longitudinally generalize derelict patterns from childhood through adulthood. Personality categories such as "scapegoat" and "family hero" lose their ominous meanings and are replaced with functional meanings that sort the mutiplicative cause and effects into experimentally replicable variables. Researchers can vary them as independent and dependent variables and show correlative and causative relationships in predicting why ACOAs have problems.

Once these variables are known, they become operational in redefining assessment and treatment protocols.

The natural transition in science from raw data to governing principles appears in every heuristic discipline from chemistry and archeology to medicine. Gathered artifacts, such as herbs suspected of historic or medicinal value, undergo testing to further assay their unknown properties. Analytical findings may reveal properties that are benign or significantly iconoclastic, which revolutionizes thinking and provides a new solution to old problems. For example, the Hubbell telescope, despite its costly setbacks, transmitted astronomic data disputing common beliefs about distant galaxies and showed closer galaxies exist with possible inhabitable planets. The Mars-plant missions equally upset traditional thinking and folklore with scientific innovations. Just as NASA projects employ science to operationalize studies of the cosmos, so can mental health providers employ science to operationalize studies of unusual human pathology.

Why a Behavioral Approach?

Revisonary thinking requires instincts and scientific integrity. Instincts in ACOA research refer to natural compassion felt about the topic. Researchers ranging from recovering alcoholics and ACOAs, to clergy, to the most robust field scientist vicariously experience the inherent traumatic effects observed in ACOAs. Poignancy lures curiosity and sentiment attracts even objectively rigid observers to feel deeply sad or moralistic about ACOA childhood disasters. Researchers are not inhumane, and experientially confront the anguish, disgust, and joy surrounding clinical examinations of dysfunctional people.

Behaviorally acute researchers are no exception. They are often tempted to rescue their subjects. Predictive knowledge clearly enables behavioral practitioners to intervene effectively and solve impeding problems before emotional casualties abound. Caring, however, has the distinct disadvantage of destroying scientific integrity, which allows science to supply the empirical principles that define causal interconnections between ACOA behaviors and determine the rules governing why ACOA patterns respond to certain stimuli. Behaviorally minded practitioners guided by this paradigm provide unusual insight for ACOAs. Behaviorists remove the mystery, fears, and superstitious beliefs long associated with drinking-related family disorders and give ACOAs incredible hope for recovery.

A behavioral analytic perspective achieves this goal in two ways. First, units of behavior represent samples of quantitatively larger behavior groups examined for learning links. This explains how the behavior sample was acquired, how it was maintained in a person's repertoire, and eventually how it transferred or generalized exponentially throughout the natural environment. Carryover effects from childhood to infinitely multiple adult situations can be subtle and untraceable. Magnifying these effects involves diligent recording methods that behavioral practitioners employ to "run a trace" on operant, respondant, and intermingling variables. Technical methods sort causal from accidental or "adventitious" conditioning and produce precise measures to estimate the probability of behavior units varying under different situations—that is, the "chance" of a person reacting precisely the same or in similar way given same or similar conditions. Recording mechanisms traditionally used include self-reporting, frequency counts, duration and latency measures, intensity and magnitude measures, biofeedback, and now computer-assisted, multiple response counters. Sophisticated computer devices record sequential or concurrent response patterns over a designated period of time.

A second way behavioral analysis achieves recovery goals for ACOAs is by logically explaining how operational behaviors fit into the real-world or "the bigger picture." Targeted, operational behaviors that undergo scrutiny include not only behaviors of the ACOAs themselves, but also those of significant others impacting their lives. Naturally, realistic contingencies differ from in-session contingencies, and "test" the accuracy and social validity of targeted behaviors. It is rare to find a perfect match between operational behaviors and tested behaviors. In most cases, deviations from the operational behavior occur through unexpected or "artifactual" variables in the person's life. Clinically defined behaviors must then be revised to properly fit these deviations and secure a greater chance of their running smoothly in the next round of interactions.

Treating "caretaking," for example, may begin by operationally defining three patterns observed by the provider and client. One part is submissiveness. Another part is accommodating other people's needs by pleasing them and never imposing selfishness. A third part may entail encouraging maladaptive behaviors in other people (e.g., drinking, hyperactivity, domestic violence) simply to appease or maintain civility. No matter how operationally precise the definition of this behavior, or the client's understanding of the definition, real-life intervention may produce surprises disqualifying or limiting the definition and begging for behavioral revisions. Caretakers, in addition, may anticipate conflict by exerting laborious effort to placate a person in advance of impeding conflict. Excessive avoidance also occurs in refusing to travel outdoors or in public because of phobic reactions of elevated anxiety bordering on panic attacks. Fear associated with making mistakes, looking stupid, or enduring abrasive reprimands from significant others all conspire to emotionally paralyze caretakers.

Real-world tests of caretaking behaviors may reveal these new findings and serve as vital input in revising the operational definition of caretakers. Consequently, the more informed ACOA caretakers are about their response patterns under predictable situations, the faster they grow as self-monitors, self-changers, and self-healers.

Because ecobehaviorism is decisive, samples of behavior extracted from ACOA populations and studied scientifically can be used to predict changes in the ACOA population. Data generated from samples of behavior supply a blueprint for rapidly assessing at-risk or maladaptive behaviors and accurately alerting providers to the best interventions for affecting change.

Until recently, ACOA personality classifications were derived from personal experience and calculated guesses. Correlations presumed among victimized children and their later adult lives were drawn from testimonials, biographies, and intergenerational oral history partly attesting to family histories of mental illness or alcoholism. Alcoholic grandparents automatically had alcoholic children; likewise, families with with alcoholic parents automatically spawned stereotyped children who either were arguers, conflict resolvers, peacemakers, bystanders, or defiant absconds (Black, 1982; Levy & Rutter, 1999; Wegscheider-Cruse, 1986). Experimental research even attempted to support such instinctive family role players. Lyon and Seefeldt (1995), for example, attempted to validate 13 common characteristics of ACOAs using personality measures and interview checklists. Results showed the sampled ACOAs were indifferent to family relationships and did not perceive their role consistent with symptoms they exhibited. Categories were invalidated, and the study raised questions as to the categories' scientific veracity. Similar disconfirmations were reported in other replication studies (e.g., Baker & Stephenson 1995). Consequently, these personality categories were poor launching pads for systems behavioral analysis.

Alternatively, tracing the ontogeny of ACOA behavior using measurable units of response not only makes scientific sense but is clinically more efficacious for designing treatment intervention. For starters, then, we will examine the etiology of the ACOA syndrome through the behavioral concepts of functional relationships, functional characteristics of punishment, superstitious characteristics, avoidance and escape characteristics, and ecobehavioral characteristics.

Functional Relationships

Several functional relationships exist between drinking parents and the emotional behaviors of their offspring. Let us consider some initial hypotheses, followed by a discussion on similarities and differences among these hypotheses:

Hypothesis 1. Among alcoholic parents, there is direct relationship between parental discipline and frequency of child acting-out behaviors.

Hypothesis 2. Among alcoholic parents, there is an inverse relationship between parental contact and child acting-out behaviors.

Hypothesis 3. Among alcoholic parents, there is a direct relationship between parents' drinking and child acting-out behaviors.

The first and third hypotheses propose similar interactions. Hypothesis one proposes that as parental punitive discipline intensifies, so will acting-out reactions among children. Hypothesis three proposes that increases (or decreases) in parental alcoholic consumption can increase (or decrease) child acting-out behaviors. Both hypotheses thus share common properties. Both statements are nonreciprocal, because acting out behavior alone may or may not cause harsh disciplinary action or increased intake of alcohol.

Both statements do have a deterministic and a causal value. Punishment contingencies, shown experimentally, can induce attention seeking or aggressive responses in children (Abramowitz & O'Leary, 1990; Bennett & Cherek, 1990; Charlop, Burgio, Iwata & Ivancic, 1988). Intoxicated parents clearly are more prone to punish. As the effects of alcohol increase parents' intolerance to child misbehavior, discipline becomes rigidly aversive and potentially abusive. Intoxicated, angry parents may have a short fuse for a defiant or incessantly inquisitive child. But effects between an agitative child and parental aggression are not linear; they are bilinear or reciprocal. Maladaptive parental reactions are both the cause and effect of reciprocally maladaptive child reactions.

Parent–child acrimony may produce highly reinforcing consequences for the child. Positive reinforcers include parental attention for a child who otherwise goes ignored. Negative attention may involve opportunities for the removal of abuse and adversity. Frequently, for example, punished children know that after their parents volatilely explode, adversity immediately ends. A child may incite parental aggression, knowing "it will all be over soon." The relationship is *positive* insofar as increases (decreases) in one variable (parents) proportionally affects increases (decreases) in the other variable (children).

The second hypothesis is a bit different. Increases in parental contact in the form of (a) physical proximity and (b) frequency of interaction may decrease child misbehavior. Alcoholic parents are typically aloof from mainstream family needs and usually respond only when levels of misbehavior exceed a tolerance point. Because this tolerance point is low, negative traps ensue, with parent and child wasting what few contacts exist in unpleasant ways. However, when physical proximity increases, as in touching or verbal affection, attention is provided for appropriate attention-seeking behaviors.

In view of this potential, the statement is different from hypotheses one and three. There is a *reversible* relationship. Reduced acting-out tendencies can just as easily produce an increase in physical proximity and frequency of parental contact. In addition, while still deterministic and sequential, the types of interaction are very much contingent upon (a) durations of parents' sobriety, (b) the child's risk-taking potential, and (c) the number of successful and reinforcing family transactions without punishment.

Support for These Hypotheses Testing these hypotheses using a grounded theory method is perhaps putting the cart before the horse—that is, data is collected after the establishment of some preliminary theories. But at least the support offered can indicate if the concepts are socially valid. The empirical indicators derive from clinical intake evaluations that record referral reasons for seeking counseling. Two hundred cases of ACOAs seen from 1997 to 1999 disclosed biographic history revealing information on family contingencies. The primary referral reasons, along with contingency dysfunction and ACOA fear levels, appear below in Table 1.

A major referral reason repeated throughout the interviewing process is that families inherently are afraid to deal with presenting problems. Fear itself is quite prevalent despite parents blaming children or children blaming their parents for the communication breakdown. Family decay attributed to children further evinces a need for control. By contrast, parents unafraid of control usually can admit fault in themselves as equally as they might ascribe fault to others. An alcoholic family feeds on control and protection of self-vulnerability, even if it means fabricating accusations or ignoring personal problems.

Beside childhood contingencies, functional relationships hypothesize multicausal reasons underlying ACOA symptoms. Earlier examples of caretaking showed the discernment of actual interrelationships among anxiety, avoidance and appeasement. Similarly, any pronounced symptom is amenable to functional reinterpretation by dissecting field events in three ways. First is to operationally target the exact response pattern under question. Second, carefully identify historical antecedents and consequences surrounding prior occurrences of the response pattern, including unusual permutations of the pattern as the variables change. Historical antecedents address the "reactional biography"

TABLE 1 Referral Reasons of Clinical Cases (n = 200) and Levels of Ground Theory Concept

Referral Data	Contingency Dysfunction	Fear Level
1. Our children are perfectionistic.	Excessive use of punishment	Fear of mistakes
2. Everybody wants control.	Inflexible with rules	Fear of vulnerability
3. My wife is too passive.	Spousal aggression	Fear of rejection
4. My husband drinks too much.	Normalcy of family drinking	Fear of stress
5. We never solve arguments.	Conflict avoidance	Fear of conflict
6. The kids are too dependent on us.	Overprotective, aggressive	Fear of abandonment
7. The kids are disruptive at school.	Severe family acrimony	Fear of social disapproval
8. Our parents ignore us.	Severe response inhibition	Fear of love
9. Our parents yell at us.	Aggressive discipline	Fear of criticism
10. The kids think they're adults.	Distrust and excessive anger	Fear of losing control

or developmental continuum of maladaptive behaviors learned from addicted parents and common triggers of that behavior. Third, isolate any preconceived beliefs, rules, or social contingencies the client strongly adheres to as self-governing and perpetuating the targeted response pattern. Rigidly moral, religious, ethnic, or cultural indoctrinations are potential variables that blend indiscriminately into the behavior repertoire but exert powerful evocative effects.

In ACOAs exhibiting symptoms of perfectionism, functional relationships can be applied following all three steps (see Table 2). Note the resounding number of "phobias" associated with perfectionistic comments. Traditionally, perfectionism belonged to the nosology of obsessive–compulsive disorders, marked by the client's ritualistic intensity and intolerance for mediocrity. Hypersensitivity to trivial details presumably implied an irresistible preoccupation with rules, efficiency, procedures, and being around dominant people. Stubbornly insisting on self-discipline and exclusion of pleasure, moreover, attributed to varying reifications, from anal retentive theory to egocentric needs for control (Masterson, 2000; Neziroglu & Yarjura-Tobias, 1999). Ironically, fear–attribution probably was an accurate assessment, although the causal explanation missed the point. Perfectionism is not reinforced by self-stimulatory preoccupation with details. That assumes, functionally, that obsessive fear is innately self-gratifying.

Fortunately, perfectionism is a different class of behavior than self-injurious behavior. In autism, for example, self-stimulatory head-banging behaviors maintain durability and frequency by the reinforcing neurosensory effects produced by repetitive physical contact. Unlike self-injurious behavior, perfectionism evolves from chronic anticipatory fears of *punishment, not reinforcement.* Elevated fears rapidly escalate as the perfectionistic ACOA faces imminent confrontation for some infraction perceived as catastrophic and consequently emotionally immobilizing. Table 2

TABLE 2 Functional Analysis of Perfectionism Employing Operational Definition, Antecedent/Consequences, Belief System

Referral Data	Operational	Ant/Cons	Belief
1. I have an eye for details.	Phobic of mistakes	Random punishment	Mistakes equal stupidity.
2. I think in extremes.	Impulse decisions	Interrupted and punished	There is one right way.
3. I hate criticism.	Phobic of conflict	Deprivation/punishment	Criticism means rejection.
4. I don't trust people.	Phobic of obedience	Mixed contingencies	People are bad.
5. I like to be in control.	Phobic of dependence	Client was caretaker	Do it right by yourself.
6. I hate making decisions.	Phobic of adaptivity	Punished for all decisions.	I hate change.

shows under "Antecedents and Consequences" that infractions received random and capricious forms of punishment and deprivation. Punishment means the consequences entailed verbal or physical aversive stimulation. Deprivation means just the opposite. Stimulation of any sort was absent in response to transgressive behavior, which produced confusion and excitatory fears. In other words, fear invoked by delaying or no delivery of the punishment contingency (i.e., deprivation) produced effects that were just as bad as punishment. Behaviorally, these residual punitive effects resemble a state called "conditioned suppression" (Malloy & Levis, 1988; Myer, 1968; Seligman, 1975).

Functional Characteristics of Punishment

Functional characteristics of behavior shaped by parental punishment begin in childhood and evolve unchanged into adulthood, when contingencies remain static. Dysfunctional circumstances experienced during childhood may persist while dating, during marriage to alcoholics, or when engaging in alcohol oneself. In childhood, side effects of punishment are manifold. Child behavior research enumerating post-punitive behaviors typically includes the infamous oppositional defiance and attention-seeking behaviors (Browning & Stover, 1971; Gelfand & Hartman, 1968; Meyer, 1999). "Bad children" supposedly rebel against fiercely aggressive parents. So, too, demanding children may coerce aversive attention from nonresponsive parents or teachers (Ruben, 1983).

Defiance, however, is but a drop in the bucket compared to variations of punishment effects investigated through a systems behavioral perspective (Macciomei & Ruben, 1999; Ruben, 1993a & b). Traumatic reactions go beyond defiance and negative attention to include suppression of appropriate behaviors and inadvertent construction of many severely maladaptive "survival behaviors." These sordid problem behaviors include the following patterns (see Bensley, Spieker & McMahon, 1994; Gough & Reavey, 1997; Kazdin, 1994, 1995; Steinhausen, 1995):

1. *Child learns to react to punishment for attention.* Attention-seeking responses are instantly fueled by negative or aggressive parental discipline. Child learns yelling, anger, interrupting, and tantrums, or noncompliance as his only response to obtain gratification, regardless if the consequences are adverse.

2. *Child learns to pair or "associate" the properties of punishment with the person administering the punishment.* Repeated anger, aggression or negativity by parents turns the parent himself into an aversive event. Properties defining the parent—such as tone of voice, physical stature, odor, and facial features—acquire threatening messages avoided by the child.

3. *Child learns to stay away (avoid) anticipated or actual punishment.* Repeated exposure to aversive situations oversensitizes a child to obvious and subtle stimuli surrounding the parent or punishing situation. Hearing a drunken parent return home late at night might cue the child to hide in his room or remain silent. However, hearing that parent return home at any time, drunken or not, may cue the same response.

4. *Child inhibits appropriate behaviors in anticipation of punishment.* Anticipation of aversive situations interrupts appropriate and inappropriate behaviors. Not only does the frightened child hide underneath his bed during a loud marital argument, but the avoidance prevents him from also (a) saying goodnight to his parents, (b) brushing his teeth or going to the bathroom, and (c) changing clothing. That is, appropriate behaviors that never were punished but are collateral or sequential to punished (avoidance) behaviors now undergo inhibition. Unless corrected, inhibitions develop into routines in which the child simply omits steps (a) through (c), even into adulthood, whenever he goes asleep.

5. *Child learns inappropriate behavior in anticipation of punishment.* Suppression of some inappropriate behavior from punishment does not prevent the spontaneous learning of other, more discrete inappropriate behaviors. Inappropriate behaviors "spontaneously" arise for two reasons. First is to replace necessary appropriate behaviors that are inhibited. Second is to replace inappropriate behaviors receiving punishment.

A spanked child aggressively told to stay in his bedroom at night and who fears asking to use the bathroom may (a) urinate in his bed (enuresis) out of biological necessity, (b) sneak into the bathroom in late evening or early morning hours, forcing himself to awake at odd hours (insomnia), or (c) void the following day on household objects, or outside on the shrubbery. A second example deals with eating food. A child severely hit or verbally assaulted at mealtime (regardless of why punishment happened) may (a) avoid meals altogether, (b) sneak food into his bedroom and leave it under his bed or in secret places, or (c) eat inappropriate or inedible substances (pica) out of biological necessity.

6. *Child never learns behaviors appropriate for peer group.* Social or interpersonal behaviors suppressed at home prevent learning basic peer skills. Children punished for speaking or freely playing never learn to (a) express feelings, (b) share objects, (c) trust people, (d) make mistakes, (e) ask questions, (f) explore their curiosity and imagination, and (g) dismiss criticism.

7. *Child learns sensitivity to and generalization of avoidance and escape in punishment situations.* Avoidance and escape responses learned at home instantly transfer to other situations where there is no need for avoidance and escape. Abused children refrain from talking, risking changes, and playing with friends at school. Confronted by these deficits, the child may cry, act out, or aggressively attempt to escape the confrontation.

8. *Child learns inappropriate reactions that interfere with normal behaviors as well as "opportunities" for normal learning.* Afflicted children suffer two repercussions from constant suppression. One,

already described, is development of spontaneous alternative behaviors, many of which are inappropriate but subtle. A second repercussion occurs when inappropriate behaviors delay, interrupt, or entirely prevent access to learning opportunities for socially appropriate behaviors. For example, aggressive, attention-seeking children tested for special education who spend the majority of school in a resource or contained classroom lose precious interactions with peer groups. Mainstreaming into regular classrooms restores some opportunities, but by then prerequisites for proper peer dialogue and play are way below standards.

An abundant laboratory and applied body of literature with both human and nonhuman subjects indicates that delivery of punishment causes decisive short-term changes and recurrent long-term damage up subsequent behavior (Azrin, 1970; Azrin & Holz, 1966; Azrin, Hutchinson & Hake, 1967; Azrin, Hutchinson & Sallery, 1964; Cherek, Spiga, Bennett & Grabowski, 1991; Sidman, 1962; Ulrich, 1967; Weiner, 1969). Punishment used for clinical purposes follows a wide variety of procedures (e.g., visual reprimand, overcorrection, time out, contingent slap, water mist, electronic shock), aimed at an equally wide variety of inappropriate behaviors (e.g., tantrums, aggression, self-injurious behavior, self-stimulation).

Although the clinical effectiveness of punishment clearly has been demonstrated, side effects frequently arise that defeat any positive benefits of punishment and seriously jeopardize the person's functional skills. By-products of aversive control outlined by Hutchinson (1977) includ aggression, post-shock in physical and sensory responses, avoidance and escape, and decrements in response-generated effects long after aversive stimulation. Analysis of these by-products offers a critical interpretation of the behavioral dynamics underlying the pathology of most ACOAs.

Parameters of Aversive Control Aversive control is essentially any aversive stimuli (electric, noxious, social) which support responses that eliminate or reduce such stimulation. A contingent relationship between aversive events and responding further denotes a *discriminative* and *consequential* effect, so that cues forewarn of ensuing stimulation, whereas outcomes produce an increase or decrease in responses. Discriminative cues may signal the onset of aversive stimulation in the form of *time* (when it will occur), *intensity* (how bad it will be), *duration* (how long it will last), *frequency* (how many times it will occur), or *latency* (how much time will elapse before the next onset). Time between termination of one aversive episode and onset of another aversive episode is called *inter-trial interval (ITI)*.

Conditioning of *cues* can be primary or secondary. Primary aversive stimuli (cues) cause naturalistic, biological, or unlearned reactions, such as electric shock eliciting pain or a loud noise eliciting a startled reflex. Secondary cues, also called generalized aversive stimuli, are the product of repeated pairings between primary aversive stimuli and neutral events, during which the latter acquires many elicitive properties and can produce exactly the same behavior as the primary stimulus. Most generalized conditioned aversive stimuli are social manifestations in subtle or obvious forms ranging from verbal reprimands (paired with loud yelling) to a glaring stare (paired with painful spanking). Intensity, duration, and other noted properties of the primary stimulus also transfer over to the generalized fearful stimulus, until, after many years of intermingling, both stimuli become nearly indiscriminate. ACOAs simply cannot tell them apart.

Consequences directly alter properties of responses over a period of conditioning. Consequences occur on a *schedule* or order of presentation. Schedules are either *response-contingent* or *time-contingent*. Response-contingent punishment is when aversive stimulation follows an exact (fixed ratio) or average (variable ratio) number of responses without delay. Time-contingent punishment is when aversive stimulation follows an exact (fixed interval) or average amount of time (variable interval) depending on whether at least one response appeared before the time interval ends. Schedules of punishment have a second feature, as well. They rarely occur in isolation.

Most contingencies, whether schedules of punishment or schedules of reinforcement, occur one after the other, or simultaneously. Multiple schedules make it more difficult to predict punishment and are the reason that complex obsessions and fears slowly develop. Prediction is possible by naming the four basic types of multiple schedules. These include *multiple, mixed, chain,* and *tandem*. Multiple schedules are generically two or more contingencies having their own cues and consequences. Mixed schedules involve two or more contingencies having one cue and two consequences. Chain schedules include two or more contingencies having two or more cues but only one consequence. Tandem schedules involve two or more contingencies having one cue and one consequence. Table 3 schematizes the relationships and gives examples in an ACOA's life.

Finally, consider "response properties." Response properties are similar to discriminative properties and include *intensity* (strength of response), *duration* (length of response), *frequency* (number of responses) and *latency* (time between end of response and onset of aversive stimulus). Properties unique to responding also involve *inter-response time* (time interval between two consequent responses), *response concurrence* (simultaneous responses producing identical consequences), and *response sequence* (responses following a distinct pattern that produces the consequence).

Manipulation of these properties abounds in punishment research and has accounted for both fascinating and frightening conclusions regarding the operant or respondent effects of aversive control on human subjects (Axelrod & Apsche, 1983). Among these findings are certain predictable relationships between stimuli and behavior that are briefly described here, followed by a closer examination of the stages of *post-traumatic stress disorder.*

TABLE 3 Multiple Punishment Schedules (in terms of two contingencies)

Type	#of Cues/Consequences	Example
Multiple	Two cues, two consequences	Told to help siblings; spanked for doing it wrong. Right after, told to clean up, and spanked for being sloppy.
Mixed	One cue, two consequences	Told to make dinner; first spanked for not setting the table, then spanked (right after) for not cooking meal correctly.
Chain	Two cues, one consequence	First told to make dinner, then right after told to clean the house. Spanked for doing neither correctly.
Tandem	One cue, one consequence	Told to make dinner, the person also cleans his siblings' rooms without instructions. Spanked for doing something without being told first.

Findings suggest that:

1. Rapid, intense punishment effectively suppresses behavior.
2. Variability of punisher effectively suppresses behavior and maintains suppression.
3. Superimposing one punisher upon another punisher or upon a reinforcer causes conditioned suppression of the reinforced response.
4. Entire situations or the transitions between different situations come to be perceived as entirely aversive.
5. Pain produced by aversive stimuli induces aggressive and defensive (escape/avoidance) responses.
6. The probability of escape behavior under pain is greater when the person has an opportunity to physically or emotionally attack.
7. Punished behaviors occurring concurrently with or sequentially to other behaviors may have specific or general effects

upon the other behaviors. This is also true for identical behaviors under two different schedules of punishment. People exposed to multiple schedules of punishment develop distinctly different patterns associated with each schedule, despite similarities in the behaviors.

Findings of nearly five decades of applied and experimental research clearly are more extensive than the preceding list, but these represent the most relevant data for ACOAs. In sum, aggression, avoidance, and escape are punished-invoked behaviors that appear largely learned. They are maintained by primary and secondary aversive stimulation, and they remain unaltered because reinforcers for alternative, healthy behaviors are absent or too elusive for the ACOA habituated to punishment and learned helplessness.

Childhood years of punishing experiences that induce fear responses leave an emotional scar of inhibition in early adulthood. The response deterioration rapidly permeates all segments of the person's life, not only destroying opportunities for healthy recovery but also turning the punished person into a person who punishes others. The process from start to finish may be called *post-traumatic stress disorder.*

Post-traumatic Stress Disorder Post-traumatic stress disorder (PTSD), behaviorally speaking, is the after effect of shocking, aversive stimulation either entirely unpredictable, unavoidable, and inescapable, or predictable but not at the level of severity and density encountered. Symptoms reportedly suffered span cognitive, emotional, and behavioral reactions—including nightmares, flashbacks, disturbance of thought, memory impairment, trouble concentrating, sleep disturbance, fears, obsessions and phobias, and chronic feelings of detachment.

Foa, Stekette & Rothbaum (1989) reviewed models explaining this phenomena and the delineations made between categories of trauma. With *combat trauma,* those exposed to life-threatening experiences become conditioned to a wide variety of stimuli present during the trauma. Reexperiencing these stimuli, even long after the direct experience, triggers terrifying memories of the traumatic event (Keane, Zimmerlin & Caddell, 1985; Mayor & Ruben, 1991; Wolfe, Keane, Lyons & Gerardi, 1987).

Rape trauma equally evokes fear and anxiety. Sexual assault violates the safety and predictability of familiar surroundings, inducing a constant distrust and life-threatening panic in new situations. Like combat trauma victims, rape victims may be triggered into terror by hearing words, sounds, or experiencing other sensations (odors, tactile force) reminiscent of the traumatic event. Unlike combat PTSD, symptoms endemic to assault victims include hyperalertness, guilt, symptom intensification around rape-related cues, attempted suicide, and sexual dysfunctions (Fairbank & Brown, 1987).

Other victims suffering transportation accidents, death of loved ones, natural disasters, and fires—to name only a few—react with a similar symptomatology. In particular, child victims of abductions, animal attacks, exposure to nuclear accidents, and other violent situations react with sizable fears and vigilantism. In abuse cases, traumatically exposed children may undergo shock from the unpredictable terror and show rapid signs of behavioral suppression while their cognitive and emotional capacities slowly deteriorate. Even after an interim of calmness and control, repetition of fear-induced (physical abuse) cues will trigger old memories and identical behaviors to those displayed under earlier adverse conditions.

Understanding the PTSD "condition" of unavoidable, inescapable, unpredictable abuse (shock) is crucial to the link between PTSD and punishment in ACOAs. Substantially increasing the number or amount of exposure to parental physical abuse in a given time period (i.e., childhood) will *increase the duration and intensity of stressful reactions in adult victims*. But how this happens is more bizarre. The probability of ACOAs currently perceiving harm as adults depends on four interactions between availability, escapability, and predictability that occurred during childhood. These interactions, adopted from Foa et al. (1989), include:

1. The more punishment contingencies contained in the family structure, the more difficult it is to identify and predict them.
2. Anxiety reactions that decrease over repeated exposures to abuse (habituation) and are then reactivated by new punishers at a later childhood time (facilitation) develop into more severe generalized anxiety and somatic problems.
3. Absence of predictability leads to inferences. Inferences produce exaggerated probabilities associated with the feared consequence. When probability estimates come true, no matter how exaggerated, erroneous perceptions continue. Reductions in fear and erroneous perceptions depend on stable, consistent, and predictable interactions.
4. Highly fear-aroused children who display excessive physiological activity are afraid to calm down unless escape is possible or there are clear signs of abuse termination. When these signs are ambiguous or simply do not occur, arousal continues until physical weakness sets in and the person faints or collapses. In adulthood this might cause a propensity for major medical complications, particularly from abdominal pain, constipation, or diarrhea. Such symptoms occurring without any diagnosable physical cause are called *irritable bowel syndrome* (e.g., Blanchard & Schwarz, 1988).

Superstitious Characteristics

ACOAs also display erratic or idiosyncratic behaviors, which at times are discretely connected to ongoing situations. Sensitivity to the suppressive or potentially suppressive environment triggers them to act in ritualistic ways that can be explained behaviorally as *superstitious behavior.* In experimental analysis of behavior, Skinner (1948) first showed patterns of stereotyped responding by food-deprived pigeons given grain on fixed-time schedules of reinforcement. Pigeons developed behaviors not intended by the reinforcer, although the behaviors recurred every time that reinforcer was available. Skinner characterized the acquisition of this responding as a "sort of superstition," because responding followed a ritual and by accident received strength from the reinforcer (Ferster & Skinner, 1957).

Superstitious behaviors have been found in humans for the same reasons (Ferster, Culbertson & Boren, 1975; Hollis, 1973; Skinner, 1977; White & Liu, 1995). Of particular importance were pathological obsessions, compulsions and phobias (e.g., Herrnstein, 1966; Zeiler, 1972). For adults, superstitious or ritualistic behaviors spontaneously emerge for three reasons. First, they occur if accidentally paired with target behaviors for reinforcement. For instance, while waiting for a cab, if adults smoke two cigarettes, pace up and back, and sing to themselves and the cab arrives sooner than usual, the exact same sequence or ritual of behaviors occurs next time a cab is called. Second, superstitious behaviors occur if they immediately follow reinforcement ("adjunctive behaviors"). The person waits for the cab, for example, without peculiar actions. Moments after the cab arrives early and a person enters the cab, dialogue immediately starts with the cab driver where previously no dialogue occurred. A third reason for superstitious or ritualistic behaviors is avoidance and escape behavior. Superstitious rituals derive strength from the delay or removal of aversive events. In avoidance situations, for instance, the person stays inside a building, out of the rain, while waiting for the cab. Habits that form include always waiting inside a building, never on the curb. In escape situations, the cab driver, speaking in a loud or nasty voice, may push the person back into the building or away from the cab. Escape from confrontation becomes a conditioned ritual.

Ultimately, the learning of compulsive, ritualistic or avoidance and escape behaviors arises from mistaken or adventitious conditioning occurring during childhood, as we have already discussed

(Wagner & Morris, 1987). Substance-abusing parents who angrily shock the child into submission and develop generalized fears in the child are also accidentally teaching repetitive, stereotyped actions to that child, who believes superstition will avert the impending punishment.

This author cannot overstate the principle governing ritualistic or superstitious behavior based on perfectionism. A young child's behaviors never occur for specific reinforcers. Superstitious behavior is not reinforcer-driven. Behaviors are not learned for a specific reward or reinforcer simply because (a) there are few or no reinforcers available, (b) if available, they are random, arbitrary and unpredictable, (c) reinforcers always pair with punishers, and (d) reinforcers never are trusted as being reinforcers. For example, after an aggressively violent mother cools down and offers her child ice cream for smiling and being happy, that ice cream hardly functions to motivate smiles and happiness. A very frightened child is doing everything possible to show smiles and happiness to avoid the mother's repetitive violence. Nothing about the ice cream is reinforcing (i.e., increasing smile and happiness behavior).

Avoidance and Escape Characteristics

The terms "avoidance" and "escape" are common in behavioral literature. Traditional learning theorists (e.g., Dollard & Miller, 1950; Mowrer, 1950; Solomon & Wynne, 1954), as well as their applied counterparts (e.g., Eysenck, 1979; Stampfl & Levis, 1967; Wolpe, 1958) have proposed that psychological symptoms can be conceptualized as avoidance behaviors when they produce two changes: Either responses prevent contact with an aversive event, or, in the case of escape paradigms, responses immediately cause termination or suspension of aversive conditioned stimuli (Denny, 1991; Domjan, 1996; Falls & Davis, 1995; Ulrich, Holz & Azrin, 1964).

Human laboratory experiments attesting to this phenomena (Banks, 1965; Mallow & Levis, 1988; Maxwell, Miller & Meyer,

1971; Sidman, 1962) repeatedly show that persistence of avoidance and escape patterns even in the absence of danger, relates to a history of conditioning and intermittent contact with fearful stimuli. Operationally, avoidance and escape refer to response-producing changes that terminate the fearful, aversive event. *Termination* takes several forms. Responses may:

1. Delay the impending aversive event.
2. Alter the impending aversive event before it arrives.
3. Eliminate the impending aversive event before it arrives.
4. Interrupt the aversive event while it occurs.
5. Alter the aversive event while it occurs.
6. Eliminate the aversive event while it occurs.

Ecobehavioral Characteristics

Within the ecosystems model, certain propositions explain the extent of family adaptability and cohesion depending upon the openness or closeness of boundaries (Ruben, 1992b). A boundary, defined simply, is a region between systems that separates one system from another one in either physical, material, or symbolic form. Open boundaries (systems) allow for interaction and transaction with other systems. Closed boundaries restrict or prevent interaction with other systems. Boundaries also may be random (arbitrarily closed and open). Given these variations, note the following six propositions on family ecosystems:

1. The adaptability, and hence viability, of a family system is related positively to the amount of variety in the system.

2. Undue energy demands upon a family result in a lessened ability for adaptive, creative behavior, and can result in stress on the family system.

3. The rigidity of the boundaries around a family system will influence the family's to adapt to stressful situations.

4. The ambiguity of the boundaries around a family system will influence the family's adaptability.
5. The family members who control the information coming into the family and who control the family "memory" have greater ability to control the behavior of other family members.
6. Family systems that are moderately cohesive but allow for individual autonomy are more able to adapt to change and stress than those in which family members are very tightly bound to each other or those in which there is little cohesion and everyone goes his or her own way.

Propositions 2, 3, 4, & 5 are particularly germane for ACOAs. Boundary regulations limit children from autonomously expressing opinion and from having transactions outside of proximal boundaries. For instance, suspicious parents may question their children on what other adults said to them about their behavior, and will presume the children are lying. Alcoholic families limit boundaries by limiting "resources." When resources communicated to children are ambiguous, the children never properly develop or satisfy basic needs that likely are met in nondysfunctional families. One type of a regulated resource is "exchange" of interaction. Exchange pertains to parenting styles or discipline used on the children.

In ecological terms, exchange of resources usually means that parents grant money, gifts, or special accolades to children for many reasons. Noneconomic resources such as love and caring also may be transferred. In both cases the exchange is unconditional or noncontingent; the child owes nothing in return for the gift. In alcoholic families the exchange not only is contingent, but noneconomic resources such as love and caring are a scarcity. Affection and love, if given, come at a stiff price of compliance to rigid, unrealistic expectations. Such high expectations, however, are rarely reached and instead children receive punishment.

On a systems level, punishment disrupts this exchange system. Denial of support, of affection, and of noneconomic resources distances children from parents, from siblings and from the human behavioral environment outside the family. Punishment also closes boundaries around a child's potential, forcing unavoidable and inescapable fear. While dysfunctional parents believe this maintains family control, in effect the control invalidates the child's self-purpose, stifles his learning opportunities, and largely instills hostility toward the parents. Anger that reaches a certain peak takes the form of acting-out behavior.

Family discordance thus intensifies when noneconomic exchange of resources is infrequent. In alcoholic families, systems theory elucidates the steps of this gradual deterioration by viewing each member in relation to one another. As barriers to adaptation increase, intrafamily relations crumble and the child has a non-goal-directed perception of the world. Families torn by this chaos lose their core values and their interest in saving the family system. This inevitable decay sets the stage for children to repeat learned defective intergenerational patterns in their own family life cycles.

Application of Exchange Theory to ACOAs In alcoholic families, where one or more members are alcoholics, resource exchange is both conditional and unconditional. Goods and services are transferred or not transferred and may involve a high price for the barter. Effective and reciprocal exchanges maintain equilibrium. Ineffective and inconsistent exchanges disrupt the family balance, causing gradually progressive deterioration in interpersonal relationships.

Using Foa & Foa's (1974, 1980) social exchange theory, early indicators of family alcoholism are plentiful. From the perspective of a child, patterns may arise based on the rules of exchange and become very noticeable to observers. Teachers, other parents, and clinicians may discover warning signs over time rather than from isolated episodes. Warning signs reflecting a breakdown of family exchanges is possible to predict if we make a slight change in Foa

& Foa's model. While Foa & Foa call love, money, and status "positive resources," we will call them "rewards" (rewarding exchanges). While they consider physical abuse, verbal abuse, and hate other resource, we will call them "punishers" (punishing exchanges).

With these changes in mind, consider the following revised "rules of the game" for a clearer picture of intrafamily dynamics coexisting between parent and child in terms of rewarding and punishing exchanges.

1. *The larger the amount of rewards possessed by a person, the more likely it is to be given to others.* An abundant supply of resources selfishly guarded by parents is a form of control. In dysfunctional families, abundance of supplies does not threaten resource shortages and egocentric parents can afford giving rewards to children without feeling themselves "robbed" or sacrificed. Self-sacrificing love, money, or other accolades are inconsistent with addictive parents or family members strongly protective of their own needs.

2. *The smaller the amount of rewards possessed by a person, the more he or she is likely take it away from others.* Limited resources in a selfish family member's possession are guarded. Family members are greedy, fearful of losing their supply, and selective about which resources to donate. Hoarding resources, in effect, protects the parents from feeling vulnerable, out of control, and risking that their children will grow "spoiled," thereby demanding more resources from the parents' supply.

3. *The nearer two rewarding resources are, the more likely they are to be exchanged with one another. The nearer two punishing resources are, the more they are to be avoided.* Rewarding resources never occur in isolation. Money and love, for example, become united holistically as a larger reward. Children may grow accustomed to receiving one rewarding resource with another resource. Failure to supply one resource without the other feels unnatural. For example, frequently dysfunctional parents show their love exclusively

through gifts rather than physical or verbal affection. Gifts paired with "love" are dually exchanged, so that the occurrence of one reward invokes expectations to receive the other reward.

By contrast, giving punishers may occur by proximity and contiguity. Proximity refers spatially to object closeness, whereby one punisher follows sequentially after another punisher; order of sequence is both reversible and irreversible. Verbal yelling, for example, may precede spanking, or vice versa. Contiguity refers to simultaneity. Two punishing resources coexisting simultaneously in time and space exert greater impact on receivers. Yelling and spanking occurring together, for example, frighten a child more than when both punishers are sequential.

Still, whether they occur sequentially or simultaneously, receivers (e.g., children) are prone to avoid the punishing resources. Avoidance may take several forms. One form is silence, withdrawal, and recession of any behavior to private levels, that is, thinking. A second result of oppression is outward aggression; children who argue, debate, or passively-aggressively sabotage communication may hate conflict but find their yelling terminates adversity immediately.

4. *The nearer to love a rewarding resource is, the more likely it is to be exchanged with the same resource. The nearer to love a punishing resource is, the more love and the punishing resource will be avoided. Love is exchanged for love except if punishers are present.* Love displayed as a physical, verbal, or material resource along with another rewarding resource is apt to be mutually exchanged between giver and receiver. These rewards carry similar "weight" and pose little risk for a dysfunctional parent to give to his or her child, knowing the same amount of reward is received in return. When love is contiguous or proximal with punishers, children avoid both rewarding and punishing resources in spite of a past history of seeking and attaining the rewarding resource. Eating a meal, for instance, is a rewarding resource (e.g., food). However, when food intake frequently coincides with angry parents verbally or physically assaulting the child at the table, food is avoided.

Varying conditions may increase or decrease this propensity for avoidance. For example, children who are extremely hungry (i.e., in a state of deprivation) may approach the punisher faster and endure the punisher for a longer duration than nonhungry (satiated) children.

5. *The nearer to love a punishing resource is, the narrower the range of resources with which it is likely to be exchanged.* Love paired with punishing resources discourages a family member to exchange that love for another resource. Avoidance of punishing resources not only prevents contact with family members giving those punishers, it also suppresses love, affection, or any rewarding resource typically exchanged for love. Punishment inadvertently has three effects, none of which encourage love: (a) it decreases overall effort and caring; (b) it inhibits asking the punishing resource giver anything; and (c) it produces inappropriate, aggressive or passive-aggressive responses, further replacing love and affection.

6. *For resources closer to money or any other rewards, the amount lost by the giver tends to approach the amount gained by the receiver (so that one's gain is another's loss).* A serious problem in dysfunctional families is resource imbalance. Breakdowns in family economic systems occur when a disproportionate amount of rewarding resources is allocated to family members. One child may receive more love; others may receive no love. Distribution of rewarding resources is arbitrary and random in response to the impulsive lifestyles of addictive parents. Children find it difficult to predict when they are in favor or when they will be deprived. Teens who complain of their drinking parents' unreliable payment of allowance or food for dinner, for example, usually are confused from one day to the next.

7. *When a rewarding resource is not available for exchange, it is more likely to be submitted by a less particular person than by a more particular person.* Rewarding resources are rare commodities in a dysfunctional family economy. When they are presented, rewards are superficial, temporary, and lack enthusiasm. Less particular in

a giver means the resource is uneventful and that givers are casual, nonchalant, or even aloof about reward exchanges. In nonaddictive families, rewards are given with intentionality, caring, and affection.

8. *The simultaneous transmission of love and a rewarding resource increases the value of the rewarding resource, or facilitates its transmission. The simultaneous transmission of love and a punishing resource decreases the value of both resources, or terminates their transmission.* As suggested earlier, variables of simultaneity and proximity greatly determine the value of resources exchanged. Rewarding resources paired with love intensify the rewarding resources, further attracting interest and enabling equitable transfers of the rewarding resources between family members. Love paired with punishment has the opposite effect. Punishers delay and prevent family members from wanting an exchange; they avoid exchanges in spite of their state of deprivation.

9. *Taking away any resource (including love) produces a loss of love and produces punishers.* Families who place a premium on resources instead of sharing them equally are prone to penalize members who jeopardize the resources. When rewarding resources are limited, removed, or contaminated (e.g., ruined), the penalty is retribution. Dysfunctional parents aggressively blame, shame, and physically torment children believed to be the culprits of reward cessation.

10. *The optimal range (neither too little or too much) of a resource is narrowest for rewards, and increases progressively for resources closest to money. Punishers in the way of money decrease exchange of resources closest to money.* Rewarding resources are distributed sparingly. Optimal ranges of resource exchange in dysfunctional families is either too little or too much depending on the parents' impulsive needs at the time. Parents who run out of marijuana, for example, may spend money replenishing their supply rather than on dinner for the kids. Few options are considered. As money increases, rewarding resources are more generously given and, for example, purchases of both marijuana and dinner occur.

Punishers exchanged with money follow a different trajectory. Punishing resources paired with monetary resources can sabotage or terminate the exchange from the outset. For example, if asking for money means a child must receive a beating, be interrogated, or be shamed into thinking that money will be misspent, requests for money immediately stop.

11. *In the absence of an exchange, the amount of love possessed and rewarding resources decrease, and the amount of love is lower for people closer to love.* Troubled families scarcely show exchanges of love. Reduction of love exchanges to the point of nonexistence has two effects. First, any rewarding resource in general—whether paired with love or not—deteriorates to the point of oblivion. It simply loses its potency and no longer functionally occurs between family members. Second, loss of love, affection, or compassion in the primary family prompts a search for rewarding resources outside families. Examples are when neglected and abused children "adopt" a surrogate parent or fiend's parent, who generously invites the child over frequently for meals and nights, or when neglected and abused spouses engage in infidelity to fill a void of love in their marriage.

12. *Other conditions being equal, the probability of occurrence of a given exchange (rewards and punishers) is contingent upon the family economy in which it may take place.* This is a general postulate stating that family dynamics entirely control the frequency and value of rewarding and punishing exchanges. In alcoholic families, exchanges are unilateral, inconsistent, unreliable, and consist primarily of punishing resources based on a context of distrust, greed, and impulsivity. In nondysfunctional families, balanced exchanges derive from a cohesion between family members and equal use of punishing and rewarding resources.

13. *The probability of reward and punisher exchange is higher in small families. The opposite is true for larger families in which different members of the family may serve as surrogate-parent givers of rewards and punishers.* Size of the family is a critical variable in

predicting distribution of resources. Small, close families of four people (parents, two children) risk little competition and obstacles in equally benefiting from resources. Members receive individualized exchanges from the primary parent. In larger families, distribution of resources from primary parent may be tedious, and resources can be exhausted before all the children receive equal amounts. In dysfunctional families, size of family also plays a role but is complicated by nepotism. A child from either a large or small family perceived as a "helper" will be given preference and receive resources before another member perceived as a "scapegoat" or "follower." Labeled children who fall out of favor are relegated a lesser number of resources and fewer rewarding resources.

When "helpers" are mobilized to act as surrogate parents, they may not be sympathetic to neglected siblings who are scapegoats and followers. Rather, helpers replicate parental attitudes and behaviors snubbing the unfavored siblings and may withhold rewarding resources for themselves. Or, they may put the unfavored siblings through extensive labor before the favored child receives rewards. When received, rewarding resources are "leftovers" or inferior portions of the rewarding resources.

In sum, social exchange theory provides a viable paradigm to explore the interplay of economic and social factors in family life. Love, fear, and other qualities transfer from one family member to the next, with expectations that similar qualities will be equally reciprocal. Failure of this reciprocity means there is family disparity, marked not only by poor communication but by decomposition of love, affection, and general caring. In the case of alcoholic families, resources deliberately withheld or randomly allocated disrupt family trust and inherently engender a search outside the family for rewarding resources.

Exchange theory further provides the behavioral systems tools required for developing the line of thinking that ACOA families operate on a contingency. It spells out the scientific logic predicting family dysregulation and early childhood maladaptivity. From operationalism to laws of exchange, ACOA etiology judiciously undertakes the mission of debunking myths, folklore, or reifications spiraling from unfounded theories. It shows that ACOAs are both easily understandable and potentially very treatable. The chapters ahead will focus on personalities and family behavioral dynamics that pose unique problems in assessment.

CHAPTER 3

Behavioral Patterns of the ACOA Syndrome

Robb's (2000) satire on people labeling themselves members of a "problem" group reflects a common fallacy believed by many clients and professionals alike. The belief is that human fallibilities are symptoms of a disease acquired simply by association with other people exhibiting similar fallibilities. For example, victims of domestic violence uniformly share their misandry with other victims; conversely, falsely accused domestic perpetrators commiserate in their misogyny. So, too, recovering narcotic abusers identify with others abstainers sharing similar addiction backgrounds. Probationers and parolees, as well, do the same thing. Released prisoners gravitate toward other ex-cons who understand miscarriages of the judicial system or share stories of survivalism while incarcerated. "Belonging to the "politically correct" group is a universal phenomenon predictably observed among factions of people with common denominators—from similarities in ethnicity, culture, and religion to medical conditions (e.g., cancer, diabetes, liver disease, etc.).

Grouping people by similar diagnostic attributes, on the downside, risks stereotyping personalities. Gross generalizations about group behaviors can distort empirical analyses and mislead practitioners into unfounded conclusions about treatment choices. Professional guides designed to reduce this observer bias, such as the DSM–IV, provide taxonomic definitions presumably based on research studies that correlate similar emotional and personality disorders. Criteria-based response typologies replace subjective interpretation in symptom evaluation. To reach this objective standard, personality research usually begins with heuristic theories that sort idiosyncratic from causal response patterns. Personality theories that employ operational definitions systematically rule out irrelevant and inconsistent response patterns, and quantify the functional relationships among relevant and consistent response patterns. The end product, naturally, is to validate behavioral symptoms for making accurate clinical assessment.

In studying ACOA response patterns, careful attention must be paid to evaluate functional interrelationships among response sequences and complex contingencies. Functional analysis avoids the trap of stereotyping personalities. As such, current investigative efforts take a scientific approach but lack clear functional analyses (Brown & Lewis, 1999; L'Abate, 1998). This chapter, alternatively, facilitates several functional analyses on ACOA symptoms by dividing pervasive patterns into twenty behavioral categories, which largely comprise the ACOA syndrome. Personality categories integrate complex developmental and social contingencies shaping the ACOA since childhood. ACOAs exhibiting these patterns typically are oblivious to the detrimental effects of their maladjustment and have habituated to the normalcy and infinite labyrinth of avoidance behaviors.

Pathological Response Patterns of ACOAs

Caretaking or Enabling

Caretaking means avoidance. Adults afraid of conflict or acting selfishly for fear of peer disapproval will resort to accommodation. Compromising personal needs occurs so frequently and habitually that no longer is the forfeited need considered a loss. Sacrifices become a natural, familiar operation in daily interaction, much like breathing, eating, and sleeping. Without realizing it, caretakers operate entirely on negative reinforcement. Pleasing, satisfying, or absorbing grief for people delays, alters, and destroys impending aversive events and consequently encourages the same behavior in the future. Confirmation comes in the (a) amount of time elapsed before another conflict (the longer, the better), (b) the mild or diminished intensity of arguments when they occur, (c) the shorter duration of arguments, and (d) the recuperative capacity of the arguer.

Because dealing with aversive events is awful, false alarms are common mistakes and are acted upon in the same way. False alarms involve believing there is a potential argument brewing and intercepting it beforehand. Avoidance this far ahead creates the false inference that had steps not been taken, conflict might arise. Ensuing conflicts may or may not occur, whereas avoidance automatically speeds into motion long before risk of conflict. Predators on the receiving end of this intervention are neither perplexed nor willing to reverse the caretaking tactics. A fearful husband, for example, anticipating his wife's critical words over a recent office purchase, lavishes his wife with bouquets, "I love you" cards, and takes her out to dinner. All efforts assumingly are designed to avoid his wife's cynical remarks long before she learned of the purchases. This may be called *anticipatory caretaking*. Planning ahead seems safe but it is no guarantee of conflict elimination. In fact, his wife may thrive on the voluminous reinforcers and may expect this complimentary treatment to be repeated, regardless of her intentions of conflict. Evoking her husband's repeat behavior may be as simple as uttering sarcastic remarks or always finding fault in him. His passive obedience in response to conflict-warning signals negatively reinforces excessive, overcompensatory behaviors.

So, too, caretaking—also called "enabling"—functions on variable schedules of establishing operations. Discriminative cues signal not only impending conflict but are antecedents to elevated autonomic arousal or "anxiety." Escalated fears activate sensory and cardiovascular effects, producing increased respiration, circulation, and perceptual acuity. Bordering on panic attacks, rising anxiety is stopped by insisting on altruistic actions. Terrified ACOAs may persist indignantly and obsessively, and almost appear aggressive in their stubborn determination to pacify the perceived predator. Persistence rises as the perceived predator resists or criticizes the benevolent overtures. For example, expecting that her boyfriend may yell at her, an anxious woman may insist that she and her boyfriend go out for dinner despite the boyfriend's repeated protests against dining out. The motivational force underlying the woman's insistence is to reduce her anxiety brought on by anticipatory fears of confrontation.

Anticipatory caretaking usually is a methodical, systematic, and incredibly calibrated effort. ACOAs insightfully evaluate potential for aversive contact and immediately disinfect the situation in much the same way as ecologists pour cleaning solutions into polluted waters. Every connected step in the avoidance sequence has a history of effectively altering one, many, or all of the predator's responses leading to confrontation. Synchronicity becomes imperative. A wife expecting her drunken husband to be physically abusive may, ahead of time, rearrange the furniture, call a friend (witness) over, evacuate the children to their bedrooms or get them out of the house, and prepare a meal of his liking. These tasks all have specific functional reasons and must occur in this precise order. Calculated risks are not tolerated in the overall scheme of avoidance. Failure to produce these sequentially coordinated activities may or may not delay punishing outcomes, since the predator's behaviors could be unpredictable. Consequently, ACOAs develop ritualistic, superstitious, or obsessive behaviors when estimates of aversive control are unreliable or inconsistent.

Caretaking also entails an unusual degree of empathy. *Empathy* enjoys wide recognition as a human asset. Empathizers who are sensitive to people's emotions come to vicariously experience the feelings, sufferings, or situation of another person without these feelings being communicated by words. Love, anger, elation, sadness—all apparently observed independently—are internally identified, presumably without the empathizer being exposed to similar stimulus conditions or without his having a similar reactional biography as the other person. However, in the case of ACOAs, empathy occurs at an alarmingly high rate, with uncanny precision. ACOAs are not simply vicarious; their vicarious arousal is amplified through a compulsive drive to absorb the entire suffering inside another person. Attraction to people in distress and subsequently trying to erase the sufferer's misery is called "rescuing."

Rescue behaviors arise for three reasons. First, what appears *vicarious* is actually a conspicuous form of stimulus generalization. ACOAs respond urgently to distress signals in people displaying pain or suffering mood swings, since these patterns precisely duplicate the ACOA's own past history of misery. Because the ACOA's history of symptoms involved highly charged aversive consequences, the act of vicariously experiencing another person's trauma includes fear. This mobilizes ACOAs to rapidly eliminate the person's hurt feelings so they can eliminate their own anxious feelings. Fears associated with "self-rules" may propel stronger rescuing efforts, which will be discussed in the next chapter.

A second reason for excitable vicarious responses is *conditioned protection*. Dysfunctionally raised children scolded for neglecting care of their younger or even older siblings may suffer additional punishment by witnessing the unsupervised siblings being spanked, criticized, or abused. Blamed for the siblings being beaten, the young ACOA unequivocally learns responsibility for the punishment and subsequently becomes hypersensitive to close friends and relatives tormented by life traumas. ACOAs feel obligated and responsible to rescue the other person from suffering before both the person and ACOA gets blamed for negligence. ACOAs may strategically and excessively protect perceived victims by escorting them to therapy or nurturing their emotional wounds, thereby fulfilling a duty and freeing themselves from recriminations.

A third reason for vicarious caretaking deals with pride. Personified meanings of pride typically abound as "self-respect," "dignity," and "delight in self-achievements." Pride historically involves "feeling worthy," "deserving," and self-efficacious. Pride for ACOAs takes on a very different connotation by its unusual prohibition of selfishness and obsession for social approval. Inherently, pride is tantamount to conceit and arrogance. Rather than feeling deserving, ACOAs never feel deserving or even special, but they can redeem themselves by the value another person places on them. Perceived self-esteem rises when people the ACOAs rescue are grateful and praise the ACOA for being dedicated. Verbal reinforcement, *functionally,* is a powerfully evocative stimulus for response overexertion. ACOAs invest countless hours and unlimited energy in solving mild to severe life problems for other people without serious exhaustion or frustration.

Contrary to the ratio strain theory of response diminishment (Green, Sanders & Squier, 1959), ACOAs do not slow down their pace or stop rescuing efforts despite exhaustive or oppressive responding. The consequences for response decrements may be unbearably humiliating, and thus they act compulsively to control these unpredictable contingencies. As verbal reinforcers increase, ACOAs recover from fatigue and renew their laborious, workaholic efforts. This rapid recuperative behavior is analogous to conditioned suppression effects of dogs under forced exposure to reinforcement. Helplessness in the dogs dissipated over time, but complete recovery occurred when responses that activated reinforcers competed with avoidance and escape behaviors (e.g., Seligman, Maier & Geer, 1968).

The potency of rescuing typically is confused with love. A 35-year-old man tired of dating uncaring women discovered he repeated the mistake of mislabeling caretaking as falling in love. His cyclical pattern of making a good first impression involved (a) over-spending on the first date, (b) immediately offering his home-maintenance services, and (c) catering to the female partner's incessant requests, no matter how unusual or inconvenient. As partners reinforced his generosity either romantically or by lavish praise, the client felt emotionally intoxicated with pride and perceived his being indispensable to the partner. Rescuing overtures tripled over the next several weeks, proving his unsurpassed loyalty and affection, but largely, he felt his efforts represented his degree of caring. Predictably, rescuing responses never were reciprocal, and eventually he felt insulted by manipulative partners benefiting from his caretaking while they dated other men.

Aggression

As alluded to previously, caretaking can look like aggression. Why is this? ACOAs are not impervious to anger but they rarely get upset unless several contingencies intermingle. First, anger arises in response to loss of control; ACOAs are afraid of exposing their vulnerability. *Vulnerability* means skill deficits that are blatantly conspicuous despite concerted efforts to conceal them. Second, anticipating conflict, anger triggers the predators to stay away (avoidance) or terminate conflict (escape). Anger rarely involves disclosure of emotional frustrations as might occur in most people expressing anger. Non-ACOAs accept vulnerability as a mature outgrowth of being fallible. ACOAs, on the other hand, carefully suppress anger manifested from vulnerability, and only release anger to eliminate conflict. Threats of physical retaliation, profuse vulgarity, hostile demands, and abrasive criticism on the surface may resemble aggression and thus lure the listener into fierce battle. But just the opposite is occurring. Insulting attacks intend to dismantle the listener from responding in any way.

A byproduct of mismanaged anger is *anticipatory aggression*. Less calculated and more reflexive are aggressive assaults made in anticipation of conflict. Like *anticipatory caretaking,* conflict looms on the horizon but is not definite. ACOAs' history of conditioning and inability to escape from anxiety compels overreaction. They become hostile while waiting for conflict. Poor control over emotions sets off a series of physiological, cognitive, and behavioral responses that sequentially follow this format: (a) autonomic arousal (rapid heart beat, tightness of chest, perspiration, shallow breathing, etc.), (b) negative, paranoid-like statements ("who does he think he is," "nobody will blame me for anything," etc.), and (c) outward aggressive actions (yelling, hitting objects, stomping around, etc.).

Arousal is impulsive, progressive, and lacks sensitivity to immediate consequences. In the end, hostile actions produce one of three outcome in listeners. First, listeners never approach the aggressor out of shock and perplexity. Explosive anger stifles them into submission. Second, as the conflict emerges, listeners stop the argument instantly, appearing offended and perplexed by the rude interjections. Or third, annoyed listeners pursue the conflict perpetuated inadvertently by ACOAs. Escalating conflict accelerates aggressiveness in both parties until the ACOA, now desperate for escape, resorts to physical property destruction, injury toward another, or threats of self-injury. Family court cases of domestic violence, for example, frequently include intraspousal altercations that begin with one spouse provoking reciprocal assaults from another spouse. Ironically, neither spouse may have physical abuse histories or come from violent households. Instead, one spouse, the ACOA, may react in a hostile manner to derail anticipatory conflict, thus setting off the passive, docile spouse who never planned to get angry.

Anticipatory aggression stems from indiscriminant learning. Randomly punished children develop anxiety symptoms in adulthood over the uncertainty of which stimuli—relevant or irrelevant—may signal onset of aversive conditions. For example, a twenty-year-old son living at home explosively blows up at the mere mention of his getting a job. His parents appear stunned by the disrespectful outburst, considering that their son has no history of reactionary behaviors. However, oppositional behavior is no surprise when the son's past career efforts backfire and his parents shamelessly reprimand him for every job loss. He comes to expect abrasive criticism on a continuous schedule. Lacking healthy interpersonal skills, the oppressed son rapidly exhausts his limited repertoire of responses. Once he is helpless, anger substitutes for healthy skills and serves to terminate (escape from) discussions about jobs or careers. Years later, one facial expression or word hinting onset of career topics triggers the son's agitative responses.

Anxiety and Panic

Negative reinforcement occurs in a third way. When conflict is pending, panic and anxiety typically arise. Reduction of anxiety by avoiding and escaping conflict does not obliterate the problem; rather, it fortifies the problem. Responses that terminate anxiety reinforce more anxiety or panic in future situations. Panic, as in panic attacks, builds from unregulated excitement of the sympathetic nervous system under fearful situations. Dizziness, loss of breath or rapid breathing, weakness in limbs, tachycardia, ear and eye sensitivity comprise symptomatology that triggers an urgent need for escape. Failure to leave the situation prolongs the physical misery and turns into *catastrophizing* thoughts; fears abound about fainting, being disabled, or being dreadfully embarrassed.

ACOAs who expect conflict therefore react by suffering panic attacks moments before or just after conflict starts. Displays of panic pivot the predator's actions from possible assault to sympathy. ACOAs who report panic episodes at the outset of arguments receive compassion from even a callus spouse, in turn eliminating adverse conditions and restoring peacefulness for the ACOA.

Lack of Communication

Anxiety-producing avoidance may also silence the ACOA. No communication occurs when ACOAs remain mute under any impending threat of conflict. Attempts to penetrate this silence are met with poor eye contact, crying, or staring into space. Self-inhibition accomplishes two goals. The first goal is preventing further antagonism from perceived predators. ACOAs withhold opinions hoping to avert acrimony and to create a diversion for confronters. The diversion is stimulating predator compassion by crying or appearing depressed, which inadvertently reinforces the predator's motivation for being angry. Reasons for predator anger may include subverting, shaming, or subjecting the ACOA to submission. For example, docile spouses who easily cry when critically confronted for infractions either may deflect the angry spouse to repulsion, or empathy or agitate the spouse into domestically abusive rages where the spouse appears to "feed off of the ACOA's passivity."

A second goal of intentional self-inhibition is protecting a myriad of avoidant behaviors deceptively interconnected and unknown to the predator. ACOAs who establish a complex matrix of response sequences spanning days, months, or even years may be especially cautious to guard against exposure of these secrets, the revelation of which may cause emotionally irrevocable consequences. One middle-age woman, for example, carried on an affair for two years before divorcing her husband. She kept the infidelity secretive both during the marriage and for 10 years after the marriage by meticulously arranging meeting places where the romantic couple was inconspicuous. She either remained silent or lied about her whereabouts to friends and families with such aptitude that her lies became truths in the minds of others. By the time she decided to marry her lover, and when faced with exposing her decade of lies and deceptions, she refused to proceed with the marriage and deemed that the lies must be preserved to prevent confrontation.

Running Away

Running away means an ACOA takes refuge by physically escaping to another location. Relocation can be to their parents' house, a friend's house, a bar, or driving long distances in unspecified directions. Runaways emerge longitudinally from adolescent conditioning, where argument defusal involved the child literally leaving the house. Destinations varied, although they typically were at same-sex friends' homes. But they were always engendered by escalative parent-child altercations. After a period of self-imposed "time out," the returning child typically gained sympathy (verbal reinforcers) from worried parents, and consequently the reunion restored family equilibrium. As the grown-up child eventually marries partners resembling one or both parents, repertoire reproduction effects are inevitable. Runaways generalize their escape behaviors when faced with marital discord, regardless of how minor the argument is.

Self-removal from perceived hostile conditions progressively increases as four factors occur. First, as in childhood, the spouse is apologetic, sympathetic, or compassionate following the ACOA's return. Second, the refuge sought is sympathetic, nurturing, or provides anxiety relief. That is, the ACOA's friends, family or whoever harbors this fugitive remain unconditionally reinforcing. Third, duration of time away from the hostile environment synchronizes with the ACOA's ritualistic and sequential actions of (a) verbalizing himself as a victim, (b) intensifying work or personal productivity, (c) executing unilateral decisions, and (d) restoring perceived self-control.

For example, a recent newlywed prone to runaways left her home every time her husband questioned her about overspending the credit card limit. His inquiries typically were civil, affectionate, and respectable, but nonetheless simulated a conflict situation. She either interrupted his inquiry to leave the house or left in anticipation of their financial discussions. Her protectors, childhood girlfriends, comforted the ACOA, reassured her, and inspired her to take charge of her life. While away from home, the ACOA always completed her backlog of work-related reports, communicated astutely and intellectually with other professionals, restored a vigilant exercise regimen, and overall felt invincible from anxiety. She repeated this cycle every time marital arguments arose.

Substance Abuse

Abusing substances may escalate to such rarefied heights that every drink, smoke, or pill-taking response becomes cosmic, Inebriation eliminates not just fear but the most fearsome tyrant—the person himself or herself. Contingent use of substance abuse usually means the ACOA only engages in substances under emotional duress or when conflict is unavoidable or inescapable. Two predictable benefits of poyldrug abuse occur. First is risk reduction; the second is tranquilization. In the first case, alcohol or drug consumption disinhibits nearly asphyxiating levels of anxiety. Artificial courage replaces cowardice. Drug-using ACOAs feel invincible to social criticism and spontaneously become audacious and gregarious. They rampantly circumvent interpersonal phobias suffered when not using drugs, and emit responses out of their ordinary repertoire. Maintaining an engrossing focus, disinhibited ACOAs transform behavior into a psychological free-for-all where they are impulsive, inventive, and stunningly original. Self-assertiveness explodes in sly wit, allurement, and fortitude.

This uncustomary behavior, however, does have some origin. While typically absent in sober behavior, this burst of sultry and tenacious behavior arises from the supplier of most verbal transcripts that later get converted into self-rules: the parents. Shamelessly critical parents whose confrontations literally scared their children into passive submission during childhood left an indelible behavioral impression. Antipathy played a role, perhaps, but the more multicausitive effect was providing an intraverbal sequence of responses "coded" with evocative reactions. The "coding" loosely refers to inherently subtle but powerfully controlling variables that come into play when ACOAs unknowingly imitate a parent's aggressive behavior. Imitation evokes concurrent responses in the ACOA, including: (a) auditory cues, which sound like the parent; (b) cardiovascular cues, which feel like the ACOA pictured his parents feeling; (c) cardiovascular cues, which feel like the ACOA felt as a victimized child listening to the cues; and (d) visual cues of the listener's submissive or aggressive reaction. To the extent that any of these auditory, cardiovascular (or other sensory), and visual cues feel "normal," motivation occurs for repeating the sensory effects via alcohol or drugs.

A second underlying effect of polydrug abuse is sedation. Normally anxious, aggressive, obsessive, or emotionally excessive ACOAs may enjoy the sensory relaxation acquired from effects of muscular and glandular dilation. These effects create a temporary euphoria, so that the tense person can think more slowly, more calmly, and feel impervious to emotional pain. Catalytic changes transform rigidly moralistic "prudes" into sultry, exotic lovers, or defuse the vitriolic machismo aggressor into a tamed, sensitive caretaker. Opposite personalities unfold that otherwise are anathema in the ACOA's nondrug using state. This happens because the sedative side effects of intoxication are only reinforcing when the person cannot experience aversive consequences of the side effects. Happiness, cheerfulness, and vulnerability are reinforcing sedative effects; but in abstinent states, these behaviors may provoke odious consequences. For example, emotionally elated and optimistic ACOAs were sharply criticized in childhood for appearing irresponsible, inefficient, and "apparently enjoying themselves when there is real work to be done." An infusion of guilt associated with healthy self-efficacious thinking scared the ACOA out of enjoying "too much fun" and taught him to always anticipate that "happiness" brings untoward consequences "if you're not too careful." Consequently, cheerful and spontaneously bohemian behaviors pose grave fears of impending doom and are avoided, or greatly diminished, at all cost. The only time ACOAs become slightly slapstick, humorous, playful, and unintimidated by unforeseen emotional dangers is when alcohol or drugs inoculate their fears.

The case of Laura illustrates this metamorphosis. A 25-year-old obsessive-compulsive ACOA raised by alcoholic and rigidly religious parents, Laura learned to passionately abhor socializing. She regarded peer "get-togethers" as wasteful, petty, immature, and beneath her self-ascribed intelligence. She also avoided dating men for the same reason. However, she frequently reported a "hidden" desire for sentiments of Woody Guthrie's communal song "This land is your land," and the Norman Rockwell picture-perfect paeans to the American experience. She forbid herself to attain these goal in a sober state but not when she drank. Binge drinking habits formed over a two-year period, shifting her perspective. While inebriated, she thrived on uplifting, feel-good movies such as *October Sky, Liberty Heights, The Straight Story,* and TV docudramas of original heroes and heroines. When drinking, she stopped exclusively watching CNN, CNBC, and news shows *20/20, 60 minutes, and Nightline.* But her usual TV habits and focus on serious rather than light hearted topics, were restored the moment intoxication wore off.

Emotional Paralysis

Studies on learned helplessness (Seligman & Johnston, 1973) and tonic immobility (Ratner, 1958; Ratner & Thompson, 1968) have application here. The "fight or flight syndrome" operates on the confronted person who feels totally helpless under inescapable or unavoidable circumstances. Lacking adaptive alternatives—they can neither fight nor flee—the person's only repertoire is emotional paralysis, catatonically remaining in the situation without realistic orientation or thoughts. Self-induced numbness overwhelms sensory receptors and inhibits all activating emotional responses. Appearing as if under an hypnotic trance, the immobilized ACOA becomes listless, apathetic, dysphoric, and nonresponsive

Emotional paralysis builds on the learned helplessness and tonic immobility models of complete response cessation under forced exposure to shock. Behaviors "shut down" as the ACOA's thinking circuitry, so to speak, is interrupted by overwhelming skeletomuscular tension. However, just because behavior stops does not mean it extinguishes. Singular or repeated absence of behavior means the behavior still exists but is competing with fear behaviors. No behavior ever extinguishes. It is just in varying degrees of privacy in one situation and subtly generalizable in other situations.

Adolescent twin girls, for example, were subjected to repeated molestation by penile penetration from ages 12 through 15. The alcoholic stepfather was the perpetrator. The girls grew to despise their bodies and hated not only the stepfather but any male peers making sexual overtures toward them. In adulthood, one twin became homosexual, whereas the other twin drank heavily as a platform for excessive sexual promiscuity. However, both girls reported identical symptoms of "going into a stupor, fog, or feeling paralyzed" when confronted sexually by men. They depersonalized themselves to the point of feeling transparent in the situation. Numbness vanished for one twin when inebriated and sexually aerobic. The other twin avoided this emotional paralysis by aggressive sexual advances to women. Their femininity and proclivity for sexual behaviors did not vanish, but rather came under unusual discriminative control.

Selective Attention

This is the opposite of emotional paralysis. Discriminative abilities became sharper under threats of conflict, criticism or rejection. Astute perceptions in thought, sensation, and observation alert the person to subtle behavior changes in the predator that appear modifiable. Once the ACOA determines which responses these are, aversive stimuli can be avoided or escaped. Awareness, for instance, that her spouse forgot to call home ahead of his arrival must mean he stopped at the bar. Inferring this, the wife can alter the environment ahead of his return and demobilize confrontation. Prone to enabling, she rushes to clean the house, orders the kids to start their homework, and creates a "productive and efficient" atmosphere. Sensory arousal heightens when her husband actually gets home. Visual, auditory, and olfactory senses detect alcohol on his breath or behavior irritability. From these behavior samples, she commences a sequence of strategic, damage-control responses, including anticipating her husband's needs and distracting his moods until he is happy or busy.

Passivity

Quietly assuming a passive posture functions like aggression to expedite unwanted predatory attacks. Persons who selectively withhold comments wait for the aggression, criticism, or rejection to end; then they resurrect pleasant topics or divert the discussion rapidly to safe territory. This shift begins by selecting topics interesting or rewarding to the predator, on which he can monologue without relapsing into arguments. Emotional docility gains strength from negative reinforcement of escaping aversive conflict, and from the variables affecting emotional paralysis. However, transactions between the submissive person and antagonist go beyond the two stimulus and response causes. Two other field-integrative interactions occur as well. First, the antagonist's anger escalates in direct proportion to the ACOA's silence. Response properties of docility—such as duration, latency, and intensity—reciprocally covary with the aggressor's response properties.

For example, longer durations perpetuate yelling, while shorter durations reduce anger; a longer time between docile episodes avoids anger while short periods between docile episodes rapidly provoke and maintain anger magnitude; docility accompanied by crying, pleading or fear (e.g., intensity) exacerbates aggression, while docility involving only silence produces episodic rather than continuous outbursts

Furthermore, anger abatement in the aggressor produces conflictual fears. Passive ACOAs who insist they hate aggressors typically experience fundamental comfort around such aggressors; they do not necessarily want the aggressor to stop yelling. When the predator's anger dissipates, the resulting "calm" may engender hysterically grandiose perceptions of impending disaster; ACOAs believe the angry person "is not done with his or her punishment and will return with worse ammunition." Anticipatory fears induce ACOAs to belabor and intensify passive responses to incur an uninterrupted flow of reactionary hostility. Motivation for reinforcing aggressors' behaviors are mixed: They consist of (a) avoidance of and escape from more anger and (b) avoidance of and escape from ephemeral silence predictive of more anger. Consequently, ACOAs cannot imagine not being passive and therefore feel traumatically helpless and out of control.

A college senior ACOA succumbed to this dichotomy. She never overcame shyness from childhood and was interpersonally ineffective at meeting other men and women. When finally together with a male partner, she obediently bowed to his wishes to avert conflict and his disapproval. Her concessional behavior disturbed her boyfriend, who contested it and insisted she "show some anatomy." Avoiding his request, she began crying uncontrollably and could not make eye contact with her boyfriend. His impatience escalated, became frantic, and he scolded her for being weak and inferior. As his sermon subsided, the ACOA's tearfulness reemerged, and whimpering heavily, she ran into the bathroom and locked the door. In response, the boyfriend's attenuated reaction spontaneously reverted to shouting.

Implications of conflictual causal variables for domestic assault are obvious as well. Contrary to victim advocates who almost exclusively blame men for the incidents, case examples strongly support the antithesis. Many passive-dependent ACOA women inadvertently provoke and perpetuate violent male behaviors. Worse yet, they are fearful of living with nonviolent transactions. Diplomatic and healthy communication poses a fear that the violent assailant really does not love them when he is inattentive or nonaggressive. Rather, verbal and physical arguments signify depth of caring and love. Not surprising, victims of domestic abuse who divorce their perpetrators largely risk repeating marriage to homogenic abusers.

Accusation

Accusing the predator of inappropriate behavior ahead of the conflict either starts the conflict or defeats it. Accusations primarily arise for two reasons. First, anxious and annoyed, ACOAs may have improperly inferred information from the predator or environment. Inferences motivate the ACOA to blame perceived predators for violations that the predators question, especially when insufficient evidence supports the heinous accusation. Defensive inquiries rapidly evolve into heated arguments. Second, accusations may emotionally injure or intimidate the alleged predator and thereby disable retaliation or further confrontation. So-called predators stunned by this attack are equally dumbfounded when they "bite the bait" and politely inquire about proof for the accusation. ACOAs retort with vehemently abrasive jabs that entirely ignore peaceful problem-solving efforts and only serve to provoke confrontation. Even reconciliatory efforts from antagonists go unnoticed, since the ACOA is engulfed in self-protection and feels he or she must prove their point just as they did growing up.

Accusatory behavior is also a progenitor of domestic abuse. Rather than remain docile, many ACOAs who fought for attention from their parents in childhood developed a superstitious and distorted mode of interpersonal dialogue. Close verbal intimacy, they believe, involves loud, Socratically debative arguments persistently fought until they exonerate themselves from wrongness or guilt. Anger is explosive, irrational, and directional; the purpose is to incite retaliatory aggressive anger in partners. Disputations, as a result, never recover during a lull or because of both partners' fatigue. Tired challengers are perceived as "weaklings," and "giving up the fight too easily. ACOAs fervently persecute these perceived inferior challengers through verbal and nonverbal scoldings. Escalated reactions occur until the challenger fights back.

Thus, the controlling variables are conspicuous. First, ACOAs' establishing operation of feeling unloved and "at fault" is relieved through combative efforts. Second, ACOAs generate reinforcers associated with love and family by duplicating hostile altercations in challengers, (i.e., that which they experienced growing up with a parent.).

The harrowing look at what led a 15-year-old Oregon boy to murder his parents and then open fire on his fellow students in 1998 offers a good example of learned aggression. The trouble youth's writings and unsettling police videos reveal a predictable tragedy because of parent-endorsing intrafamily violence. Father-son arguments from early childhood were coupled with a growing noncompassion for authority and peer relationships. The youngster learned early on that the only way to acquire nonverbal affection or caring was by verbal violence. As explosive verbal outlets lost luster, the assailant resorted to higher caliber threats and acts of aggression, expecting similar reinforcing outcomes. Just as gambling amounts increase proportional win-loss ratios (reinforcement schedules), so the teen offender increased his "bets of behavior" from innocuous misdemeanors to a shooting spree. Murder became a repertoire-enlarging from of violence to which he was habitually conditioned during his entire life.

Feigning Ignorance

Passivity and emotional paralysis serve to encourage withdrawal from perceived conflict. Another avoidance tactic is pretending one simply is ignorant of facts presented in the conflict. Ignorance liberates the anxious person from justifying answers, coming up with solutions, or dealing in any way with surface anger. Usually the "feigned" reply from ACOAs is offering sympathy, empathy, or just listening as the predator ventilates aggravation.

Pretending ignorance produces another immediate consequence: likeability. Self-effacing ACOAs who outwardly, although deceptively, expose lack of knowledge may be perceived as vulnerable. Ineptitude creates an impression of subordination. The ACOA appears emotionally dependent on controlling predators, who favorably accept the ACOA as inferior and uninsightful. ACOAs who curry favor from friends and lovers alike may actually be quite intelligent but fear that demonstration of their aptitude may provoke conflict. By suppressing intelligence, by faking stupidity, or by deliberately answering questions incorrectly, the smart ACOA avoids unpleasant consequences.

A Ph.D.-level social worker specializing in therapy for sexual dysfunctions presented an unusual case of feigning ignorance. Her therapeutic acumen was impressive, and consequently she enjoyed a growing clinical practice. However, intense sexual phobias entirely transformed her personality from competent professional to an uneducated parasite. Erotophobia and especially eurotophobia (fear of female genitalia) as male partners made advances stimulated hypersensitivity to what her partner would think of her silly fears about sex and body parts. Anxiety-distracting effects inhibited both sexual pleasure and capability for building a subsequent romantic relationship with lovers. Outwardly she masked her fears by laughing it off and purporting to have no idea what was causing her sexual problems. Childhood memories of her drinking mother denouncing her underdeveloped breasts, big hips, and masculine-looking genitalia made her fear that partners would surely see the same thing. It is interesting that her vigilant academic study of sexual aberrations and near perfection of treatment methodology still did not emancipate her from shyness and fear.

Impostorism

One progressive response product that comes from feigning ignorance is impostorism. This is a very serious type of avoidance and escape. Fear of incompetence or of exposing faults that may incur excoriation may force a person into a disguise that masks his true identity. Rather than fake ignorance, the ACOA does just the opposite and fakes wisdom. Faking knowledge or agreeing with things about which the person knows very little or nothing creates the impression of strength, pride and intelligence. However, underneath this charade is the anxious ACOA, fearful that other people will spot their stupidity and discover they are impostors.

The level of actual integrity, of education, or of career advancement is an irrelevant variable in determining how sensitive a person is to impostorism. One woman, a financially secure, executive director of a company with more than 200 employees, and a confident and outspoken lobbyist, struggled against the incipient fear of being discovered by her constituents as incompetent. There was actually nothing incompetent about her other than her self-imposed, persuasive belief that an approving public wanted her to be error-free. Within seconds of presenting speeches, she experienced an undercurrent panic sensation that all eyes were on her and somebody out there would know what she did wrong.

Generalizablity of impostor fear stems from two variables. First, confidence-shattering remarks occurred since childhood on random and arbitrary schedules. Second, anticipated reinforcers were concurrent with punishment, the latter of which left more indelible consequences. Sarcastic, acidic comments delivered unpredictably and inescapably during childhood by addicted parents for any number of appropriate or inappropriate child behaviors damages self-trust. ACOAs consequently never can trust that good efforts produce good outcomes. Rather, distrust magnifies into the cataclysmic belief that "something bad will happen—mark my word on it." Even behaviors generating absolutely good results cannot be trusted. Happiness always must have a sad ending. ACOAs resist positive consequences, knowing the praise is short-lived compared to the imputable, dehumanizing, and emotionally devouring assault yet to come.

Victimization

Self-affliction takes many forms. ACOAs may believe strongly that they are visible targets of cruelty and persecution by other people. Unlike paranoia, ideations are neither grandiose, ruminatory or unrealistic. Functionally adaptive ACOAs who carry on their lives normally simply blame every self-mistake on their inescapable and unavoidable subjugation to external controls. Accusing other people for one's own downfall gains multiple sources of reinforcement. First, externalizing fault liberates the ACOA from taking responsibility for mistakes and thereby suffering elevated episodes of anxiety or depression. Second, outside blame reduces the establishing operation of feeling vulnerable, during which error-prone behavior may occur. ACOAs remain in control and inoculated from fragility by saying somebody else caused their grief. Third, fault-attribution sets up the blamed recipient as fallible, incompetent, and needing a caretaker to remedy his or her shortcomings. ACOAs may unknowingly craft a weak, imperfect partner to reinforce their enabling compulsions, in much the same manner as many Munchhausen-diagnosed child providers induce sickness in their offspring to reinforce paternal compulsions.

Dismissal of culpability appeared in a 45-year-old man raised by alcoholic parents. His repeated job losses, interrupted attempts at higher education, and duplicative relationship failures began taking a toll on his emotions. In a "globalization moment," he came to the conclusion that his problems must be due to bad employers, egregious faculty, and a crop of nasty, unloving partners. Alleging unfair treatment by the world appeared as his ultimate truism. He firmly believed powers beyond his control lay in deceitful, predatorial outsiders determined to ruin his life. When faced with his obvious blunders—for example, that yelling at faculty is politically destructive—the ACOA instantly invented another excuse for why perpetrators "had him by the balls." Denying self-flaws acted as damage control not only to positively reinforce his perfectionistic self-image, but also to negatively reinforce his hyperarousal of distrust and victimization.

Normalcy of Chaos

One of the most severe repercussions of ACOA childhood on marital relationships is *normalcy of chaos*. ACOAs raised in volatile, acrimonious families replete with witnessed episodes of verbal and physical abuse, come to expect identical measures of abuse within their own adult relationships. Conditioned aggression is only one example. Provokers of hostile altercations may turn a passive partner into a domestically assaultive partner by replicating contingencies mistakenly interpreted as love and caring. However, two additional side effects evolve from normalcy of chaos. One may be called *family intensification*. A second hybrid is *reactionary intensification*.

Family intensification involves a calibrated and excessively unrealistic amount of family structure inciting constant rushing and unmet deadlines. Hyperorganization entails rigidly militaristic time management exploiting the 24-7 time clock and the expectation that all family members will conform to this order. Intensified planning creates the false perception of the family not only being in motion but in disequilibrium. Reinforcement occurs as the family matches images of household disorder in the ACOA's childhood. A second reinforcing variable is caretaking as *troubleshooter.* Overplanners who turn the family household upside down thrive on generating temporary solutions to restore family balance. Despite its ephemerality, achievement of order conditions the ACOAs to repeat superfluous planning in the future.

Reactionary intensification, affectionately called histrionic personality disorder in psychiatric circles, describes chaotic family households in which ACOAs become hysterically frantic and exaggerate the degree of disorder. Hyperbolic reactions impulsively arise from increasing helplessness (i.e., loss of contingency control), anticipatory fears of being criticized, and low tolerance of frustration. Helplessness over ending the mad thrust of schedule overload engenders an establishing operation of vulnerability. This emotional deprivation elevates awareness of personal mistakes. As the establishing operation intensifies, escalated fears of being perceived incompetent evoke sporadic, superstitious, and ritualistic behaviors effective at eliminating the establishing operation. ACOAs overreact by aggressively accusing others of mishandling responsibilities, of being unproductive and inconsiderate, and of forcing them to solve the convoluted situation. Zero tolerance accounts for a burst of energy of short duration, during which household congruency is restored.

Sadly, career overachievers reared in alcoholic families reflect this pattern. An engineer working a day job and moonlighting at a local factory recalled arriving home about the time his children awoke for school. Every day, at precisely 7:00 a.m. when he stepped inside the doorway, he mobilized the entire household—first by waking his wife, then the children, and then rushing to prepare breakfast and the children's lunches. He assumed there was no preexisting morning routine and dismissed his wife's parenting competencies. Instead, he charged head first into multiple and simultaneous tasks that both confused and disturbed family members. As they voiced resentment, the ACOA exerted more effort, believing he was the quintessential martyr.

Chrono-sexual Behavior

Dating persons excessively older or younger than one's chronological age is chrono-sexual behavior. ACOAs typically attract partners 10 to 15 years older or younger, depending on the ACOA's behavior and function of the relationships. Partners who are 10 years older than ACOAs fulfill motivations for attachment with the ACOA's mother or father. Behaviorally, attachment is not an intrapsychic process. Disconnected parent–child relations during childhood that result from excessive parental punishment, emotional deprivation, neglect, or absence produces partial discriminative conditioning; a child learns some relevant, but mostly irrelevant, responses to confusing and random human contact stimuli. Interrelations with a parent never properly form, leaving the ACOA child one of three contingencies: (a) to select a surrogate parent (e.g., grandparent, friend's parent, lead gang member), (b) to imitate the paternal behavior and become the parent himself or herself, or (b) to aimlessly exhibit attention-seeking behavior around friends and adults, none of whom become surrogates.

For example, class clowns or arrogantly demanding peers may be like parasites searching for a parental host.

Failure to find and secure nurturance probably would be unimportant except that emotionally deprived children witness other children receiving nurturance. Observation of family reinforcement elsewhere alerts the ACOAs of a critical missing link in their own lives. ACOAs envy peers who receive parental affection, support, and a balanced emotional household economy. The picture formed in the young ACOA's mind of a perfect parent, partly derived from their own parents (relevant stimulus properties) and mostly derived from friends' parents (irrelevant stimulus properties), remains embedded in memory until the ACOA grows older. The choice of an older partner typically satisfies the parental profile stored in memory and based on distorted facts.

The choice of a younger partner occurs when ACOAs compensate for no parents by assuming the parent's identity. In all families, intergenerational features such as religion, ethnicity, and social values are evident. Highly reinforcing rituals and responses pass down through generations with great momentum. Therefore, it is not unusual for offspring to exhibit characteristics endemic to their parents. With ACOAs, however, emulation of parent behaviors goes beyond environmentally inheritable responses. ACOAs literally become a "clone" of their parents, despite how reinforcing or punishing the biological (or step) parent was toward the ACOA. From education and careers to nonverbal gestures and verbal expressions, recreation of the parent systematically occurs through self-reinforcement, exactly like a child imitates a cartoon voice until the impersonation sounds perfect (e.g., Ruben 1979). As the behaviorally reincarnated parent, the ACOA is very susceptible to choosing partners who remind him or her of how the ACOA was as a child when the parent was absent. That way, the ACOA can now nurture this partner (child) the way the ACOA wanted nurturance years ago from a parent.

Admittedly, analysis of this time-delayed contingency resonates a "cognitive" or unempirical interpretation and may initially seem "unbehavioral." However, according to field integrative analysis, behaviors do not occur in isolation and consequently may endure over time as long as four conditions occur: (1) contact with some of the relevant stimulus properties persists; (2) contact with irrelevant stimulus properties exists but maintains response generalization; (3) concurrent or sequential responses similar in properties to the initial responses that develop and generalize: (4) a condition that pertains to rule-governed behavior, which is covered in the next chapter. In short, then, choice of considerably older or younger partners occurs as a function of deprivation of consistent parental contact; neglected, abused, or foster-children duplicate desirable parental features either in themselves or in the partner, a process which progressively matures over time.

The trouble is that by the time ACOAs realize partner selections replace emotionally lost parents, they have already suffer years of debilitating marital problems and cannot understand why the relationship is discordant. A couple married for 14 years, presenting problems of poor communication and a dissatisfactory sex life, exhibited a worse problem. They had antithetical personalities; the wife was gregarious, socially and vocationally achieving, and highly energetic, while the husband was docile, unambitious, and withdrawn. To add fuel to the fire, the husband was 15 years younger than his wife, and depended on his wife's income after frequent loss of jobs. Described as procrastinative, unproductive, and child-like, the husband admitted he was disorganized and lacked confidence. The ACOA wife lamented that she was raising another child in her husband and was tired of it. Family histories revealed that the ACOA wife's father, a docile alcoholic and unemployed gambler, never was home and never formed a parent-child bond with the ACOA.

Shame and Guilt

Discussion of shame and guilt relative to self-rules appears in the next chapter. For now, realize that shame behavior as avoidance and escape functions to release predators from their burdens (Ruben, 1993b, 2000b). ACOAs relieve predatorial conflict by blaming themselves for causing the conflict, thereby accepting full responsibility. Self-culpability provides anxiety relief in three ways. First, ACOAs volunteer their faults at the *outset of conflict,* hoping their faults match the predator's perceived accusations. Whether or not the faults match the accusations, predators accept the confession rather than start an argument.

Second, ACOAs interrupt predatory attacks by apologizing and reexplaining the conflict, naming themselves as culprits. Again, escape from conflict is nearly guaranteed as the predator accepts the ACOAs self-incrimination. Few predators are disputants; those who do refuse the ACOA's apology, blaming themselves instead, are viewed as challenges. ACOAs fervently plead for the predator to accept their apologies and may expend considerable compensatory effort until predators succumb. Compensatory actions vary infinitely from offering sexual favors to passively conceding to the predator's arbitrary wishes.

Third, ACOAs blame a third person, who is not present during the conflict, for the damage. By again absolving the predator, ACOAs regain control over the situation and eliminate their own guilt for upsetting the predator. Shame occurs, then, as a manufactured effort to avert confrontation without the ACOA realistically feeling ashamed.

Diane, a 25-year-old married homemaker, celebrated another wedding anniversary by surprising her husband with her singular brand of cooking. She prepared a four-course gourmet spread replete with delicious wines and candies. Thinking sensually, she believed her husband's ultimate appreciation would assure an auspicious platform for their anniversary. Instead, her husband stumbled in intoxicated and babbled about Diane's insensitivity and libertarian attitudes destabilizing the marriage. He critically said that her latest projects of attending law school and late night study groups amounted to a psychological free-for-all and selfish abandonment of the family. His explosive anger and criticism at first stifled Diane, emotionally caught between feeling defensive and guilty. Shame for upsetting him instilled anticipatory fear of being rejected on her long-awaited anniversary. She immediately confessed her egocentric wrongdoing, promising to quit law school and remain homebound. Despite her husband's inebriety, his accusations subsided within minutes and he embraced Diane for her abiding love.

This example typifies the paralyzingly periphrastic way in which ACOA's employ avoidance to eliminate self-guilt. Negatively reinforced "my fault" statements proportionally increase as the predator's allegations decrease. Reciprocally, attenuated predator allegations rapidly decrease with the ACOA's rising anxiety, sense of culpability, and obsessive thinking about how to rectify the situation. The behavior of both people in this stimulus-response contingency emanates from their own unique histories. The ACOA operates under fear of anticipatory conflict, her own self-imposed verbal punishers, and the magical mand (discussed in Chapter 4: see Skinner, 1957), that by enjoining her husband with apologies he might reconsider her jubilant anniversary meal. Her husband uses the occasion for guilt-producing remarks (stimuli) and is reinforced when Diane capitulates to his needs.

Artistic and "Psychic" Powers

Introspective ACOA clients seemingly possess a gift of the sixth sense. They are intuitive, perceptive, and cleverly describe events pre-dating the actual occurrence of these events. They appear gifted with "premonitional telepathy" and can foretell the future or empathetically sense intimate details of people's lives without ever meeting the people they describe. Astute insight earns them a reputation of being "psychic" or of manifesting supernatural powers supposedly inexplicable by modern scientific technology. Artists fall under the same myth. Incredibly life-like portraits with meticulous attention to detail, portend more than a great masterpiece. They suggest the artist's talent is somehow inside the person; they are born with it. Their honesty and vitality somehow originate from mysterious mental mechanisms that seem occult and radically different from the rest of the population.

Precognition poses a very unique aspect of ACOA behavior. Their unusual abilities are neither magical, spiritual nor mentalistic; instead, explanations for artistry, palmistry, numerology, astrology, or other preternatural phenomena lay within behavioral analysis (e.g., Ruben, 1987a; Ruben & Ruben, 1985a). The perceptive ACOA possesses these so-called talents for four reasons. First, severe childhood exposure to arbitrary and random punishment produces highly discriminative sensitivity to relevant and irrelevant events within a stimulus field. ACOAs are vigilantly aware of subtle stimulus properties forced upon them during fear-induced autonomic arousal. Oppressed children cultivate their auditory, visual, olfactory, and other senses in anticipation that the more stimulus details known, the greater the chance of preventing confrontation (aversive stimulation).

A second reason for elevated sensory awareness stems from excessive ruminatory thinking. ACOAs who deliberate for hours over past events invent alternative scenarios of behavior–consequence options and the multiplicity of effects they may produce on significant people. Visual imagery arouses elevated anxiety, which intensifies as reconstructed memories are analyzed and reshuffled until the perfect scenario appears. Overthinking, as it where, attunes the ACOA to minor, irrelevant stimulus properties misperceived as vital to effective responding. Self-absorbed, repetitive thoughts may dissociate the person from reality in an inner world shut off from a meaningful and functional lifestyle. ACOAs caught in this isolated dream state suffer chronic dysfunctinality but are amazingly creative.

A third explanation for so-called psychic and artistic behavior among ACOAs is *self-reinforcement*. Automatic reinforcement describes a self-conditioning process by which approximations to a target response are emitted in logical sequence, followed by the behaver's feedback. For example, impersonators shaping their performance "fine tune" their voice and body gestures until the total effect copies a targeted person. Likewise, ACOAs shape approximations of highly perceptive or visual reconstructive thinking with vigilant perfectionism. Meticulously repetitive responses undergo trial and error until the product—making predictions, art, etc.—reaches expectations.

A fourth reason is an extension of vicarious reinforcement. Earlier we said that symptoms of caretaking emerged from ACOAs abnormally empathizing with feelings, thoughts, and experiences of distressed individuals. Caretaking overtones recur in premonitional and artistic behavior as ACOAs subtly imitate sensory or emotive experiences perceived in other people in order to (a) relieve the sufferer's agony by absorbing their emotional pain and (b) anticipate consequences of the agony based on the ACOA suffering vividly relevant expenses and wanting to spare the sufferer anticipated pain. Replicating another person's "internal emotions," either through graphic artistry or by "psychically" predicting their behaviors, is a measure of *vicarious aptitude*—a repertoire developed superstitiously during childhood by focusing more on appeasing or fixing emotional disturbance in others than on managing emotions in oneself.

Sarah, a journalist and TV show host, was featured on a longstanding cable talk show on paranormal activity. She regularly invited guests to expound on topics ranging from crop circle designs to extrasensory perception. Several years ago the author appeared on this show representing the "scientific voice" on a panel with a reputed psychic. Performing her "magic," the psychic voiced a premonition that the author's wife, in the first row of the audience, would get pregnant within 6 months. Crowd reactions of "oos" and "ahs" made her a hard act to follow, although the author offered the following behavioral explanation for the psychic's prediction.

First, the psychic identified the author's wife, wearing a then-fashionable, oversized sweater and stretch pants, creating the perceptual illusion of largeness. By way of stimulus generalization, the author's wife's outfit relevantly resembled maternity clothes. Second, the relative age, physical status, and posture of the author's wife's also conformed to stimulus generalization laws. Third, the psychic vicariously identified with the verbal and nonverbal behaviors of the author's wife, believing them similar to what the psychic said and did around the time the psychic became pregnant years ago. Debunking the psychic's spellbinding powers was less important than providing a simple lesson in behavioral conditioning. Incidentally, the author's wife never got pregnant in 6 months, or after that.

Alien Abduction

Strangely, the tabloid commercialism of the *X-Files* focus on alien abduction and government conspiracy has become a national obsession. Today's generation of TV-addicted viewers, along with educated and degreed professionals, actively engage in serious contemplation over the existence of extraterrestrial beings invading human lives and causing irreparable post-traumatic stress. Whether we blame public hysteria or legends of unanswered Roswell-like questions over several decades, experimental and clinical research documenting the alien abduction phenomena is reaching credible status.

The reason this sociologic phenomenon is noteworthy here is twofold. First, many individuals claiming to be victims of alien abduction—that is, involuntarily beamed into a space ship and experimentally probed like guinea pigs—report stories with uncanny similarity without knowing one another or even believing in UFOs. Testimonials further document a multiplicity of common experiments, ranging from ovary and semen removal to implantation of miniature telecasting devices, all of which endure fairly identical laboratory procedures. Report consistency and accuracy unquestionably sparks some curiosity about the social validity of the data. Moreover, current biophysical research conducted on glassy particles found in households of abudctees increasingly show noncellular, nonplant structures with unusual wire-like strands resembling the internal mechanisms of a transistor (Pinelandia Biophysics Laboratory, 1999).

Taken literally as proof, advocates of alien abduction research persevere in their investigations to find the truth (Hough & Kalman, 1997; La Vigne, 1995). While their crusading efforts may unveil intriguing findings between the controversial rhetoric and sensationalism, there is a more important reason for considering the abductee testimony. Behaviors characteristic of alien abductees are similar to those of ACOAs. Reporting abductees typically suffered childhood maladjustments ranging from random physical and verbal abuse to disruptive parental bonding because of addicted parents. Boylan & Boylan (1994, pp. 30–45) further cataloged twenty post-abduction adult symptoms consisting of:

1. Unexplained persistent anxiety or restlessness.
2. A strong fearful reaction when confronted with objects, pictures, stories, films and other media associated with alien encounters.
3. Persistent insomnia.
4. Repeated daytime thinking about UFOs or aliens.
5. Compulsive behavior concerning UFOs and aliens.
6. Unexplained moodiness or irritability after an anomalous incident.
7. Body symptoms or marks characteristic of alien encounters.
8. A substantial, inexplicable period of "missing time" following an anomalous incident.
9. The sudden, unexplained onset of feelings of social oddness—like one is strange or doesn't belong.

10. A new cosmic awareness.
11. Sudden development of feelings of affinity for aliens.
12. The sense that one has received telepathic messages from aliens.
13. A sense of sharing the space in one's mind with aliens.
14. The beginning of psychic abilities or a marked increase in pre-existent psychic ability.
15. Attraction to a spirituality or religion based on the indwelling of the supreme source in all nature.
16. A longing for a particular alien.
17. An obsessive sense of mission acquired during the alien abduction.
18. A strong urge to travel to a specific area.
19. A sense of partial alien heritage with a strong belief that one (a) shares the alien's perspective of Earth, (b) had sex with the alien and is a biological parent to alien offspring, and (c) had been born elsewhere.
20. A sense that one's destiny is with the aliens in the galaxy as prophesized during an encounter with them.

A superficial reading of this list invariably will elicit a chuckle from most serious researchers who view the symptoms as "hocus-pocus" and grossly unscientific. "Sensing parital alien heritage," for example, does require a leap of faith beyond empirical reasoning that sounds like a reification. Outwardly this lunacy may seem superfluous, but the abduction syndrome both matches the ACOA personality, as well as characteristics of many post-traumatic-stress-disordered (PTSD) individuals who diagnostically exhibit flashbacks, compulsive behaviors, retrospective fears, cyclical mood swings, insomnia, recurrent intrusive thoughts, memory impairment, estrangement, avoidance, and intensification of symptoms by exposure to events believed symbolic of or surrounding the traumatic event. Acute and chronic onset of symptoms producing physical and cognitive malfunctions overlap with ACOA behaviors, suggesting either that ACOAs are susceptible to perceiving themselves as abducted by aliens or indeed have been subjects of unknown terrestorial or extraterrestrial experimentation.

Like any challenging natural phenomena, evidence based on unconventionality of the data source cannot be dismissed unequivocally or vilified as perverting science. Rather, as ecobehaviorists, responsible researchers must examine the integrated field of interaction between many public and private events. Some events may be immediately observable and measurable, whereas other events may be corporeal but unobservable because the researcher is in ignorance of them to varying degrees (Ruben, 1985).

Depression

Kazdin's (1990) comprehensive review of childhood depression insightfully describes many convergent symptoms as *comorbidity*. That is, many children meet criteria for more than one disorder, including overlapping criteria for anxiety, conduct disorders, and oppositional disorders. With the onset of adulthood, unrelieved childhood fears, anxieties, and disorders act as weak immunity against stressors of conflict, rejection, and criticism. Unchanged emotional disabilities, as we have seen, may also increase the adult's susceptibility to avoidance and escape behaviors. Thus, a diagnostic problem arises: How does a clinician delineate between avoidance and escape from conflict, and avoidance and escape from endogenous depression? Most ACOAs who suffered arbitrary and critical punishment in childhood struggle with depression in later years. Symptoms arise slowly or rapidly but typically follow repeated episodes of uncontrolled anxiety or entrapment in inescapable, unavoidable situations.

One way to distinguish avoidance–conflict from avoidance–depression is by the diminished effects of caretaking in depressed ACOAs. Caretakers prohibited from or significantly limited in functionally engaging in altruistic behaviors and who lack sufficient personal resources to problem-solve alternatives may feel depressed when:

1. Their efforts are disrupted, violated or replaced by another caretaker or enabler.
2. Their enabling efforts are refused by recipients which is misinterpreted as rejection.
3. Their efforts are stifled by absence of any available recipient.
4. Their caretaking or aggression fails to avoid or escape conflict, criticism, or rejection.
5. They develop generalized anxiety escalating to panic attacks after physical exhaustion and anxiety subside.
6. They are forced to sit, relax or remain immobile either when alone or around a predator.
7. They suffer removal or interruption of food, alcohol, or drugs after habitual or excessive use either before, during, or after conflict, criticism, or rejection.
8. They suffer removal or interruption of running away or hiding either before, during or after conflict, criticism, or rejection.
9. They are forced to outwardly express angry, vulnerable, or personal feelings around a predator even if mediated by the therapist.
10. They suffer prolonged guilt or shame from repeatedly upsetting people or inferring disapproval.
11. They suffer prolonged guilt or shame from repeatedly asserting personal ideas, disagreements, or refusals and inferring disapproval.
12. They suffer prolonged guilt or shame from repeatedly finding fault in self, treating self as a scapegoat for others' problems, and regarding loneliness as abandonment and rejection.

Tragically, depression can incapacitate an otherwise vivacious person in mid-career. Forty-five-year-old Robert, a night-shift assembly line worker, typically rushed home after his shift to prepare breakfast for his children and wife, and gladly drive his children to school. His unemployed wife expected this routine and rarely praised Robert for his Herculean endurance of remaining awake after 12 hours of work. Benevolent Robert, on the other hand, entirely perceived his efforts as providing quality parenting time and proof of his marital commitment.

Value derived from appeasing his wife and children far surpassed selfish needs for sleep. However, after 15 years of this routine, Robert's wife commenced a job and drove the children to school herself, unintentionally relieving Robert of morning caretaking. Rather than grateful, Robert felt emotionally devastated, inadequate, and rapidly lapsed into a depression where he ate irregularly and slept the entire day before rising for work. Detachment from his family intensified as Robert appeared irritable and forlorn. Unavoidable cessation of caretaking purged his reinforcement contingencies and left him feeling helpless, hopeless, and useless.

Consequences of ACOA Behavioral Patterns

Predictable outcomes of avoidance and escape responses thus far have included removal of aversive stimulation and restoration of reinforcement. But this is not always the case. In fact, consequences for avoidance and escape may be the opposite. ACOAs who seek removal of aversive stimulation may produce more aversive conditions; ACOAs who seek reinforcement may either get punishers or reinforcers for irrelevant behaviors. The irony is that non-ACOAs exposed to punishment or reinforcement for wrong behaviors are instantly trainable; they would decelerate caretaking, enabling, or even aggressive reactions. Research showing response attrition under schedules of punishment clearly supports this result. But ACOAs respond with greater immunity to punishment contingencies.

ACOAs perceive aversive contingencies differently. Impending or confrontable aversive consequences may be perceived not as threats but instead *as challenges*. ACOAs persistently emit the same punishment-producing behaviors because they strongly believe their persistence will pay off if they just work harder. Variables controlling this behavior lie with rule-governed learning (discussed in the next chapter) and habituation to reinforcement intermittency. Delayed schedules of reinforcement, although typically evoking weak response topographies and frequencies, serve to motivate the ACOA to stronger response forms.

Continuous versus intermittent reinforcement affects ACOAs differently. During childhood, coercively punished ACOAs develop acute behavioral sensitivity to intermittent reinforcement. The chronology of conditioning is predictable. First, children are exposed to variable ratio and variable interval punishment schedules generating low rates of responses (e.g., lack of motivation apathy, crying, procrastination, disorganization, noncompliance, etc.). Second, conditioned escape and avoidance responses (e.g., caretaking, doing everything right) averted punishment but also occasionally triggered irrelevant and remote source of reinforcers. Placating responses—for example, obedience—prevented or delayed criticism from a parent but also generated compliments from a teacher or friend's parent impressed by the child's appropriate manners (irrelevant and remote sources of reinforcement). As lower density of reinforcement intermingled with higher density of punishment, two contrast effects typically resulted: First, children habituated to punishment and, second, they exerted superstitious or higher rate behaviors for delayed reinforcement. Similar parameters of successive and simultaneous behavioral contrast effects are reported in the experimental literature (e.g., Firestone & Douglas, 1975; Kollins, Lane, Shapiro, 1997; Sonuga-Barke & Lea, 1989; Wertheim, 1965).

Consequently, dysfunctional reactions to punishment emerging in adulthood are the byproduct of unusual behavioral contrast effects. ACOAs astutely responsive to spatially remote and quantifiably inconsistent reinforcement typically exhibit or experience the following side effects:

Exploitation Caretakers subject their generous behaviors to the hostile manipulation of "users." Unreciprocal predators exploit caretakers by coercing higher amounts of altruism as proof of love or commitment. As demands grow, ACOAs may feel resentment and possibly indirectly express their dissatisfaction, but as a rule will remain obediently silent about the demands. Outspoken protest only makes the ACOAs feel guilty; shame-induced fears then propel higher rates of caretaking behaviors.

Superstitious Behavior in the Predator One peculiar consequence of *anticipatory caretaking and anticipatory aggression* is that they reinforce whatever the predator is doing before a conflict. Recall that conflict may or may not be impending and efforts to appease the predator may end up accidentally shaping strange or unwanted behaviors. For example, one husband claimed that his wife always greeted him with excessive affection after work to prevent him from opening the mail and discovering her compulsive overspending on credit cards. Ironically, he came to expect her luscious affection and noticed feeling sexually aroused and wanting intercourse every day after work. His wife, of course, never expected her husband to turn her affection into a sexual response. When his wife stopped the erotic affection, thinking her husband's stimulated libido might dissipate, she observed residual behaviors. Her husband now perceived her cessation of affection as rebuking his sexual advances because she found him physically undesirable. In other words, his superstitious behavior persisted, despite actual changes in the operant contingencies or even rules modified about his wife ("She doesn't want sex now") (Pisacreta, 1998). Consequently, the wife now had the burden of engaging in new avoidance behavior (e.g., lovemaking) to prevent criticism from her sexually rejected husband. Stereotypical behavior shaped inadvertently in her husband compelled the wife to increase the labyrinth of avoidance responses rather than to thin them out.

Overachievement First, a primer on why behavioral principles may appear contradictory. Reinforcement does not always directly increase behavior; nor does punishment always directly decrease behavior. Operant effects are reciprocal and interconnective to multiple sources of stimuli expanding the learning field. Consequently, the same stimulus may be reinforcing to one behavior but punishing to another behavior or simultaneously be reinforcing and punishing to the same behavior This is particularly true in the case of overachievement. ACOAs receiving abusive criticism for being stupid, inefficient and ugly, for example, may aggressively perform some skills while displaying chronic deficits in other behaviors. In childhood, abnormally high discrepancies occur between academics and interpersonal skills. Verbally punished children may excel in education, produce honor grades, and rapidly ascend to gifted levels of performance. Later in adulthood, they obtain masters and doctorate degrees, and subsequently pursue precision vocations such as medicine, dentistry, law, and engineering.

The reason for their ascendancy rests uneasy with the behaviorally minded thinker. Punishment contingencies stimulate such incredible fear (avoidance) of criticism about mistakes that ACOAs become obsessive–compulsive by overcontrolling their lives to minimize mistakes. Calculated efforts to look infallible require the ACOA to engage in any response class which contains clear and concise criteria for performance. Tasks or careers defined by rigidly clear standards are preferred since the ACOA, in meeting the standards, can reduce errors and guarantee reinforcing peer feedback. Whereas, tasks or subjects with vague or varying performance objectives set the stage for punitive peer feedback. Law, medicine, and engineering, for example, are predicated on technically precise rules that are immutable. ACOAs can perform exceptionally well in these disciplines knowing the contingencies are reachable and self-controllable without punishment obstacles.

Does that mean that reinforcing a child on predictable schedules with love, affection, and nurturance, minus punishment, will not produce a high achiever? Does that mean the reinforced child will not pursue medicine, law, and engineering? The answer, sadly, is *yes*. High achievers typically experience profound deprivations, severe punishment, and arbitrary or intermittent reinforcers growing up. In adulthood, motivational forces for becoming financially prosperous, prolific, or a celebrity usually can be traced to unavoidable and inescapable exposure to aversive conditioning. By contrast, developmental research that propounds reinforcement over corporeal punishment in shaping adaptive behaviors (e.g., Bijou, 1976; Gelfand & Hartmann, 1984; Ruben, 1992c) are perfectly correct in saying reinforcers build healthy, emotionally balanced children. But a healthy, emotionally balanced child may never suffer the emptiness and inferiority evoked by punishment, which triggers and fortifies excessive perseverance.

Rejection Extensive caretaking dissatisfies the manipulative, demanding predator whose needs are insatiable and who expects unconditional favors. Denigrated ACOAs never quite understand reasons for this rejection, and attribute the predator's anger to the ACOA's own inadequacy. Self-blame eliminates the predator as instigator and blindly catapults the caretaker's rescuing efforts into action; he or she engages in extraordinary apologetic behaviors, hoping to reverse predator opinion. Instead, ACOAs' frantic overcorrection of a perceived problem backfires by further infuriating the predator and maintaining adversarial reactions.

Inattention to Appropriate Behavior Not all partners are predators; frequently significant others are appreciative of caretakers. Spouses and other partners may acknowledge the caretaker's generosity and properly reciprocate with rewards, although the ACOA rebuffs the rewards. Resisting reinforcers indicates two conditions. One condition is that the ACOA distrusts appropriate behaviors in other people, no matter how much caretakers insist they want appropriate behaviors. A second condition involves ACOAs' panic over the sudden "center-stage" attention received for their kindness. Feelings of stupidity, mediocrity, and impostorism elevate anxiety, causing humiliation and catastrophic thinking. ACOAs uncomfortable with compliments may deflect them by discrediting the praise or being sarcastic to stop further laudable remarks.

Hatred of compliments, viewed as conceit and selfishness, turned a family upside down when they tried to please their mother. A controlling wife lamented that her family never helped out with household chores. On the father's initiative, the family surprised the caretaker by doing the laundry, preparing dinner, and finishing other odd chores. Rather than appreciate this surprise, the mother immediately found fault in all family participants for improperly doing the chores. Assessment of faults suppressed further initiatives by family members to help out with chores or even think of repeating similar surprises in the future.

Why do ACOAs seemingly sabotage good-natured gestures by those whom they accuse of being unhelpful? The answer is threefold. First, helping out is perceived as exposing incompetence; it signals that the caretaker could not do it alone. Perception of fault transforms into believing he or she is being criticized. Second, helping out is distrustful; treating the caretaker nicely must have underlying motives believed to invalidate the kind gesture. Nobody ever did things in the past for this person, so why are people doing them now? Third, expectations for reciprocity far exceed realistic criteria for people returning favors or acting correctly. Helping out is never as good as it should be. ACOAs invest such excessive efforts, even at perfectionistic levels, in helping other people that they expect people to reciprocate with identical response intensity. When reciprocal intensity does not occur, ACOAs misinfer that they did something heinously wrong and are undeserving of another person's respect.

Provoking Aggression Although caretakers want equal love and respect, demands for attention may involve ACOAs becoming aggressive. Again, misconstrued theories about domestic violence figure prominently here. Docile male spouses provoked by an ACOA's insults, criticisms, teasing, and repetitive threats do not remain immobile. They ultimately turn against the ACOA, using verbal and physical abuse as a defense. In fact, physical and emotional abuse of men is something rarely talked about. Feminist advocates of battered woman's rights sharply profess that abuse is always male-dominated. Interbehaviorally, the reverse is equally true. Female violence against men typically arises for the same reasons and follows the same pattern as male battering, including objects being thrown, kicking, biting, hitting, and assault with a knife or other object.

There is a critical reason that caretakers provoke aggression. Historically, they expect and know how to "deal with" aggressive attention. Enduring physically or verbally abusive attacks during childhood formed a repertoire for aggressive interactions. Habits were formed that prepared caretakers to anticipate and cope with random episodes of hostility as part of home survival. Consequently, conflict must occur for them to feel normal. Conflict that does not occur naturally, that is, by another partner causing a fight, results in the ACOA contriving an altercation simply to restore familiar contingencies. Once conflict is produced, ACOAs regain control, redeem their confidence, and ritualistically feel comfortable, in much the same way as couples who gain comfort in repeating certain religious or ethnic rituals learned in childhood.

Procrastination Avoidance and escape nearly always produce a delay or termination of tasks the ACOA feels are (a) difficult to do, (b) outside their repertoire, or (c) prone to cause conflict, criticism, or rejection. Rarely, if ever, does the ACOA admit deficiency when confronted with impossible odds regarding a task or even a small favor asked of them. They politely accept the task rather than refuse to do it and face instant rejection. As time passes the task remains incomplete. Reminders to complete the task are responded to with honest apologies and temporary compensatory efforts that relieve the accuser of anger. However, none of these ephemeral solutions complete the task; promissory behaviors and appeasements serve only to extend delays.

Faced with ensuing deadliness, ACOA procrastinators ravage through their limited behavior repertoire to produce four reactions. First, they show fierce anger and aggression or vehemently deny their commitment to complete the task or fulfill a promise. Second, they distract the accuser by shifting to incompatible, irrelevant topics likely to upset or please the accuser. One distraction is turning the topic around to blame the accuser for not reminding them to do the task, so it is the accuser's fault for forgetting. Other shifts, also called "roadblocks," are to start a new conversations, offer sex or food treats, or simply walk away.

Third, they sink into spontaneous depression characterized by crying and self-criticism, vowing to stop whatever they are doing at that moment and fulfill the promise. Naturally, sympathetic partners hearing this "11th hour" proposal refuse the spontaneous remediation because it seems preposterous, illogical, and impractical. In other words, for the person to "stop whatever they are doing now" may also interrupt the partner, who is unwilling to stop whatever he or she is doing. Finally, combinations of these reactions are very common. For instance, spontaneous acts of remediation ("Fine, I'll do it now") may accompany aggressive, defensive remarks.

Blaming Others when Embarrassed Attribution of fault represents a common reaction when ACOAs feel vulnerable. They externalize the locus of control as the first line of defense against anticipatory fears of criticism. Randomly punished youngsters generalize anxiety responses not only to relevant discriminative stimuli, but, as already indicated, to irrelevant (metonymical) stimuli; response generality in adulthood particularly occurs when none of the relevant antecedent stimuli are present. Since anxiety elevates so rapidly and discretely, cessation of anxiety requires an aggressive or curt response.

A 45-year-old ACOA wife was feeling cheerful walking with her husband down the dairy aisle at the local grocery store. As she nonchalantly picked up one box of butter from the freezer, she accidentally knocked four other boxes onto the floor. Neighboring shoppers did not even notice the fallen boxes, and the aisle was not crowded with people. However, the ACOA impulsively exploded at her husband saying "You stupid idiot, didn't you see the butters were hard for me to get? Why did you make me get them?" Her harsh verbal blast shocked her spouse, who looked at her dumbfounded and then walked away.

Miscommunication One of the severe repercussions of avoidance and escape is miscommunication. Fear of conflict, criticism, and rejection prevents inquiry into suspicious behaviors of other people, resulting in inferences about why and how people do things that are inconsistent with the real reasons. Such impure inferences distort and affirm stereotyped beliefs that never get clarified (Ruben & Ruben, 1984). A man exploded in a rage over somebody giving him a gift he did not want. He assaulted the gift by destroying it with a hammer, thinking that the gift was left on purpose to spite and hurt him. Never did it occur to him prior to his destructive actions to check out why the gift was left for him and whether the reason was inconsistent with his inference. Failure to confront assumptions may seem intuitively harmful, but, functionally, it avoids the risk of looking stupid or arousing unwanted conflict.

Termination of Friendships "Cutting your nose off to spite your face" is a proverb. It typically describes an adult who aborts or destroys something thinking it might annoy another adult which is personally gratifying at the time. This "annoyance" is retaliatory and, it is hoped, will hurt the perceived predator as much as it upsets the sacrificer. In childhood, examples of self-aborting activities are manifold. Imagine a child munching on a juicy hamburger. Told he must eat his vegetables or not get dessert, the stubborn child might stop eating his meal altogether and proceed to dump the entire plate of vegetables and hamburger into the garbage can. Consequently, his parents yell at him, deny him more food, or in some way punish these actions.

In adulthood, similar behavior patterns occur in response to inferred deprivations of selfish needs. Remember the hammer-smashing person? He was so infuriated that he not only blew a gasket, he boldly terminated a relationship with the gift-giver, despite friendship for over 10 years. Why did the ACOA cut his nose off to spite his face because of one upsetting episode? How could he believe this action truly would hurt the person just as similar actions hurt his parents during childhood? The answers lie in the need to avoid conflict, criticism, and rejection. The ACOA would rather maintain avoidance and escape patterns than attempt solutions that would defuse false inferences and ensure continuation of rewarding friendships. On the one hand, forfeiture of accumulated personal rewards at "the drop of the bucket" illustrates severely deficient coping mechanisms. On the other, dispensing with rewards rapidly relieves compounded anxiety, impure inferences, and eliminates having to apologize to the offended friend for acting abusively.

At the forefront of ACOA clinical assessment are discerning questions about the unusual behavior of ACOAs. Etiologically, the answer thus far involves two reasons: a history of punishment contingencies and an intermittent reinforcement history producing severe deprivations and response generalization covarying with an unstable stimulus field. The scientific triumph of identifying these variables serves many purposes, among them the demystification of mentalistic, unfounded explanations for ACOA behavior. Depersonifying the ACOA syndrome is necessary so that the syndrome becomes a scientifically valid construct, amenable to further applied and experimental research. In the next chapter, we discuss the *rule-governed effects* of ACOA behavior, the foundation for which has already been laid by research.

CASE ILLUSTRATION

Complexity of psychopathology varies depending on how perceptive the observer is about the reasons underlying the pathologic behavior. Identifying causal variables is not a terribly arduous task, once predictable behavior patterns are known, and detected among concurrent and sequential responses. Without this knowledge of behavioral principles and operational responses, the myriad of ACOA symptoms can appear chronically obtuse and untreatable. Such was the case with Mark S., a 45-year-old engineer who repeatedly sought counseling over 20 years. Mark's choice of therapy ranged form psychodynamic to humanistic approaches, none of which directly ascertained reasons for or offered practical solutions to his perpetual interpersonal deficits. The case of Mark S. presents an illustration of compound symptoms that boggled therapists, his own family, and resulted in a psychotropic cocktail of assorted antidepressants and anti-anxieties. Medications provided symptomatic relief but bypassed an assessment of intricate conditioning factors repeatedly producing similar symptoms. Re-emergent symptoms elevated his fear of being incurable and validated his "illness" would be a permanent handicap.

That is when he received a referral to a behavioral psychologist.

Presenting symptoms

Mark S. suffered a labyrinth of symptoms psychiatrically diagnosed as bipolar disorder. That is, he experienced swings of elevated energy bursting into hypermania, overconfidence, excitability, and indefatigable work habits. Projects began with unrealistic deadline dates and involved unachievable tasks that were beyond his skill level. His charisma persuaded other people to follow his lofty plans, eventually surrounding himself with believers who invested time, energy or dollars into his crusading ventures. As he undertook new projects, impulsively shifting from one priority to another, arousing more trust in investors, Mark S. repeated the same pattern. First he found fault in others people impeding his progress on a project; second, he lost momentum trying to overcome new obstacles and abruptly aborted the projects without consulting the investors; third, he evaded financial, legal, or social obligations incurred from the projects and instead withdrew into a depressive stupor; fourth, he cocooned himself in a paralyzing suicidal state of mind, isolated from family and friends, and outwardly appeared too legitimately ill to bear responsibility for his debts.

Complicating his cyclical mood swings was binge alcoholism during manic stages and cannabis use during depressive stages. Hypermania relied on alcohol-induced effects to disinhibit his fears and artificially enabled courage for entrepreneurial undertakings. The cannabis acted to anesthetize self-criticism for miserably failing the project and helped Mark avoid confrontations with angry investors. Polydrug use also served a third purpose; intoxication inhibited appetite and allowed rapid weight loss during hypermanic stages.

Behavioral history

A cogent integrative-field analysis begins with variables in his childhood. Historical data track the ontogony of multi-causal links among stimuli and inappropriately learned responses. Faulty conditioning that is traceable to the developmental environment reveals defective units of behavior and their consequences before response and stimulus generalization occurred; it also pinpoints the defective parental models of behavior, from who imitative and rule-governed behaviors evolved.

Mark S. grew up the oldest of three children raised by dually employed parents. His father, an alcoholic, drank 5 to 10 beers nightly and became aggressively volatile over minor household transgressions. Angry outbursts evolved rapidly into threats of physical violence and frequently the father accused one of the children of gross misconduct, regardless of their actual culpability. Mark, the timid one, received the brunt of his father's rage. He recalled many incidents of randomly being abrasively scolded for uncleanliness, laziness, and stupidity. For example, he cited an example of sitting on the couch watching cartoons, when his father burst into the family room in a fury, blaming him for his messy room and making the house dirty.

Subsequent verbal assaults occurred whether Mark was obedient, disobedient, or simply nonresponsive. Angry reprimands arbitrarily identified an imperfection no matter how many times Mark apologized or sought his father's approval. Even overachieving in Math and English, with all A's in AP honor courses, failed his father's test of acceptance. Corrective feedback either was insultive or aspirational; "That grade is fine but how long will you keep it up?" Or, "Why can't you always get the "A," instead of just on certain exams." Abiding his father's requests, for example, by earning straight "A's" and volunteering chores around the house, Mark met opposition from his rigidly stubborn and cynical father, who ridiculed Mark's efforts with undercutting remarks that Mark was just "brown-nosing him." Underloved Mark even feverishly praised his father and competed with his siblings for solitary time with "dad." Alone or in public, his father's caustic repudiations of Mark's feeble efforts disastrously shrunk Mark's confidence and emotionally paralyzed him.

A self-employed bridge construction operator, his father always was busy and efficient with time. Long arduous hours of typing and telephone calls went into the late evening and overlapped onto the weekend, frequently supplanting time with the family. Mark perceived his father's work as paramount and admired his industrious completion of multiple projects. Fascinated with his father's energy, Mark impersonated his father's speech patterns, erect standing position, and even his gait, discovering that vicariously simulating his father felt like he was with his father. When his father discovered Mark's emulative secret, the father was furious and verbally chastised Mark for his infancy, mediocrity, and unoriginality.

By comparison, Mark's mother was a reserved, docile, and conservative individual raised by alcoholic parents. Although working a full-time job, her flat, blunted affect and conspicuous indifference toward her appearance and household chores left housekeeping duties to the children. Mark recalled her durable episodes of depression characterized by excessive sleeping, detachment form the family mainstream, and self-effacing remarks. Even on holidays including her birthday, his mother's deflated grimace and doomsday skepticism alienated him from a close bond with her. His father's intolerance and disparaging remarks worsened the problem. His patronizing vilifications drained Mark's mother of residual energy and plunged her deeper into periods of disabling guilt and catatonia. Stuck in a stupor for hours, dissociated from the family mainstream, his mother sat silently staring out the window unwavered by the passage of time. Mark felt bad for his mother, but hated her apathy in contrast to his father's workaholism.

By age 15, with conflicting goals of wanting paternal approval and self-individualization, Mark experimented with beer during weekend parties. He found inebriation could excite his motivation to pursue long-shot ideas and attract onlookers hooked by his bubbling enthusiasm. Male friends and girlfriends trusted his articulate language and compassion for goals way beyond their own skill level or imagination. Mark portrayed himself as ingeniously and vigorously creative, and capable of fulfilling lofty promises such as gaining longer lunch periods, more diverse food selections, or even methods on income generation for the high school newspaper. His exhortations enticed many loyal followers who lionized him as sensational and enviable. As he fulfilled one or two easy promises, the harder and more desirable promises fell by the wayside but went unnoticed. Rising rapidly to the top of the high school popularity charts, Mark gained a flood of boyfriends and girlfriends absorbed by his infectious charisma. Into his twenties, having aced his grades in college, he majored in engineering fascinated by the mathematics of problem solving. Aspirations to be precise, logical, and attain his sizable goals became an obsession.

Mark married a deeply religious, conventional-thinking wife who was a social worker. Her restricted Christian upbringing marked a contrast to Mark's riveting and adventuresome persona. She escaped from her monotonous life by living vicariously through Mark's adrenaline-arousing, impulsive lifestyle and portfolio of projects he assaulted with great vengeance. Together they had three children synchronized to be two years apart and Mark persuaded his wife to remain unemployed while raising the children Adoring and passionate, she found her favorite times alone with Mark was during his depression when both would smoke marijuana together. This intimate privacy reunified their personal communication and bolstered romantic lovemaking.

Behavioral analysis

Analysis of Mark's symptoms was possible by identifying five patterns common to ACOAs. Each of the five symptoms entailed multi-causal contingencies occurring both within Mark's immediate field of events and, *interbehaviorally,* across preceding fields of events from which his current behaviors evolved. First, Mark exhibited classic symptoms of *anticipatory aggression.* Anxiety over investor conflicts when he reneged on promises was relieved by forcefully blaming people and places for obstructing his goals. Hyperbolic reactions diagnostically called "histrionic personality disorder" described his exaggerative, overly dramatic excitability over minor transgressions. His over-reactive hysteria about failing people's expectations produced three consequences. First, it escaped impending aversive contact with investor criticism. Second, it manipulated the investors to sympathize, empathize and positively reinforce Mark for incalculable time attempting to materialize an idea. A third consequence generated automatic-reinforcers for simulating his father's arousing verbal or nonverbal excitement about a project (autoclitic-tacts). Sounding and feeling like his father, in other words, reinforced the delusive belief that Mark worked hard like his father, despite the barriers encountered.

Second, Mark displayed *running away behaviors.* The inescapability of angry investors resulted in Mark imitating his mother's depressive role. Mark plummeted into the "sick role" feigning somatic complaints and immobilized in bed for days on end. Running away behavior received multiple sources of reinforcement. First, escape from aversive investors negatively reinforced the facade of illness. Second, his empathic social worker wife rushed to Mark's bedside nursing his fabricated emotional ailments and positively reinforcing his time-out from reality. Third, self-reinforcement from emulating his mother's behavior allowed Mark to artificially and temporarily feel a close bond with his mother. Just as widows wear their deceased husband's watches to feel a close memory, so, too, Mark *wore his mother's behaviors to feel a close and reinforcing memory.* The establishing operation particularly evocative of this imitation was feeling deprived of a mother-son bond during childhood due to his mother's depression. By imitating her behavior, Mark satisfied this deprivation in experiencing what her behavior must have felt like when he wanted closeness with her years ago.

Third, Mark suffered a *substance abuse*. Alcohol dependent effects disinhibited his anxiety and self-effacing cruelty. His emotions springboard with tenacity, and risk-taking feelings of invincibility both lifted him out of depression and restored courage for new entrepreneurial undertakings. Inebriation provided three effects. First, it self-medicated fears, doubts, and destabilizing self-criticism formed as rule governed behaviors from his father's years of assault. Mark suppressed obsessive, invasive fears of failure and idealized grandiose schemes based on skills he did not have. Second, ethanol effects autonomically aroused his verbal and nonverbal behaviors, allowing him to talk fast, think fast, and use impeccably logical reasoning in presenting his ideas. Third, stimulatory effects magnified the accuracy and consistency of social behaviors that would incapacitate him when sober. Deviant verbal etiquette such as interrupting people or impulsively and brazenly volunteering opinions, flowed rhythmically and without hesitation when Mark drank too much.

Inebriety reversed suppressive behaviors and catapulted audacity. However, cannabis-dependence did just the opposite. Mark regularly smoked marijuana during depressive episodes to decelerate his autonomic momentum and escape the uncontrollability of helplessness. Cannabis thus served three major functions. First, it acted as a mood stabilizer, sedating Mark's fire-cracker excitement, and kept him from drifting deeply into suicidal ideation. Second, THC-effects elongated mild depression and allowed Mark to escape impending aversive confrontations. As investor's anger wore thin, or they rallied behind Mark's emotional recovery, self-terminated use of cannabis permitted Mark to recycle his enthusiasm for another business endeavor. A third function lies with reciprocal reinforcement form enhanced sexuality and sharing with his wife. Time alone with his wife was sparse unless Mark descended into depression and smoked cannabis.

A fourth and fifth behavioral variable were *emotional paralysis* and *accusation*. Needless to say, recession to solitary confinement, apathy, anhedonia, and dyphoria all comprised emotional paralysis. Replicating his mothers' behavior, as well as to escape punishment, Mark externalized locus of control to outside forces and believed himself helpless. Perceived victimization produced two consequences. First, it removed self-deprecatory beliefs (i.e., rule-governed statements) about his repeated failures echoing his father's torrent of criticisms. Second, it generated concurrent positive reinforcers from his wife and investors for his sickly role. As for accusations, the previous explanation for anticipatory aggression clarifies these variables.

However, a unique contingency acting on behavior included a paradoxical effect of positive punishment (e.g., Long & McNamara, 1989). Although positive punishment, by definition, decreases behavioral responses, research evidence shows it can increase behavioral responses for several reasons relevant to Mark's accusatory behaviors. First, Mark's awareness of random association between criticism (punishment) and praise (reinforcement) from investors for his business efforts means he has a 50-50 probable chance of confrontation. Given his history of aversive conditioning in childhood, he errs on the side of caution (avoidance) by acting aggressively to eliminate *any chance of criticism*. Second, Mark's accusatory behaviors are resistant to extinction. Faced with either criticism (punishment) or no responses at all from investors (extinction), Mark chooses to get angry and thus endure aversive stimuli by directly accusing the investors of ruining his efforts, rather than say nothing. Response generation partly is due to reinforcer-strength gained from critical investors paying attention to him tantamount to his father paying attention to Mark, although it was painful afterwards. Finally, accusational behavior is negatively reinforcing because it provides fear reduction by eliminating the perceived predator.

A third reason for paradoxical effects is habituation. Aversive stimuli repeatedly presented under inescapable conditions lose their power to exert fear after a while. Diminished effects from human adaptation means a person grows immune to punishment and responds according to ritualistic or superstitious contingencies. For example, Mark is so accustomed to blaming people for his mistakes, he may disregard harsh rebukes when responding angrily. Explosive anger may or may not silence the predator for brief durations, since this reprieve is both ephemeral and unpredictable; just the same, the chance that this reprieve *may occur* superstitiously conditions Mark to automatically react defensively when he is under attack.

Etiologically speaking, Marks' elaborate web of compound contingencies represents a severe case of ACOA pathology. Reinforcing and punishing variables are interwoven insidiously and can go easily undetectable from the traditionally trained clinical eye. Nonbehavioral assessment clearly would reveal Mark's bipolarity, substance abuse, and even spousal codependency. Dynamic-oriented assessments especially might identify Mark's blatant developmental dysfunctions and father-child (Oedipal) equivocations. But rendering the data into a theoretical interpretation is only half the battle. Collected data must first undergo functional or operational analysis, so that responses are a *scientific product of the human organism under study, and not a byproduct of the observer's opinion*. That way, assessment is an empirically supported process in the continuum of treatment.

CHAPTER 4

Family Rules and Contingencies

In communities across the country, there are families beset by tragedy that are developing coping strategies to help through transitions of recovery. For example, a 6-year-old boy accused of gunning down a little girl in a Michigan elementary school forced two families into emotional crisis. Death of shooting victim Kayla Rolland damaged a family unit while stirring public outcry over unsafe schools. The assailant's family, foisted into the limelight, was less surprised but publicly scrutinized nonetheless for neglecting a troubled child. In both cases, juxtaposing the mad and the mundane, intrafamily reactions to violence engendered beliefs and rules about how to survive the tragedy.

The question thus arises: How do we establish verbal rules governing coping behavior? This chapter explores principles of self-talk and its implications for ACOAs who transform aversive childhood experiences into rigidly inculcated beliefs about self-suppression. First, we provide a brief background contrasting nonbehavioral with behavioral formulations of verbal behavior.

Where Does Verbal Behavior Come From?

Production of beliefs—whether ethical, moral, legal, social or religious—involves an uniquely systematic process of conditioning. Historically, cognitive theorists disagreed with this position, arguing that thought development entailed internal mechanisms phylogenetically evolving from birth. Linguist Noam Chomsky's *Language Acquisition Device (LAD)* (1957), for example, sympathetically resonated Piaget's theories of underlying competence and creativity that allowed people to think. Language acquisition focused on a set of complex and abstract rules governing word formation and comprehension. Different from stimulus–response principles, language and ideas presumably underwent a myriad of grammatically complex stages before surface structure or "meaning" resulted. For instance, children uttering the word "fish" only understand its aquatic reference once a relationship has occurred between action and agent, or source of action. In his scathing review of Skinner's book *Verbal Behavior,* Chomsky (1959) further argued that terms like "stimulus," "response," and "reinforcement" used outside the laboratory lost all of their technical meaning and were simply vague metaphors.

Ironically, the Chompsky–Skinner debate revolutionized research studies of human language, giving momentum to operationalzing Skinner's verbal behavior paradigm. Laboratory as well as applied investigations supporting operant- and respondent-based verbal performance (Ferster, 1973; Salzinger & Salzinger, 1967; Winston & Baker, 1985) advanced the behavioral conceptualization of language. Empirical studies showed not only that language was environmentally learnable as opposed to innate but that words, thoughts, and even moral beliefs were scientifically predictable. Bijou (1975, 1976; Bijou & Baer, 1978), for example, outlined systematically the operant units integrated in morally analyzing a person's experiences. His later research (Bijou, Umbreit & Ghezzi, 1985, 1986) expanded methods for teaching "referential linguistic interactions," based partially on Kantor's *Psychological Linguistics* (1977), and the speaker–listener model of speech Skinner called *intraverbals* (see Vargas, 1982). Like Bijou's pioneering efforts, other behavioral crusaders affirming operant causes of verbal behavior, have demystified mentalistic vagaries of "preprogrammed language" by defining and replicating procedures on how humans form words and thoughts.

Accordingly, plaudits poured in from the scientific community which hailed verbal behavior research as seriously departing from sorcery. But the cognitivist critics were recalcitrant about one problem they believed behavioral scientists failed to solve: How does learned verbal behavior remain stored inside the organism without exposure to operant or respondent contingencies? Automatic reinforcement provided one explanation—that self-producing consequences evoked verbal and nonverbal responses and maintained durations of behavior sequences. Another solution derived from Skinner's concept of *autoclitic tacts and mands*, formulated to show convincingly that self-evocative behavior changes independently of listeners. Autoclitic tacts are self-verbal relationships between surrounding nonverbal stimuli and evocative verbal replies. Saying "it is snowing outside" occurs after visual (photoreceptor) detection of snowfall functions as a discriminative stimulus. Controlling discriminative variables may also be inaccurate or irrelevant, such as saying "it is snowing outside" purely on hearsay or by watching the Weather Channel forecast snowfall.

The autoclitic mand is slightly different insofar as its evocative sources. Self-verbal or nonverbal responses are triggered by *self-statements* and *establishing operations*. The speaker's own verbal statements enjoin changes partly because of hunger, thirst, curiosity, worry, or some state of deprivation or punishment, and partly from relieving the establishing operation once manded responses occur. A child whispering to himself, "Oh my God, Dad is drinking again," followed by "I better leave the house," is reacting both to visual (photoreceptor) sensations of his father drinking, and the establishing operation of fear (impending punishment). The rejoinder "I better leave the house," and actually vacating the premises, negatively reinforces the autoclitic mand to occur in the future. The speaker responds without directly experiencing consequences from the inebriated father's behavior. In other words, that child may rush out of the house governed by autoclitic mands, never knowing whether his father might *really* get angry at him for staying in the house. Past history of the father's anger is all the matters in forming autoclitic mands.

A third remedy was Michael's (1983b) revisionary categorization of variables controlling verbal behavior into *evocative and repertoire-altering effects*. Hypothetically, behaviors triggered by antecedent stimuli without consequences constitute evocative effects. Observed changes may be immediate, momentary, and lack sufficient response strength. Loud noises, for example, may signal hypervigilant responses in adults raised among acrimonious parents. Autonomic arousal may stimulate histrionic, overreactions such as spontaneously yelling at the people causing the noise. In contrast, "repertoire-altering" effects arise when behaviors change from reinforcing or punishing consequences, regardless of the events preceding the behaviors. The noise-punished adult may still overreact but in hopes of instantly terminating the noxious sound. As the noisemakers stop, reinforced behaviors of overreaction probably will recur under similar circumstances.

Rule-Governed Behavior

A fourth reason for self-mediating thinking deals with a precocious behavioral phenomenon called *rule-governed behavior.* (Hayes,

1989; Zettle, 1990; Zettle & Hayes, 1982; Zettle & Young, 1987). Rules are set up like discriminative stimuli or "cues" that parents give to their children when a certain behavior is called for, such as "Don't touch that; it will burn you," or "Taste this; you'll like it." Most people follow rules specifying direct behaviors, whether behaviors are proactive or avoidant. Rules prohibiting action—such as "Don't do that!"—originally gain support from direct-acting contingencies or experiences where the parent presents instances of right and wrong behavior followed by punishment. A parent sets up a training situation (deliberately or inadvertently) in which good or bad behavior verbally is described. For example, abusive parents might shout, "See, I told you not to do that," or "You did that all wrong." Stated rules describing the child's actions and its consequences lay the initial foundation for rule imitation.

Rule imitation occurs when the learner repeats the rule to himself. This is especially important if rule-following action occurs without the rule trainer (parent) being present. Self-generated rules usually begin with the question, "What rule is most appropriate here?" This question gives rise to various words and phrases, until the person says something that in turn cues the right or relevant rule. Recalling our earlier discussion of autoclitic tacts and mands, self-mediated statements help the speaker to search for rules. For example, on finishing a task, an adult asks himself, "Did I really finish this task, or is there more to do?" Rules that question incomplete tasks imitate parental rules about unfinished homework or chores and the anticipation of impending aversive consequences. This snapshot example of explainable cognitive processes may seem obvious, but it is crucial to understanding the damage that rules can have on brutal self-evaluation.

Self-Evaluatory Rules

One classic symptom of ACOA is obsessively severe self-criticism. Reasons for self-criticism equally explain the frequency and topography of other dysfunctional behaviors. Rules instilled by parents produce a blueprint of questions and answers generated during a problem-solving or difficult situation. An adult faced with replanting a dying shrubbery asks herself, "Why did it die?" "Did I do something wrong?" and "Is replanting the best option?" Answers supplied arbitrarily by abusive parents for similar transgressions in childhood might sound like, "It died because you neglected it, and therefore it's your fault!" Years later in adulthood the evolving rule contains similar negativity, except the speaker instead is self-referent about mistakes. For example, "It died because *I* neglected it, therefore it's *my* fault."

Alcoholic or abusive parents who excessively punish imperfections, and both compliance *or* noncompliance of tasks, teach the child inaccurate rules. Whereas the accurate rule would be "You killed the shrubbery. Here is how to fix it," the inaccurate rule is "You killed the shrubbery. You can't fix it. You screwed up. You always screw things up." ACOAs who repeat these rules for personal mistakes consequently recite inaccurate and self-pejorative rules. Acquiring negative and inaccurate self-evaluatory rules interferes with effective reasoning and can cause serious emotional injury.

Sometimes rules fade over time. Do they vanish forever or return with intensity? Rules extinguished over time because of diminished contact with abusive parents may reacquire their strength from relevant or irrelevant environmental variables (Dixon & Hayes, 1998; Hayes, 1987). Rules become self-generative for two reasons. One is that contingencies corresponding to some or all of the relevant variables forming the rule reappear in the person's life; this type of instructional control is called *pliance*. Here the rule clearly specifies punishment or reinforcement for rule compliance. The ACOA's alcoholic mother pays him a visit from Houston, for example, and suddenly he feels anxious that "I must clean my house meticulously or else risk my mother's criticism."

A second form of rule-controlled behavior occurs from a past conditioning history corresponding to the rule and consequences, although there are no consequences at the moment of compliance. This is called *tracking*. Tracking closely resembles moralist thinking. Rules abstractly identify proper versus improper behaviors based on a host of trials and errors between behavior and natural contingencies. Self-instructions of the type. "I really should not go out this late at night" imply past untoward experiences with unsafe evening travel, although no particular consequences are immediately present as the speaker recites the rule.

A third reason for resurgent rules is a common parameter found in extinction-induced responses. Rules separated from reinforcement or punishment that, hypothetically, go into remission, may set the occasion for competing rules, that may not be any better. Replacement of one set of instructions for extinguished instructions is analogous to self-deprecatory behaviors replacing anger behaviors. ACOAs who stop reciting rules about revenge (e.g., "I can't stand being manipulated, so I will get back at him") may reverse the assault against themselves, and say, "Everything is my fault, and I must punish myself for being this stupid." Both sets of rules taught during childhood compete for probability of occurrence based on environmental conditions and establishing operations. Both sets of rule repertoires are resistant to extinction.

Central to rule resurgence is its impact on ACOA thinking. Reasoning is distorted by inflexible rules that force adults to think solutions are at one extreme or the other, either "black or white." The more naive a person is about the problem at hand, the harsher the rules. Adverse properties of rules come into play when self-statements describe why the person should have known how to do better and how their incompetence once again proves how stupid they are and how they will never amount to anything. Such disturbing statements confound logical reasoning or calmly focusing on realistic solutions. This is why ACOAs panic over minor setbacks in schedule that require spontaneous readjustment. Self-instructed anger pervades thoughts so obsessively that it is impossible to troubleshoot problems objectively.

Emotional injury builds on inaccurate rules dealing with fearful, aversive consequences. Thinking, for instance, that the dead shrubbery will look awful to the neighbors or that the spouse might be angry, carries over rules learned in childhood that mistakes are intolerable and threaten parental rebuke. Internal rules describing imminent rejection, conflict, or criticism will evoke fear and avoidance behavior. The ACOA makes the self-statement, "They'll be angry with me" and then instantly engages in a predictive series of actions. He hides the dead shrub, buys a new one from the nursery, and plants it before anybody finds out about the lethal mistake. All incriminating evidence is removed.

Avoidance behaviors such as that described here also accompany compensatory behaviors. Self-statements anticipating rejection, criticism, or conflict may describe an inaccurate rule that "one must make up for stupid mistakes or else pay the piper." Consequently, the person engages in excessive pleasing or caretaking responses toward the person from whom they expect adverse consequences. Inaccurate rules specifying these adverse consequences and the urgency for caretaking are strongly compulsive. ACOA's will resist any outsider's advice not to follow the rules.

META-RULES

Rules also arise when things parents say and do are inconsistent. Rules cannot be consistent or accurate because the rule followed today may or may not produce the same consequences tomorrow. Against this obstacle, distressed children create qualifiers or *meta-rules* that essentially govern when a rule is probable or improbable, given several different parental factors. Sophisticated as it sounds, the process of meta-rules is quite elementary.

Meta-rules consist of a pool of experiences between action and consequences *(contingencies)* that are consulted internally; that is, they are generated from autoclitic tacts and mands, or from bistimulational referential language action (Pronko, 1980, p. 465). Self-grooming rules, for instance, have many meta-rules to counter the unpredictable fluctuations in parental behavior confronted daily. The rule "I should wash my face with a washcloth before going to bed" has some reinforcing strength and effectively prompts face-washing behavior around the non-ACOA parent. Around the ACOA parent, this rule undergoes variability if other meta-rules arise dictating different behaviors. If the ACOA parent is father, here are the meta-rules:

I should wash my face with a washcloth before going to bed, but:

1. Not if dad is yelling; then skip washing my face and head right to bed.
2. Not if dad is very quiet; then wash my face twice and ask him how it looks. If he says "okay," then go to bed. If he says "no good," then get a new washcloth and do it over again. Make sure dad says "okay."
3. Not if dad yells at me while I get ready for bed: then skip washing my face and ask dad what he wants me to do. If he says get into bed, do it. If he then says, after I'm in bed, "wash your face," do it.

Meta-rules are statements specifying the additional or supplemental action needed to avoid or escape punishment or to accelerate reinforcement. Children develop meta-rules from anticipating and observing the verbal and nonverbal behaviors of their parents regarding routine or daily activities involving themselves, their parents, their siblings, or other significant family members. Rules stabilize once the additional information accurately predicts or controls parental consequences, even though the original rule does not. For example, "I should wash my face with a washcloth before going to bed," is unreliable to assure punishment or reinforcement, but any variation of #1, #2, or #3 above increases the probability of either consequence. Around the ACOA parent, meta-rules are absolutely necessary for early adjustment.

Rules of ACOA

Suppressive rules that develop from parental abuse ultimately form inaccurate self-statements about the world. As operant-shaped rules, self-statements form as imitations of punitive parental instructions linking the expected behavior to its consequences. Correspondence between behavior and contingencies may fade over time, transforming detailed-specific rules into generalities. Generalized rules lack precision about stimulus-response interrelationships and become abstract, moralistic proverbs about life philosophy. For example, from "I should do my homework and then play outdoors" comes "one ought to work first, before one plays." Rule generality converts instructions to belief systems and is less discriminative about which behaviors conform to the rule. "I ought to be a good son to my mother," for instance, clearly idealizes an appropriate intrafamily repertoire but does not specify which "good behavior" the ACOA should do. A reasonable conclusion therefore is that rule generality evokes variable or weak responses.

Unfortunately, this is not true. Recall the earlier statement that ACOA rule repertoires are resistant to extinction. Generalized rules also are resistant to extinction. Like generalized conditioned reinforcers, multiple sources of strength exert contingency control over the speaker's behavior that may or may not have anything to do with the rule recited. Generalized rules thus may produce two results. First, rules evoke a past response class learned under specific instructional control during childhood. Second, rules evoke multiple response classes (response generalization) learned from a variety of specific and nonspecific instructions encountered in childhood and adulthood.

In this first case, ACOAs who say "all good people go to church" may loyally attend Sunday morning services as they did when growing up. In the second case, this religious belief accumulates infinitely diverse reinforcing and punishing consequences from the adult community. Some of the consequences may match the ACOA's parents' consequences and thereby produce corresponding behaviors. Other adult behaviors acquired directly or indirectly through a continuum of life experiences may deviate from parental contingencies but occur with equal force. For example, peer approval, fulfillment of volunteerism, creating a positive impression for one's own children—all of these consequences figure prominently in regular church attendance. Self-instructional church rules thus mobilize the ACOA to produce incredible response efficiency, even beyond the response gradient exhibited during the ACOA's childhood.

Following are examples of generalized rules and their consequential effects upon ACOAs:

Rule 1: It's not okay to talk about problems.
Effect: Families avoid owning problems and children feel shame. As adults, blame is either entirely absorbed or attributed to others.
Rule 2: Feelings are not expressed openly. Keep them to yourself.
Effect: Child denies feelings and stores them up. As adults, conservation of thoughts and fears deny exposure of vulnerability and foster distrust toward other adults.
Rule 3: Communication is private; say as little as possible.
Effect: Innocent children become victims of self-induced fear. As adults, inferences rapidly develop about reasons, motivations underlying people's actions, and why they pose an emotional liability to the person. In addition, expression is selective, frequently edited, and rehearsed for appropriateness, and following an expression the person "replays" the interaction over and over (cognitively), looking for faults.
Rule 4: Nothing is good enough. Even imitating the parents' actions is unreliable for approval.

Effect: Child believes he always fails at tasks and that more exertion of effort will ultimately gain parental (adult) approval. As adults, intolerance to mistakes becomes perfectionism, and the person persists toward achieving unattainable goals.

Rule 5: Don't be selfish.

Effect: Self-esteem derives from altruistic caretaking. As adults, feelings of dissatisfaction are constant with a minor reprieve while embarking on a mission to help other people. Self-derived benefits never eliminate dissatisfaction, but may worsen a depression.

Rule 6: Do as I say, not as I do.

Effect: Children receive mixed messages and learn not to trust and not to take risks. As adults, action is methodical, controlled, and the person must remain in control or assume a leadership role. Failure to do so creates anxiety and social withdrawal.

Rule 7: It's not okay to play.

Effect: Child views self as unlovable, boring, and stupid. As adults, activity and productivity remain a constant gauge of self-esteem. Time for oneself is unthinkable, evokes fears of impending adverse consequences, and creates immediate feelings of shame. Adult has difficulty relaxing or acting in a childish, jocular manner.

Rule 8: Don't rock the boat.

Effect: Child withdraws from conflict. As adults, avoidance and escape from conflict become a familiar routine.

Eyeing the topic of rules superficially, skeptics are bound to denigrate the presumption that rule-governed behavior is really a holding tank of past operant and respondent conditioning. Cognitivists, particularly, may object to calling rules "evocative stimuli" that are different from pre-programmed mechanisms of language. Rules, critics may further insist, are nothing more than internally organized and sophisticated expressions of societal norms. Analyzing rules through integrative fields of contingencies may cause researchers to lose sight of traditional theories of cognitive and moral development. The infamous psychological pedigrees of linguistics and epistemology, after all, are valued professionally and receive interdisciplinary attention. So, then, why are they subordinated here?

The answer is simple: The research data supporting their conceptual paradigms are scientifically inferior to the behavioral paradigms. As clinicians, assessment decisions of ACOAs must begin with empirically predicated principles, which the behavioral position generously offers. By using these principles, practitioners can sort the real events from the notoriously hypothetical ones.

CHAPTER 5

Living with ACOAs: Spousal Reactions

Husband, wives, even significant live-in partners, may realize a loved one suffers from a dysfunctional history and that symptoms come and go sporadically. Symptoms range from conspicuous alcohol or drug abuse and unpredictable mood shifts to very subtle caretaking and avoidance behaviors. Obvious symptoms such as polydrug addiction call attention immediately to the need for treatment. Benevolently obligated partners aware of these intrarelational dynamics also discover three disturbing conclusions. The first conclusion is that loving sympathy perpetuates the partner's dysfunctionality (Brandt, 1976). A second is that unpleasurable reactions of disgust and repulsion also reinforce the partner's incorrigibility (Wills, Weiss & Patterson, 1974). A third finding is serendipitous: Complete withdrawal from the partner, thereby terminating social and nonsocial reinforcers for partner conflict, leaves the healthy partner feeling indifferent and uncaring. But it causes a rapid increase in the unhealthy partner's positive actions (Christensen, 1988).

Loving partners who grow confused by these predicaments may hunt for therapists, psychiatrists, or general practitioners. Assistance moves toward easing the rising tensions and burdens of the affected partner. Self-sacrifice, appeasements, and even self-analyzing the troubled spouse provide temporary solutions. However, partner symptoms that are well guarded or disguised by avoidance and escape, appearing as obsessions or inaccurate rule-governed behaviors, remain unnoticed or are misinterpreted. Camouflaged responses may send mixed messages such as "help me, but don't change me." Ambiguous responses also unfortunately lack a "sound-track" where the dysfunctional spouses can explain why they are exhibiting this behavior. They don't know why, and in fact view their own behaviors as normal and their partner's motivation to change them as abnormal. Without known answers, uncorrected behaviors not only damage the couple relationship but produce horrible repercussions for the presumably healthy partner.

This chapter reviews the fundamental impact of partners exposed to premarital or marital partners exhibiting ACOA symptoms. Building on Stuart's (1969) operant formulation of marital discord, reciprocal contingencies explored include the unpredictability of ACOA behavior; role ambiguity; polarity of affection; challenge to change ACOAs; avoidance of criticism, conflict and rejection; infidelity; domestic violence; and separation and divorce.

Unpredictability of ACOA Behavior

One of the worst reactions stems from not predicting how a partner behaves. Usually a cohabitant couple learns the routines, habits, and daily schedules of the other, even developing a "sixth sense," so to speak, regarding the person's reactions, given certain conditions. Development of this intuitive perception of life events is quite normal in most healthy relationships. However, living with ACOAs disrupts this intuitive sense of prediction in two ways. First, impulsive and inconsistent behaviors eliminate a correlation between what the ACOA says and does. Second, emotional instability may cause unprecipitated, cyclical mood changes from hypermania to depression accompanied by inconsistent verbal behaviors. Sometimes the ACOA is apologetic, compensatory, and compassionate. At other times the ACOA is self-critical, withdrawn, and hypersensitive to any caring gestures made by the partner. A third reaction is hostility, which includes explosive tirades that persist uncontrollably as physical aggression, and unfounded accusations that blame anything and everything on other people.

Untraceable contingencies batter the unsuspecting partner, who literally gets hit "broadside," without a clue of how to prevent or escape repetition of further adverse confrontations. Jacobson & Margolis (1979) interactional cause–effect model, where both partners continuously control the behavior of the other, assumes that changes in one partner's behavior covaries with inevitable behavior changes in the other partner. Reciprocal conditioning, in this respect, implies that healthy partners unaware of their partner's reasons for deficits or excesses nonetheless undergo measurable changes in adapting to their disturbed partner. Applying Patterson's model of coercion (Patterson & Hops, 1972; Patterson & Reid, 1970), such conditioned changes may further include interchanges where both persons provide adverse stimuli to control the behavior of the other. One result is positive punishment, when mechanisms of mutual anger intensify acrimony. A second result is negative punishment, where terminating communication decelerates partner contact and feelings of reconciliation.

In both cases, diminished interpersonal contact is conditioned by reciprocal field events without the non-ACOA spouse informed of underlying ACOA problems. Reactivity effects of anger and absconding from the relationship were evident with Judy and Harold. This newlywed couple, who premaritally cohabited for two years, presented problems of (a) violent arguments, (b) the wife's runaway behaviors, and (c) the husband threatening divorce. Closer behavioral assessment revealed Judy's upbringing in an alcoholic family, and that her parents abusively punished her for idiosyncratic mistakes. Conflict-avoidance behaviors topographically consisted of escaping discord by running away to a motel or to a girlfriend's house. Runaway behaviors transferred into dating intimate partners and systematically weakened previous long-term relationships. Fortuitously, Harold's initially passive and empathic behaviors saw her runaway behaviors differently. He attributed Judy's peculiar avoidance to emotional inexperience in relationships and thus patiently "waited until she passed through this stage."

As Judy's runaways persisted, Harold grew suspicious that her impulsive actions meant an extramarital relationship existed, and consequently his docility changed to aggression. He investigated her behavior by checking the car odometer for mileage, contacting her friends to learn of her transactions, and even by taking cloth samples of her lingerie to a police lab for chemical analysis. Why? Because Harold, previously a trusting, beneficent and carefree person, could not stand the equivocation of his wife's behaviors. Maladjustment to limited and unreliable causal variables of Judy's behavior transformed Harold from Dr. Jeckyl to Mr. Hyde, based on impure inferences and failure to regain marital balance.

Role Ambiguity

Unpredictability develops into role ambiguity. Role ambiguity is not knowing which behavior is best for the situation (Ruben, 1986a). *Best* may refer to behaviors that defuse, calm, confront, or alter the dysfunctional actions. Several options include caretaking, being aggressive, showing sympathy, avoiding or escaping. Initially the ambiguity is inconvenient and leaves the partner upset for a short period of time until prediction of behavior returns.

Prolonged role ambiguity, however, causes serious disintegration of partner trust, love, and commitment to the marriage or relationship. The partner first feels (a) annoyed, (b) then angry, (c) then helpless, (d) then seeks control and prediction outside the marriage or relationship (friends, infidelity, activities, etc.), and (e) then detaches emotionally from the dysfunctional partner. Detachment results from a paralysis or numbness at not knowing what to do or how to do it, from protracted ineffectiveness at changing partner behaviors, and from inescapable and unavoidable contact with the impulsive spouse. Behaviorally, stages of detachment refer to (a) deregulation of reciprocal contingencies, and (b) harm-reduction behaviors.

Deregulation of Reciprocal Contingencies Inconsistent partner communication consists of deteriorating verbal and nonverbal behaviors. Absence or irregularity of both verbal and nonverbal responses suspends, interrupts, and distorts contingencies reciprocally affecting a couple. Ambiguous, confusing, or perplexing verbalizations signal misleading information from speaker to listener, who may misjudge the stimuli and inaccurately respond to schedules of reinforcement or punishment. Contingency breakdown from nonverbal behavior is worse. Topographical responses such as facial expressions, eye movements, and posture may indiscriminately evoke conflicting partners' responses or no responses at all. Paralanguage responses such as voice quality (pitch, range, temp, articulation control), vocal segregates (e.g., uh-huh), and artifacts, including arbitrary movement of objects, (Jacob & Lessin, 1982; Knapp, 1982) further complicate stimulus cues, causing superstitious, adjunctive, and collateral behaviors.

Non-ACOA partners, in other words, respond favorably or unfavorably in proportion to the available reinforcers or stimuli signaling concurrent or forthcoming reinforcers. Choice alternatives depend on the predictable distribution of reinforcers and time between reinforcement delivery (interreinforcement intervals, or IRIs). Behavioral choices or *allocations* under one set of stimulus conditions may vary when IRIs vary. Consequently, an intermittently reinforced husband who waits several hours before receiving another verbal or nonverbal reinforcer, theoretically, is less likely to sustain loving compassionate behaviors.

Moore (1982) indicated a different finding, using pigeons responding to initial and terminal links of reinforcement regardless of rates of reinforcement. Results showed pigeons responding more predictably in initial links but less predictably and unusually in terminal links. By analogy, non-ACOA partners exposed inescapably to unsystematic stimulus cues with shifting IRIs, may produce better choices when first dealing with the ambiguity. But as ambiguous stimuli intensify, complicated by longer IRIs, response rate decreases and choices of behavior erode.

Harm-reduction Behavior Harm reduction technically refers to managing high-risk behaviors using behavioral principles and strategies on drug or physical abusers (e.g., Marlatt, 1998). Innovative methods emphasize alcohol abatement over complete sobriety as a more powerful deterrent to relapse. The idea, of course, is that self-paced changes that preserve some addictive habits without major life alterations will sustain recovery efforts. With couples living in ambiguity, harm reduction takes on a slightly different meaning. It means non-ACOA partners self-induce changes independently of stimulus confusion, and thereby maintain continuity of their lives. Take, for example, nondrinking spouses who unilaterally decide to change their spouse's drinking behaviors. Rather than succumb to the myriad of dysfunctional contingencies that risk enabling behaviors, the spouse may resist these enticements by first upholding self-routines and habits controlling their own daily schedules. Raising self-efficacy also allows an objective, detached perspective of the alcoholic spouse, from which intervention then becomes possible (Thomas & Santa, 1982)

Polarity of Affection

Caring and sympathy have their limits. ACOAs, as indicated earlier, may show polarity of affection in that they either are heavily compassionate, intimate or sexual, or virtually cold and distant. Cues signaling this polarity make prediction of behavior easier and the mood swings more tolerable. But when cyclical swings in affection are unpredictable—that is, when they occur for opposite cues, the wrong cues, or no cues—or verbal responses promise affection but actions never deliver affection, then spouses ultimately lose physical interest and follow the steps of role ambiguity described previously.

Opposite cues occur when ACOAs verbally prompt passion at times when they never have done so in the past (e.g., in public, around the children, or when the non-ACOA spouse first prompts it). Wrong cues are situations or conditions in which the ACOA partner and non-ACOA partner mutually agree to prohibit intimacy (e.g., in the car, at friends' homes, etc.), generally as adventitious changes arising out of discord or adverse experiences. For example, lovemaking on the family room couch—a romantic protocol for 10 years—suddenly and irrevocably changed after a neighbor knocked on the door and caused the ACOA unbearable humiliation.

No cues are when sexual arousal or sexual rejection occurs without warning, and particularly without any of the cues that previously stimulated or inhibited intimacy. For instance, a male ACOA may want intercourse after not talking to his wife for four hours following a fight. The behavior may be odd because it does not trace to any historically relevant cues understood by the perplexed wife. Finally, sexual or intimate promises that do not deliver include physical or verbal overtures toward passion made at times that are grossly inconvenient or unavailable to the non-ACOA spouse. One example is calling a spouse while out of town on business with desperate sexual demands that cannot possibly be met by the spouse. When the spouse returns, even by the following morning, the ACOA's tune changes to disinterest and sexual refusals. E-mail sexual solicitations often function in this respect. ACOAs corresponding with their partners by e-mail may write lurid stories about sex and sleaze, alluding to erotic activities planned that evening. By nightfall, as the non-ACOA comments on earlier e-mail promises, the ACOA may either outrightly deny sending sexual overtures or accuse the partner of sexual addiction that tarnishes their intimacy.

A similar couple engaged in paraphilias. They admitted to intense, sexually arousing fantasies and using pornography to accompany foreplay. Elevated erotic pleasures dominated their lives, including as arsenal of fetishes, sensual devices, and recreational positions. However, experimental lovemaking was dependent on the wife's aggressive moves, and she never accepted advances from her husband. Ironically, she perceived her husband's solicitations as invasive and predatory, which made her feel dirty and like a whore. The wife, an ACOA who suffered childhood sexual abuse, only reveled in sexual play at her own initiative, during which self-effacing fears were replaced with orgasmically driven responses. Her polarity of affection left untraceable antecedents for her husband, unable to predict or control his wife's sexual appetite. Consequently, this response inconsistency diminished his eagerness to please his wife, and progressed to impaired erectile performance. Impotency not only embarrassed the husband but drew volatile criticism from the sexually narcissistic wife, who accused her husband of deliberately depriving her of her needs.

Challenge to Change ACOAs

The adage "A little information can be dangerous" applies to the non-ACOA who gains some insight into the ACOA partner's behavior and proudly assumes the role of therapist. The challenge to change the dysfunctional partner goes beyond caretaking and becomes an obsession. Every wrong behavior—from avoidance, escape, aggression, and caretaking—is monitored, confined and evaluated; persistent effort goes into showing the partner what to do instead. Premised on good intentions, the non-ACOA vigorously delves into the spouse's background for clues to a dysfunctional childhood and endeavors to teach positive skills to replace bad habits. The trouble is, it doesn't work. Not because the archeological digging of clues and postulated etiology are wrong, or even because the positive skills are wrong; partners can be astute observers with far greater therapeutic acumen than trained therapists. The mistake is confusing partner-delivered therapy with love. Non-ACOA partners mistakenly believe that helping represents a commitment of devoted love, affection, and responsibility.

ACOAs emotionally hemorrhage when partners volunteer as change agents. The reason is reminiscent of developmental altercations with parents punished the child for asking for help. Whether about homework or life problems, ACOAs rapidly suppress questions that imminently spark criticism on why they are too stupid to solve the problem by themselves, or are so weak and inferior someone else must solve the problem for them. Aversively conditioned fears emerge in adulthood as rule-governed beliefs that literally preclude acceptance of help from anybody unless the problem is serious (e.g., needs medical attention). Remedial efforts, instead, are perceived as insults that undermine the competence of the ACOA. Outwardly this reaction appears strange, as the ACOA ruthlessly blames the non-ACOA partner for insensitivity and disrespect.

The functional duty of change agents viewed as consultants or mediators is to effectively achieve positive resolution of targeted behavior problems (Tharp & Wetzel, 1969). The trouble with this strategy is fourfold. First, change agents prefer aversive control over reinforcement methods in light of punishment they experienced in childhood, even if they are not ACOAs. Second, reinforcement is too conditional or resembles bribery offered for the change agent's selfish response requirements rather than socially appropriate requirements. For example, imposing preference for daily coitus in exchange for money is unilaterally benefiting the change agent, not necessarily the behaver. Third, external constraints limit consistency and accuracy of the change agent's contingency management. Pressure from family members to divorce, separate, or be more confrontational may sabotage effective control over the ACOA's behavior. And, fourth, insistence on equity converts the change agent's unilateral crusading efforts to demanding reciprocity from the ACOA partner.

Lisa pledged to "disinfect" her husband Rick's docile repertoire by engaging him in a host of psychoeducational classes on interpersonal skills. She also sought support from her church deacon, who agreed to talk to Rick directly and encourage Lisa and Rick's therapeutic teamwork. Politely submissive, Rick gave superficial acceptance of this intervention, which spun Lisa into a meteoric effort to network community agencies that could provide similar skill training for Rick. However, on the first day of class, Rick called his wife from work saying he was "tied up and unable to leave the job." Excuses were repeated each week, leaving Lisa with the unwelcome task of calling the teacher and canceling classes. Feeling betrayed, Lisa confronted Rick about his contradictory behavior of agreeing to attend class but always being busy. Rick reluctantly admitted his hypocrisy and charged Lisa with aggressively controlling his life and trying to transform him into a person he never would be. He further insisted that Lisa knew what she was getting into when she married him.

Avoidance of Criticism, Conflict, and Rejection

Assertive and passive partners alike may develop habits of the ACOA without knowing it. After dealing ineffectively with unpredictable aggression, partners may avoid conflict of any sort and either keep the relationship "happy" by pleasing the partner, or by withdrawal from contact with the partner. Distancing is another form of avoidance and escape for partners unafraid of conflict and disgusted by receiving little in return for their kindness. When emotional charity is exploited, assertive partners intentionally recede to isolation to maintain their own composure and to remove attention to the ACOA's dysfunctional behaviors. Calculated distancing of this sort maintains some balance in the marriage but does not advance it in a healthy direction.

Duplicating the ACOA's behavior but operating under different contingencies is called *negative partner replication*. Partners imitate response properties after cumulative, forced exposure to the ACOA model, and after discovering that their own discriminative skills are ineffective at producing desired outcomes. Replicators lack the ACOA's reactional biography (i.e., history of conditioning) and thus respond to cues unlike their ACOA counterparts. Behavioral imitation may occur for three reasons. First, reversal of aversive control may require non-ACOA partners to use means of punishment (see Balsam & Bondy, 1983). For example, children who are spanked often may employ physical force later on to exert control over people. Likewise, battered non-ACOA partners observe their ACOA partner use avoidance and escape for control and thus improperly imitate this behavior to balance the relationship.

Second, reinforcers and punishers presented arbitrarily not only affect one response but also affect competing responses. With punishment, for example, a reduction in physical affection responses is parallel to the increase in incompatible responses such as hatred of sexual behavior or exploratory sexual behavior with alternate partners. Incompatible behaviors accidentally substitute for appropriate behaviors when contingencies lose reinforcement for one set of behaviors while producing reinforcers for an opposite set of behaviors.

Third, replicatory behavior occurs when non-ACOA partners empathize or vicariously identify with contingencies observed as hurting or helping the ACOA. For example, children observing their parents pay the concierge a tip for receiving first-row seat tickets for a Broadway play may naturally imitate this behavior by directly identifying with their parents' elation (e.g., Kazdin, 1973). In adulthood, they may also pay tips to service providers giving them privileges. In the same vein, non-ACOA partners witnessing their loved ones as happy or unhappy may self-reproduce this behavior to attain identical feelings. Imitating the ACOA's happiness is a way to approximate relational cohesion and make it feel like the couple is getting along. Matching unhappy or distressful feelings, on the other hand, functions similarly to principles governing caretaking, where sharing the person's hurt is a way to remove it from the distressed person.

Reginal, a 45-year-old computer analyst, was cohabiting with Cindy for two years when they decided to seek therapy. His girlfriend Cindy, an ACOA, frequently suffered periods of depression marked by anhedonia, dysphoria, and noncommunication. She avoided discussion about her symptoms and refused individual counseling; instead she secluded herself in bed for numerous days despite Reginal's desperate pleas to help her improve. Cindy's withdrawal took a toll on the relationship, ending in cessation of sexual relations and loss of her job which, placed financial burdens on Reginal's solo income. Besides removing herself from daily interactions, Cindy contemplated suicide and openly threatened overdose of over-the-counter medicines unless she felt better.

At the end of three months, Reginal observed that his own vitality and motivation had withered away to apathy and complacency. He missed Cindy's companionship and observed sensing feelings of unhappiness that Cindy experienced. Internally depressed emotions ironically made him identify with Cindy's suffering, instantly raising his perceived value to her. Sharing her feelings, he also explained, bridged the distant gap between their worlds and eliminated fears of being abandoned. Reginal's negative partner replication of depression vicariously produced both the positive reinforcer of feeling valued, and a negative reinforcer through cessation of anxiety associated with his fears of the relationship ending.

INFIDELITY

Non-ACOA partners can destroy a principal commitment of monogamy. Detachment goes beyond polarity of emotions or deprivation of sexual intimacy. Even if coitus is frequent, the couple's reciprocally conditioned behaviors of sharing, listening, and enjoying each other's nonsexual company may be absent. Slow deterioration of physical and emotional rapport progressively loosens the closed marital boundary and increases motivation for both ACOA and non-ACOA partners to seek other intimate partners. At first, non-ACOAs threaten infidelity as an ultimatum so that the troubled ACOA partner can rapidly affect behavior change or at least admit there is a problem.

Failing at this scheme, non-ACOA partners delicately charter a path of socializing differently by flirting more with attractive single partners or engaging in social or business activities away from the couple's shared household. The result is infidelity that gradually progresses through predictable behavioral stages:

Stage 1: Friendships innocently form though casual contact with emotionally or physically attractive listeners. Conversational dialogue emerges that covers neutral topics or topics relevant to the stimulus context. Amicable exchanges generate social reinforcers preferred over the paucity of reinforcers or abundance of punishers received from the existing partner. Reinforcement also increases the future probability of recurrent conversations with the friend.

Stage 2: Platonic friendship shifts to personal advisors. Here, both parties replace superficial topics with disclosure of personal feelings and thoughts pertaining to topics such as politics, social or work problems, or the futility of dating in general. One person cathartically reveals guarded secrets while the other person empathizes with the speaker through reinforcing intraverbals. Reciprocally guiding the dyadic are confidential statements that expose both person's vulnerability.

Risk-taking remarks are transformed from covenant feelings about other people to private feelings about self. Safety in releasing these emotions corresponds to mutual continuous reinforcement schedules (CRFs) of caring and compassion.

Stage 3: Disclosure of intimate secrets builds trust. The friendship evolves from surface conversations to therapeutically charged conversations dealing with sadness and disappointments about the existing partner. Discussions broach boundary restrictions morally preventing the two friends from violating existing partner relationships. Sensitive details are trusted to remain within the confines of the friendship, at which time platonic friends turn into co-conspirators protecting potentially damaging information. Mutual commitment to guard these truths establishes a compatible motivation (i.e., safety of self-reported data) and increases the subsequently sharing of intimate matters.

Stage 4: Entrustment of self-reported data builds nonverbal affection for the friend. Just as transference is common in psychotherapy, so is transference normal after divulging emotional information to a friend. Extent of risk information disclosed typically is proportional to reinforcer density from the listening friend. Consequently, nonverbal affection arises between both friends in response to increased desires to share additional personal history. For example, revealing that one receives medication for lupus that inhibits sexual arousal may feel scary, but fear dissipates once the listener shows compassion. The establishing operation for listener approval is met and thereby relieves speaker anxiety. Such intraverbal mands generate specific reinforcers that are nonexistent in the current relationships and thus are highly evocative of repeated contact between the two friends.

Stage 5: Nonverbal affection leads to laudatory statements and augmented reinforcement systems. Friends who previously met occasionally for lunch diversify their interactions in multiple settings and share novel experiences. They eat at different restaurants, go on long drives, and engage in secret rendezvous points motivated by curiosity and enhancing generalized reinforcers. Both friends also generously lavish one other with descriptive praise about important decisions, hobbies, or high-rate responses. For example, a professor receives enormous praise from the friend about his scholarly writings and pedagogy. Attorneys hear that they are competent trial lawyers and respected in the community. Verbal compliments reinforce fundamentally important behaviors in the friends' lives. The result is response generalization of friend interaction across time and settings.

Stage 6: Reciprocal reinforcement becomes physically affectionate. Beginning with Stage 4, the couple has been courting. Their enriched reinforcement system includes safety and security of disclosures, adaptivity to new situations, reinforcers filling the void left by the existing partner, behavior compatibility, and propensity for reciprocal nonverbal affection. For relationships built on "friendship," as opposed to immediate sexual attraction, prerequisites are now met to risk mutual touching. Exploratory risk-free touching occurs with hugs, polite forehead, lip, and other facial kisses, and by gestural proximity. The latter refers to gently rubbing up against the friend, removing dust or lint particles from the friend's clothing, and making hand movements spatially contiguous with the friend's body.

Stage 7: Proximal touching potentiates higher order risks of romantic passion. Bilaterally reinforcing touching proceeds from polite contact to replications of sensual contact that previously occurred with an existing partner. Preplay, foreplay and eventually sexual intercourse are simply hierarchical steps successively reached depending on two factors. First is reinforcer accessibility for greater risks of romantic touching—that is, do the friends reciprocally give permission to make sexual advancements? Second is automatic reinforcers (e.g., sensory arousal). Self-reinforcement perpetuates romantic responses that are incompatible with romantic responses for the existing partner. Romantic feelings for the existing partner are not exclusively absent but stronger for the friend.

Differentially reinforced romantic behaviors may explain why partners carrying on affairs grow cold, detached, and distant from their existing partners. *They are not insensitive people, but instead their behaviors are desensitized from the aversive partner and reshaped by a reinforcing friend.*

Domestic Violence

Proclivity for domestic violence affects both genders and is substantially more prevalent than researchers projected several decades ago (Pagelow, 1997). Battering accounts for more than 25% of emergency room visits by women (Stark et al., 1981). For women ages 15 to 44, domestic violence is the leading cause of injury. However, sociologic research on woman battering also reveals contradictory findings about women victims—namely, that a large percentage of violence involves both husband and wife. From this arose the claims of "mutual combat" (see Elk & Johnson, 1989). Partner maltreatment, no matter who the culprit, traces to fairly predictable antecedents of escalative conflict. The profound problem lies not with *how* arguments intensify but with partners mishandling unusual manifestations of reciprocal anger. Relationships in which one partner is an ACOA run particularly serious risks of anger-related domestic abuse for reasons cited in foregoing chapters.

The point here is that patterns of domestic violence also impact non-ACOAs and spark misinterpretation about who really is victim and who is perpetrator. Within the criminal justice system, for example, battered complainants frequently are women reported as submissive, docile, and manipulable. Predatory victimizers, by contrast, receive stereotypical labels of defiance and aggression, and purportedly have a past criminal record of spouse abuse. Perceiving women as vulnerable scapegoats ignores the possibility that women may use partner violence for secondary gain (Hamberger, 1997). Men and women alike raised in drinking or punishing households may view violence as normal and therefore incite chaos among partners that is reminiscent of family life. Incitement of arguments may produce misperceived evidence of love, affection, and relational stability.

The initiation of violence in caring, easy-going or even passive partners eventually weakens their resistance. They become retaliatory simply out of self-defense and when defusal strategies fail. Arrested victimizers who blame provocation on, of all things, a drinking partner, particularly are regarded as liars. However, research studies substantially document the association between alcohol and battering (e.g., Conner & Ackerley, 1994). Intoxication-induced aggression arouses verbal and physical acrimony without the perpetrator being aware of his or her rough actions. Post-acrimony awareness even lacks the insight that under influence of alcohol the drinker is prone to fighting. Rather, drinking perpetrators surprisingly deny having reactionary behaviors and blame their poor impulse control on unsuspecting partners. Likewise, ACOAs who are not drinkers but display behavioral patterns tantamount to drinkers risk the same probability of abusive aggression.

Consequently, nonaggressive partners drawn into assaultive fighting suffer two outcomes. First, they inadvertently develop anticipatory angry outbursts when they expect the batterer to blow up. Anticipatory anger alone can provoke volatile arguments that can progress to violence. Second, in response to combatively persistent predators, they may become self-protective and reciprocate violence to terminate further fighting. Unfortunately, negative reinforcement is not the controlling operant variable. Rather, retaliatory exchanges nearly always escalate the magnitude of punishment. The only reason arguments eventually cease is either due to injury, intercession by children, or police intervention.

A 35-year-old separated woman filed a custody motion against her estranged husband. She accused him of frequent brutality and believed his outrageous temper posed emotional danger to the minor child. She sought damages insofar as terminating his visitation privileges and legally enforcing treatment for batterers. The husband reported an antithetical story. Raised by conservative religious parents, neither of whom drank, used drugs, or were violent, he presented a history of docility with glaring caretaking behaviors. He was attracted to his wife, he reported, by her excitability, impulsiveness, and extraordinary physical appearance. When the wife appeared for psychological evaluation, her leg was in a cast and she walked with crutches. She also arrived with supporters from a local domestic violence shelter. The fracture, she insisted, resulted from recent combative episodes with her husband that forced her into the shelter. Her entire testimony revolved around victimization issues, and she accused her current husband and previous lovers of physically abusive control over her.

Forensic analysis of her case background, however, revealed a different story. This victimized woman grew up in a seriously violent household surrounded by dually alcoholic parents and assaultive siblings. She also suffered repeated childhood sexual abuse by penetration and even sustained post-rape injuries in adulthood. Boyfriends since adolescent ended up in volatile altercations, provoked by her demanding and callus teasing, sarcasm, and acidic criticisms. When violence erupted, she typically sought vindication by contacting the authorities, who perceived her as the martyr and often arrested her boyfriends. After repeating this cycle of abuse, she grew accustomed to picking fights, exaggerating her personal injuries, and escaping the relationship through public sympathy.

SEPARATION AND DIVORCE

A substantial body of research supports the intuitive view that children from divorced families tend to manifest pathology (e.g., Allison & Furstenberg, 1989). Children exposed to divorcing parents basically learn two contingencies. The first is reinforcement for marital intolerance. That is, relationship decay that occurs from years of discord, infidelity, or other incompatibilities becomes an automatic prerequisite for marital separation. The divorce-generation child abhors marital problems and justifies signs of discord as reasons for terminating the marriage. A second contingency-shaped behavior is reinforcement for adaptvity. Children from divorced families transitionally adjusted without one parent present. They rapidly adapted to the awkwardness, social stigma, and additional intrafamily responsibilities and duties left by the missing partner. The eldest child, for instance, may assume surrogate parental tasks of feeding his infant brother while the single parent father is at work. Absence of a mother requires there be an understudy, or eldest child, providing caregiving. Caring for oneself or parenting another child while the real parent is gone serendipitously builds a comfortable repertoire of overcoming adversity. Adverse consequences of divorce—be they moral, legal, social, religious, or cultural—all appear surmountable and thereby reinforce initiatives to dissolve the marriage.

However, ACOAs from divorced or nondivorced families may be an exception to these conditioning principles. By separating, ACOA spouses suddenly experience panic because of fear of abandonment and loneliness. For one thing, parting lives evokes the rule-governed guilty response of "this marital failure must be my fault," and elevates anxiety until the self-effacing spouse does something. Consequently the ACOA may seek marriage therapy or desperately beg the departing partner to reconsider other means of conciliation.

Another effect of anticipated abandonment is that the lonely spouse may aggressively retaliate under conditions of helplessness and vulnerability. Retributional acts may be perceived as "malicious and controlling," but are catalysts for reinforcement. ACOAs rebuild their self-control and gain anxiety relief by positively punishing the disputing spouse through arguments. They also obstruct or distort the contingencies. Punishing spouses may wage war against the other partner through aggressive attorneys, by gossiping to friends, and by accusing the partner of emotional and physical abuses. Abuses manufactured purely for revenge produce negative reinforcement; the removal of self-blame and the adversarial spouse increase feelings of vengeance.

The self-reinforcing effects that relieve anxiety and stabilize confidence are transient. Side effects fade away when competing, unexpected contingencies surface along the marital matrix. Recalcitrant ACOAs who separate from their spouses because of conflict may reverse their decision once they discover the estranged spouse has a new lover or is enjoying himself or herself. Vindictive reinforcement contingencies vanish since, presumably, the spouse afflicted by those contingencies escaped the controlling effects. Realizing this, ACOAs may respond predictably in two ways. One way is to eagerly and strategically reunify the broken marriage by luring the estranged spouse from competing lovers. Considerable behavior intensity is expended in appeasement, self-deprecation, and apology for past retaliatory actions. Retrieval of the spouse not only terminates rising fears of permanent abandonment, but also eliminates a seriously damaging self-governing rule that becomes obsessive: "Why was I so bad that he or she wanted another person?"

A second response to recover contingencies is by belligerently discrediting the spouse's lover. Vindictive ACOAs overlook their conniving actions while perceiving the estranged spouse's choice of another partner as deceptive and betraying. Consequently, they may fabricate and disseminate lies or directly confront their spouse by phone, e-mail, snail-mail, or in person about their lover's infelicities. The ACOA collects defamational evidence by surreptitiously tracing the lover's family roots, unobtrusively talking to the lover's friends, examining telephone or Visa card records, and amassing a dossier filled with innuendoes that reveal unscrupulous actions. Exposure of this anecdotal evidence ideally functions as a behavioral contrast effect, whereby two similar stimuli (the ACOA spouse and lover) compete for the response (the estranged spouse). Additional complications arise, however, based on subtle variations in the way multiple-scheduled stimuli are presented (Kodera & Riling, 1976). For example, contrast effects may rapidly dissipate after extended stimulus training, or, in this case, where the ACOA spouse's defamational data may be on a variable ratio or variable interval schedule and thereby pales in comparison to the lover's continuous reinforcement schedule of living with the estranged spouse (see Terrance, 1966).

Additionally, matching law theory suggests that in order to modify the estranged spouse's behavior, rates of competing reinforcers must equally undergo modification. Within a singular stimulus field, such as a marital household, differentiation of reinforcing stimuli may be possible. But where stimulus fields are continuous, such as across two households (e.g., the ACOA and the estranged spouse), control over concurrent reinforcement schedules is virtually impossible. Lowering or elevating response rates to desired reinforcers further is frustrated by punishment and rule-governed contingencies. For example, at the applied level, not only does the estranged spouse hate and want to avoid the belligerent ACOA spouse, but rules emanate from punishment schedules such as "She's trying to sabotage my happiness with this new lover." Predictive and control power over spousal behaviors thus deteriorates once marital separation produces multiple schedules of reinforcement and punishment.

To this extent, legally separated spouses desiring reconciliation typically face an uphill battle because the sources of stimulus control are inextricable. Feelings of love, compassion, and even promises to change punitive behaviors exert low motivation in spouses already consumed by continuous reinforcement systems. As with any effects they have on partners, ACOAs may be uninsightful that their dysfunctional behaviors slowly are disintegrating the intimate relationship. Partners exposed to such odd and unpredictable behaviors as ACOAs exhibit may act sympathetically at first, treating the anomalies like they would a temporary physical illness. When reasonable and temporal remedies fail, and dysfunctionality persists unabated—despite love for that partner—ratio strain and eventually response decays account for loss of affection and diversion to new reinforcing relationships.

A broken partnership may only affect the adults. But what happens when ACOAs exhibit avoidance and other defective behaviors around their children? Children simply cannot choose another, reinforcing set of parents. We'll examine the effects of ACOA behavior on children in Chapter 6.

CHAPTER 6

Living with ACOAs: Parent–Child Reactions

Why does a 6-year-old boy tuck himself into bed each night while his deceased mother lies on the living room floor covered by a blanket and crib mattress? How can two high school teens gun down innocent peers over minor disputes? Do these shootings, killings, and habituation to death tragically suggest national inattention to moral decay and civil disobedience? Or, are today's fragmented families so oblivious to homelife problems that neglected children wander off into disaster? The answers, say many developmental psychologists, lay within the disrupted family microcosm.

This chapters looks carefully at one particular disruptive family system resulting from untreated ACOA parents. Intragenerational effects of parental avoidance, escape, superstition, and other maladaptive behaviors can be emotionally destructive to impressionable children. ACOA symptoms systemically contaminate parent–child interactions and account for many reasons that children grow up unloved or prone to delinquency. Infants through young adults exposed to the same arbitrary punishment and reinforcement contingencies as their parents were rapidly lose fundamental stimulus cues for feeling safe and secure. Parent–child attachment dissolves or competes with reinforcers for behaviors incompatible with intrafamily relationships. Emotionally disenfranchised children may respond defiantly, aggressively, or engage in progressively higher risk responses, rewarded by surrogate parents such as gangs, cults, pimps, and sexual partners. Escape from adverse family stimulation reflects both internal family system failures and the failure of children to accurately generalize responses across healthy stimulus fields (see Ambert, 2000).

Inside the family, children view parental actions quite differently than outsiders observing parental behavior. Children find they cope with parental shortcomings, come to expect little or no affection, attention or assistance, and outwardly act responsible. Maladapted children find they compensate for parental shortcomings in a host of ways: they try to replace the mother or father role, they become overresponsible, and they deviate from social expectations. In this way, deviance is learned or *iatrogenic*. However, deviant behaviors may take a dichotomous form. One deviant response pattern is overachievement and productivity far surpassing normal levels; gifted and high academic achievers exhibit extraordinary talents and ambition, are adored by their teachers and are accorded school leadership roles. Another deviant response pattern is taking health risks (drug use, alcohol use, promiscuity), social risks (crime, vehicular accidents), or exhibiting mental health risks (homicide, suicide, depression, panic and anxiety, etc.).

Iatrogenic deviance thus evolves ontogenetically under inconsistent operant and respondent contingencies crafted by ACOA parents. The contingencies causing the most behavioral damage in offspring include the following:

Unpredictability of Parent

Just as non-ACOA partners lack prediction of ACOA partners, so can children lose the same stimulus control. Uncertainty about when dinner is served; when bad behavior is punished or good behavior is rewarded; when clothing is new, old, dirty, fashionable; and when to speak and not to speak—all describe confusing rules the child develops in response to inconsistent consequences. Unlike adults who already have rules, children are just beginning to form rule-governed behaviors and depend heavily on connections with things parents say, do, and the consequences of action. When parental behaviors are inconsistent, rules also suffer from inconsistency. Rules cannot be consistent or accurate because the rule followed today may evoke consequences different from rules followed tomorrow. Thus, children construct defective rules (see Jahn, 1995).

Jasmine, a 6-year-old Protective Services referral, sustained emotional injury from "defective rules." Removal from his biological mother initially occurred after substantiating complaints of corporal punishment and he subsequently lived in four foster homes. His mother spanked him for misbehavior and for assertive behavior. Misbehavior consisted of Jasmine talking loudly or neglecting to turn off the television when instructed. Appropriate behaviors were affectionate gestures, requesting bathroom assistance, or requesting food when hungry. Normal assertive behaviors intruded on his mother's rigidly organized schedule and she lost her patience with his nagging for "selfish needs." Intolerance resulted in slapping, spanking or critically insulting Jasmine for his disrespectful interruptions.

Consequently, Jasmine "internalized" the aversive contingencies into rules dictating "right versus wrong" occasions to approach his mother. The right time included when his mother engaged in activities he desired, no matter when these activities occurred. For example, her eating dinner at 10 p.m. meant Jasmine waited that late until he asked for dinner himself. The wrong time for "nagging" involved any time his mother appeared engrossed in tasks. Bathroom, self-grooming, or other needs arising during these "mother busy-tasks," were ignored to avert corporal or verbal punishment. By the time Protective Services intervened, Jasmine suffered multiple symptoms reactive to parental neglect including (a) encopresis, (b) malnutrition, and (c) unhygienic care causing a severe case of lice. But problems persisted outside the training environment. Transferred into each foster home were his "rules" about proper versus improper questions, which further accounted for reports of Jasmine staying up late and exhibiting profound shyness.

Denial of Autonomy

ACOA childrearing variables equally retard individuality. Children directly experiencing hostile, moody, or overly cautious parents take fewer risks than children whose parents are predictable and less caretaking. ACOA parents who pay too much attention to their children overprotect them from errors, from normal physical falls and injury, and from the trials and tribulations accompanying healthy curiosity. Children avoid independent action because they fear punishment for leaving the parent. Emotionally quarantined, offspring develop incipient fears associated with adventure beyond the parents' boundary of contingencies. Restricted self-discovery also diminishes response strength to a helpless state, forming depression. Retrospective studies of clinically depressed children, for example, show that their parents are not only rejecting but also more controlling than parents of nondepressed children (Bifulco, Brown & Harris, 1987). Around perfectionist parents, offspring manifest anxiety bordering on social phobias (Perry & Millimet, 1977; Rapee, 1997).

A five-year-old told to sit still at the dinner table around guests was fascinated with the antique napkin ring shaped like a bunny rabbit. He moved to touch it and spilled his water glass, causing momentary confusion. The ACOA parent felt grossly embarrassed and immediately chastised the youngster for his disruption. This left the child beside himself and afraid to explore new items again. Expecting similar mistakes, the hypervigilant ACOA parent continued finding fault with her son throughout the meal. After an hour, sitting repressed and docile, the youngster sat motionless, with tears running down his cheeks.

Denied autonomy inhibits the child's appropriately directive exploratory behaviors and may cause two serious repercussions during adolescence and into adulthood. First, interpersonal communication skills may suffer developmental delay. Second, incompatible exploratory behaviors can evoke high-risk responses for inappropriate reinforcement. In the first case, inexpressive behaviors causing shyness, docility, introversion, and isolation impede social functioning. Self-insulated toddlers and teens grow dependent on their parents for simple daily living skills such as ordering food in a restaurant, asking salespeople questions about merchandise, and changing soiled clothing.

Second, deprivation of healthy autonomy extinguishes curiousity around the parent and differentially builds competing behaviors under control of concurrent reinforcement. Interest abounds for excitable, adrenaline-rushing activities generating autonomic arousal. Children drawn to these self-stimulatory responses produce positive reinforcing effects from risking more dangerous experiences. Bike jumping and playing fiercely competitive sports, for example, are thrill-seeking maneuvers requiring abnormal levels of impulsivity and personal tolerance. Exceeding self-tolerance for powerful gratifers further includes criminal delinquent acts. Here, impulsiveness is reinforced by moral and rule violations and excitement for constantly changing contingencies. Arrested adolescents involved in general theft, crimes against persons (e.g., aggravated assault, gang fights, etc.), index crimes (e.g., sexual assault, intimidation), and drug sales, frequently identify their antecedents for instigating offenses due to poor emotional and psychological functioning (e.g., Dembo, et al., 1997).

Fear of Affection

Parents who pay little or no attention to their children except for "major" accomplishments, birthdays, or special holidays transmit an inaccurate message that affection is bad, immoral or conditional. There must be a legitimate reason for affection, rather than that it feels good. Legitimizing affection forces the child to work harder in school to please the parent, hoping to reach that magical criteria for affection.

When repeated efforts for affection fail, no matter how persistent the child is, five forms of maladjustment result. First, the child fortifies appeasement by overexerting efforts for perfection on all personal activities. Excruciatingly painful and exhaustive responses are expended to placate the ACOA parent, including martyr-like sacrifices of friends, toys, or normal needs in return for morsels of recognition. A second insidious reaction occurs when the child perceives affection as inaccessible, unavailable, and absent, and consequently develops the operant rule that "families are not supposed to share affection." Deprivation of affection engenders the generalized rule that "affection is abnormal, inappropriate, immoral, or not necessary for expression of love."

Third, children dislike any form of conventional touching and perceive affectionate people as needy, overbearing, and insecure. Young adults annoyed or repulsed by touching go one step further. They imitate their ACOA parents' maltreatment by denigrating the value of affection and debasing affectionate people. Exacerbation of nonaffection includes a dislike for sexuality and preference for celibacy in intimate relationships. Rule-governed statements that typically emerge are that sex and affection are objects of inferiority that must be resisted to remain a wholly competent person.

Fourth, emotional voids perpetuate aggressive efforts to find competing sources of reinforcement. Activation of an establishing operation for physical love compels premature interest in sexuality. Prepubescent teens curious about physical contact observed in movies, plays, or among other adults, may unilaterally solicit affection from either gender and advance quickly to genital touching. Boys seeking physical love from male or female peers may initially seek nurturance and reassurance. *Platonic touching,* so to speak, reinforces initiation of expanded preromantic touching. As reciprocal touching progresses from hand-holding, hugging, and modest kisses to caressing genitals, reinforcing variables also change. Generalized social reinforcers that control simple, nonsexual touching are now replaced by unconditioned reinforcers from genital stimulation.

A fifth behavioral repercussion occurs when youngsters misinterpret kinesthetic sensory cues as sexual arousal. Naiveté about the variety of normal muscular contractions and glandular secretions associated with healthy touching can distort the meaning of internal sensations when a child grows older. Touch-deprived children lack conditioned responses to internal sensations of muscles, joints, tendons, and vibrations from central and autonomic nervous systems, also called *proprioceptive stimuli.* By comparison, healthy childrearing practices condition children at early ages to identify and label affectionate sensations. Untrained labeling of proprioceptive stimuli may confuse older children and adults touched for the first time into thinking that they are experiencing sexual excitement. Elevations in respiration, body temperature, and sensory effects may feel exactly like the sensations during normal sexual arousal. Weak sensory discrimination is common, for example, in postpartum mothers, who cry spontaneously because of mislabeled respondent behaviors (Ruben & Ruben, 1985b). Likewise, touch sensations misjudged as sexual can cause exaggeration of a friendly gesture into a sexual overture.

A homosexual male from an alcoholic family sought treatment for repeated relationship failures and found he trusted his male therapist. As months passed, goals for changing his choice of partner proved effective. The client self-reported prudent and selective care in building partner friendships over impulsively having sex.

Deeply pleased by this progress, the therapist leaned over and patted the client's shoulder and then leaned back into his chair. The stunned client believed his therapist had made a sexual pass at him. He felt a rush of tingling sensations around his genitals and sudden increase in respiration. He boldly asked his therapist if the gesture was sexual and was shocked to hear that it was not. Physical touching within his "endrogenous zones" always aroused him sexually and signified dating messages from another partner. The therapist's innocuous gesture of affection felt surprisingly odd for this client, who never previously received family affection.

NONCOMPLIANCE

Punished or neglected children are not always seeking approval or engaging in perfectionism. After futile efforts for approval, opposition may occur. A child can refuse to follow instructions, be verbally disrespectful, may even damage the parent's property, and very frequently is verbally debative. Arguments escalate when controlling parents work feverishly to restore their control by spanking, yelling or, essentially repeating the same negative discipline or neglect used for that child during infancy, toddlerhood and preteen years.

Lacking success, the parents repeat their exhaustive efforts, at times threatening the child with disownment and insisting that reentry into the family will require complete compliance with house rules. Such high demands lack sensitivity, caring, and emotional respect for the rebellious child, whose very anger started from the same inflexible control being used now. As altercations intensify, dismantling the parent–child bond, inaccurate rules develop for the defiant child regarding why all parents are ruthless, distrusting, and controlling. Insensitivity of rebellious teens' to family contingencies quickly transfers to violations of school contingencies, including a rise of incidents in homework incompletion, truancy, declines in grades, eruptive anger, confrontations with authority figures, and defection from his peer community (Herting, Eggert, & Thompson, 1996; Ruben, 1999a).

Tim's last chance before expulsion was to attend alternative education regularly without any absences or teacher threats. Since kindergarten he was the bully, agitator, and class clown in every successive classroom. Although academically gifted, he rarely studied for a test and would make fun of less astute learners, calling them "imbeciles and losers." Tim also exploded in rage at any teacher confronting him for his gross misbehavior. He even retaliated against one teacher who sent him down to the office by puncturing the teacher's car tires. Arrested twice on school grounds, Tim was no stranger to the local police, whom he also disrespected. Sadly, Tim's father was a CEO of a Fortune 500 company and his mother, although disabled, previously was a prestigious attorney in town. At home, growing up, his parents used coercive instruction and punishment to teach obedience. By age 10, Tim's argued with his parents, triggering constant altercations that evolved into physically violent exchanges. His parents figured Tim simply was a bad seed and made no further attempts to rectify his out-of-control behavior.

Fear of Retaliation

One last reaction arising in offspring of ACOA parents stems from, of all things, Freudian concepts of the oedipal complex. According to classical interpretation, young boys who feel affection for their mothers are fearful that by showing this love, jealous fathers may castrate and emasculate them. Fear, in other words, is associated with the parent's retaliation. Translated into a behavioral systems model, parental retaliation for a child who favors another parent inhibits the child's efforts to love either parent. This emotional downfall ultimately results in conflicting punitive contingencies, whereby the choice is to approach the least of two aversive stimuli. Children caught in this tug-of-war between two controlling, jealous parents (aversive stimuli) constantly doubt their true allies and consequently avoid starting conflicts between the parents. Spousal fights signify the onset of impending punishers directed at the youngster who attributes the parents' argument to his or her instigation.

This is because punishment contingencies cause an unusual form of response reduction. When asymmetrical punishment occurs, that is, one schedule of punishment is (e.g., variable interval schedule) superimposed on another schedule of punishment (e.g., variable rate schedule), corresponding decreases occur in (a) response force, (b) inter-response time, and (c) response resurgence, among other covariations (see Boe & Church, 1968). Decrements in response force pertain to topographical or frequency changes in responding relative to one aversive stimulus over another aversive stimulus. Inhibited responses under one stimulus may or may not mean responses occur at full force or even half force under the other stimulus. This is due to inter-response time (IRT). Inter-response time means the interval between termination of one response and onset of another response. Longer IRTs are predictable when concurrent punishers are unavoidable and inescapable.

Finally, response resurgence occurs when presumably extinguished behaviors under one or both aversive stimuli regenerate because of properties of the punishment contingency. For example, temporal properties account for some time delay between presentations of aversive stimuli. Spatial properties, for another, describe proximity of aversive stimuli to each other. As temporal, spatial, or other properties of punishment vary predictably, response resurgence varies respectively. As properties remain constant, response suppression (no resurgence) remains constant.

Thus children held hostage by two superimposed aversive contingencies may feel that punishers are imminent from either source. Operationally, this means the child expects retaliation and responds poorly. Consequently, the child's verbal and nonverbal behaviors with both parents are elliptical, monosyllabic, and labored. Response time is usually longer; the child procrastinates before complying with tasks or only complies after the parent delivers a harsh reprimand. Reduced response rates remain while both parents' angry and retaliatory behaviors stay the same. But when slight variations in parental behavior occur, either from the parent being absent from the house, physically ill, or "in a good mood," the child's verbal and nonverbal behaviors regenerates.

In short, concurrent punishment contingencies obviously produce suppressive effects. The question is: Do these suppressive effects change after long-term exposure to aversion? Yes. Response adaptation to punishment manifests itself in two ways. First, the child may step in the middle of parental feuds (aversive stimuli) and resolve differences by placating each parent. Mediating spousal and family peace may cause the child anxiety but will prevent predatory attacks from either parent. Second, the child may escape spousal conflict by aborting caretaking efforts, which incites resentment against the child. Betraying his parents, he is labeled as oppositional and incorrigible. Correspondingly, his parents stop fighting and join forces to deal with their troubled child. In other words, spousal unity and family peace result in both cases. One way is for the child to avoid aversive stimuli by reinforcing his parents; in return, he receives a reprieve from punishment. (negative reinforcement). The second way is to escape aversive stimuli by punishing his parents; in return, he receives compounded aversive effects but his parents get along better (negative punishment).

Love-hate relationships characterized this Renaissance child. A 15-year-old carefree youngster referred for panic attacks explained his circumstances at home. His father, a factory worker on the day shift, and mother, a nurse on rotating shifts, fought recurrently. Arguments escalated over frivolous issues, lasting several hours until one of two things occurred. Either the youngster consoled his mother, ending the discordance and reuniting the family, or he consoled his father, again prompting reconciliation. Disputants were hypersensitive to whom the child arbitrator approached. Defusing his mother meant his father harbored resentment, demonstrated when he withdrew promises or removed privileges from the child. Attention to his father, on the other hand, caused obsessive jealousy in his mother, who retaliated by refusing to drive the youngster to play rehearsal. Alternatively, he decided to take a different strategy. In subsequent arguments, he remained incognito. He remained on the sidelines, offering neither compassion nor resolution to either parent. The plan backfired as both parents felt antipathy toward his negligence and accused him of selfishness, indifference, and defiance. Retrospectively, the younger observed his angry parents got along better when he stayed out of their business, and let them conspire against his "misbehavior."

Retribution as an operational subsidiary of punishment is a common theme in many conceptual analyses of crime and impunity (Bedau, 1978). Issues arise regarding the acquittal versus retributive justification for offenses committed. In ACOA families, child offenses rarely are acquitted but rather condemned because the child ought to have known better and instead acted obstinately. That was the child's crime. Defenseless children who are juried by such punitive parents rarely are oppositional. They flounder in the confusing morass of a deregulated family system, reaching out for answers that never come. Ideally, clinicians could help ACOA parents stop their offspring from becoming second- or third-generation ACOAs, by eliminating the parents' pathologic symptoms and reshaping their dysfunctional behaviors. The problem is that interrupting a vicious intergenerational cycle is not always so easy. It requires clinical acumen about the ACOA etiology, a way to collect and assess etiologic factors, and the competence to reverse the syndrome.

Thus far we have examined the etiology underlying the symptoms. Now let us proceed to Chapter 7 to capture these symptoms in a fairly simple-to-use self-report instrument.

CHAPTER 7

Assessment of ACOA Behaviors

Alcoholics and children of alcoholics raise many difficulties for clinical assessment and diagnosis. This is especially true for self-report measures. However, self-report measures represent the most frequently administered devices for alcoholics and children of alcoholics. The reasons are obvious. They are simple to score and interpret and allow for rapid pretreatment evaluation. Advantages abound considering that alcoholic or alcoholic-like clients may be impatient, inaccessible, or available for only one of many intake assessment sessions. On the other hand, self-report measures suffer limitations due to constraints on validity and reliability (Hay, Hay, Angle & Nelson, 1979; House, Manelis & Kinscherf, 1983).

Also impairing self-reports of alcoholic or adult children of alcoholics (ACOAs) are unempirical definitions of the ACOA syndrome. Popular and research literature extensively proposes general categories of ACOAs based on an individual's role in the family system. While these taxonomies offer face validity, procedurally correlating the personality roles with factual, observable measurement proves otherwise. Validation studies fall short of confirming these categories as operationally sufficient to meet the demands of a scientific analysis. Alternatively, self-report measures designed with operationally-defined ACOA behaviors promises a more accurate assessment power.

To understand how this is possible, this chapter first reviews the economy of assessment in clinical practice. Then it examines the pitfalls of currently self-report instruments used in ACOA diagnosis. Failure of many testing protocols to assess specific ACOA target behavior accounts for the third section of this chapter, along with the presentation of recent experimental data collected on the construction and standardization of a new ACOA-specific assessment device.

Economy of Assessment in Clinical Practice

Ultimately the question becomes one of convenience. Economy of time, effort, and reasonable use of subjects can prohibit use of group comparison designs or even strategically engineered single-case designs in assessment. In using control groups, for example, there are naturalistic limitations. Control subjects cannot be matched and assigned randomly to experimental and nonexperimental groups where risk of behavior exacerbation may occur. Methodologies that delay or stagger the period of intervention, such as multiple-baseline research, may guarantee subject access to "treatment" but only for a short duration. Reversal of procedures or successive changes of treatment over time (e.g., multielemental design) also disrupts the continuity of homogeneous treatment. When therapy is inconsistent or confounded by multiple variables, assessment produces unreliable measures of post-baseline behavior changes.

In truth, few clinical settings in the natural environment enjoy this structure for pristine control and experimental groups. With weekly clients, many of whom display concurrent pathologies, in and out of session, random assignment of clients to groups would be difficult. So, too, is the difficulty of screening clients for homogeneity. Even diagnostically similar clients (e.g., avoidant personality disorder) have infinitely diverse behavioral histories, demographics, and life stressors. Classifying these clients into a unified group and presuming ideographic properties would be improbable. The solution, then, lies with sampling representative groups that possess known heterogeneity and share similar developmental variables.

Another economic convenience of clincal behavioral practice is using paper–pencil assessments. Relatively simple to administer, paper–pencil assessments include questionnaires, checklists, biographical histories, and various survey forms designed to stimulate authentic replies about personal background. Frequently these are "measures" since they serve as cues evoking realistic or semi-realistic (simulated) behaviors. Analogue paper–pencil tests are different from traditional paper–pencil tests. In analogue measures, questions attempt to quantify "general" parameters of behavior and translate them into operationally specific definitions. Two types of analogue paper–pencil measures accomplish this goal. The first type measure behaviors or situations that directly influence or precipitate target behavior. Social and organic survey schedules (e.g., Cautela, 1981) and fear survey schedules (Ryall & Dietiker, 1979) are the most common.

A second type of paper–pencil analogue directly or indirectly measures the response topography itself. For example, the Michigan Alcoholism Screening Test records written replies to questions about contexts of social drinking (Stockwell, Hodgson, Edwards, Taylor & Rankin, 1979). Or, tests like the Sensation Scale (Maisto, Connors, Tucker, McCollan & Adesso, 1980) record written responses to taste-testing trials to determine single or multiple consumption levels of alcoholism. In both cases, molecular units of behavior result from self-reported answers.

Similarly, the newly constructed ACOA Behavior Profile is designed to evoke responses directly related to experiences in eight categories of family and interpersonal functioning. Although not purely analogue by definition, the questions evoke responses about antecedents and actual target behaviors. Responses purportedly measure events causing stress and the topography of the stress, including its frequency, duration, and other qualities.

Paper-Pencil Protocols for ACOA Populations

Normative tests for screening children of alcoholics are sparse. Few studies either generate standardized data or compare scores obtained on ACOA instruments with scores obtained on both alcohol and drug devices or other personality devices (Haskell, 1993; Hawkins & Hawkins 1995). The one existing test gathering normative data is called the Children of Alcoholic's Screening Test (CAST).

CAST is a 30-item questionnaire that can be completed within 30 minutes (Pilat & Jones, 1984–1985; Sheridan, 1995; Yeatman, Bogart, Geer, & Sirridge, 1994). It can be used to identify children of alcoholics by measuring feelings, attitudes, perceptions, and experiences related to a parent's drinking. The test items were formulated from actual experiences shared by clinically diagnosed ACOAs. CAST is suitable for use with persons from nine years of age to adulthood. In addition, it has been shown to be reliable, valid, and to have good internal consistency. Its shortcoming, as Claydon (1987) points out, is poor validity with large groups of representative populations.

For example, Claydon administered the CAST and asked direct questions regarding whether a parent was alcoholic to ACOA samples of college freshmen. Results revealed that using a direct question along with CAST, identified almost 5% more ACOAs than did CAST alone. Alternatively, promising research shows higher reliability using a shorter version of the test (Hodgins, Maticka-Tyndale, el-Guebaly & West, 1995; Hodgins & Shimp, 1995). The CAST also appears limited in its capacity to identify the full range of children with alcoholic parents. It was suggested that some direct questions regarding parental alcoholism may improve the CAST. The multidimensional nature of parental alcoholism may possibly be assessed with a single or several questions pertaining to homelife and residual effects of childhood.

ACOA Behavioral Profile

Construction of the ACOA Behavior Profile involved five phases, including description of the instrument, situational description, response enumeration, response evaluation, and selection of response alternatives. A description of these phases, together with the subjects involved and procedures employed, follows.

Instrument: ACOA Behavior Profile

Improvements in multidimensionality of questions gave rise to the ACOA Behavior Profile. This 67-item questionnaire was broken down into eight sections, reflecting operationally defined patterns of ACOAs. Each question received a "yes" or "no" reply. A description of each section appears below:

Feelings Profile describing how analytical or self-absorbed the ACOA is about people's opinions. Consuming fears may become obsessive; self-talk ruminates about mistakes the ACOA made, the guilt he or she feels, and compensatory acts they feel compelled to carry out.

Relaxed Profile describing hyperarousal, overexcitability, and need for elevated activity versus the ability to be tranquil, mild-mannered, and composed. Anxious ACOAs operate on a high sensory (proprioceptive) level, equated to feeling in control, that they learned as a child when coerced to keep busy and feel guilty for relaxation, playtime.

Loyal Profile describing martyr-like devotion to caretaking another person. Self-sacrifice derives a value of esteem from the positive attention of other people. ACOAs scoring high in this category are procrastinators and neglect their own private lives while disproportionally investing energy in pampering an emotionally ill or drug-using person.

Control Profile describing a person's need to be a leader or in charge of situations rather than passively following others. ACOAs typically learn control behaviors in anticipation of unavoidable, inescapable contact with adverse events. By methodically managing their environment, contact with adverse stimulation (criticism, rejection, anger, conflict, etc.) is postponed, delayed, or attenuated. In this way, control is reinforced by reducing anxiety and fear.

Relations This section describes a past history of repeated relationship failures marked by abuse, neglect, noncommunication and romantic futility. The common denominator is largely repetition. Recycled bad relationships occur for two reasons. First is the familiarity ACOAs feel with a person who is unhealthy. Second is the narrowly confined selection of partners—either they are aggressively impulsive or passively docile.

Drugs and Alcohol Profile describing current or past use of alcohol or polydrug use in terms of frequency, intensity, and interference on adaptive or functional lifestyle. Addiction experience also includes exposure to alcohol or drug abuse during childhood or with significant partners.

Fear Profile describing specific or unspecified fears, anxieties, or inhibitions impeding normal social activities. Fears range from social discomfort under conflict to paralyzing panic episodes in agoraphobic-like situations. ACOAs suffering fear are prone to hypervigilance about social opinion and may go overboard to appease people perceived as intimidating or predatory.

Parents Profile describing discord with parents during the ACOA's childhood. Parent–child friction may vary from an absentee parent to constant acrimony to incest. Emotionally or physically battered ACOAs grow up either duplicating their abusive parents or attracted to abusive partners who resemble the hostile parent. ACOAs who are attracted to abusers and who are themselves aggressive typically may be resistant to therapy and oblivious to their dysfunctional patterns.

Situational Analysis

Goldfried (1977) states that the purpose of a situational analysis is to identify and describe the significant situations in which a given population displays the target behaviors. The process of identifying common situations that are presumed important was first completed by reviewing the literature and by interviewing available local experts or colleagues treating ACOAs.

The literature review was structured to include basic texts, journals, and current articles in all relevant fields. It focused on areas such as assessment (etiology, epidemiology) and treatment outcomes. Also explored were agencies and foundations focusing on ACOA self-help groups and characteristics these organizations identified as disruptive in adult life.

Response Enumeration

The purpose of the response enumeration phase was to determine the appropriate responses that an individual should exhibit when participating in each of the problematic situations specified in the situational analysis. This process involved an extension of the literature review and interview process to identify behaviors or behavior patterns specific to ACOAs. Identified patterns resulted in eight operationally defined behaviors that served as categories for the test (i.e., Feelings, Relaxed, Loyal, Control, Relations, Drug and Alcohol, Fear, Parents).

Response Evaluation

The response evaluation phase was designed to provide an opportunity for significant others to judge the importance of preliminary ACOA categories and questions selected for the ACOA Behavior Profile. To evaluate the importance of the questions, three experts in the area of ACOA and family studies were selected to serve as judges. These judges were selected for their knowledge of assessment, treatment, and ecological understanding of ACOAs across different settings. They included a clinical family psychologist, a volunteer in ACOA support groups and a recovering ACOA, and a business specialist who works with multihandicapped populations overlapping with ACOAs.

These experts were asked to rate the importance of each question in the ACOA Behavior Profile. Ratings were completed on a five-point scale where "0" was "not important" and "4" was "very important." Those questions (items) receiving a score of "3" or "4" were retained, whereas those items rated "0," "1," and "2" were deleted.

Standardization

Three groups of subjects participated in this study: a "high-risk group," a "medium-risk group," and a "low-risk group." Each group consisted of 100 subjects. Subjects in all three groups were multi racial 18 to 50 years old, and from lower to upper middle class families in a Midwest metropolitan city. Gender was mixed among all three groups. Subjects ranged from having advanced post-secondary education to noncompletion of high school. All participating subjects were literate and could understand the questionnaire items. The majority of subjects, 60%, worked part-time or full-time jobs either in professional or labor positions. Forty-percent received government assistance or relied on financial support by another party (e.g., child support payments, alimony, etc.).

Subjects were referrals from a wide variety of state and county agencies, physicians, and religious institutions requesting psychological evaluations or treatment. For the high-risk group (Group 1), randomly selected subjects demonstrated from self-reported clinical histories that:

1. One or both parents (biological or step-parent) drank alcohol excessively or used drugs.
2. Subject previously had alcohol or drug addiction and/or currently was using alcohol and drugs on a weekly basis.
3. Subject showed comorbidity of psychological problems and currently received psychotherapy. Psychopathologies included but were not limited to disorders of: eating, anxiety, depression, substance abuse, sexuality, parenting, or marital (and relational).
4. Subject was on parole, probation, or under investigation for either drug-using or selling, domestic assault, child abuse or neglect, child custody, criminal sexual conduct, or economic crimes.

For the medium-risk group (Group 2), randomly selected subjects met the following criteria:

1. Neither parent (biological or step-parent) drank alcohol excessively or used drugs.
2. Subject showed no previous alcohol or drug addiction and/or currently was not using alcohol and drugs on a weekly basis.

3. Subject showed comorbicity of psychological problems and currently received psychotherapy. Psychopathologies included but were not limited to disorders of: eating, anxiety, depression, substance abuse, sexuality, parenting, or marital (and relational).
4. Subject was on parole, probation, or under investigation for either drug-using or selling, domestic assault, child abuse or neglect, child custody, criminal sexual conduct, or economic crimes.

For the low-risk group (Group 3), randomly selected subjects met the following set of criteria:

1. Subjects neither reported a psychiatric history nor currently received psychotherapy.
2. Subjects showed no major cognitive, emotional, or behavioral impediments in their lives.
3. Neither parents (biological or step-parent) drank excessively alcohol or used drugs.
4. Subject showed no previous alcohol or drug addiction and/or was currently not using alcohol or drugs on a weekly basis.
5. Subjects were neither on parole, probation, or under investigation for any crimes or related legal process.

Subjects did not put their names on the questionnaire, and left no traceable identifying information except generic intake data such as age, race, gender, and educational level.

Procedure. The ACOA Behavior Profile was administered uniformly. Subjects in the high-risk, medium-risk, and low-risk groups received the test as part of an assessment protocol. After completing a face-to-face interview lasting one hour, they were sequestered in a private room and asked to complete three personality inventories. The battery of tests included the MMPI–2, Parent–Child Inventory, and the ACOA Behavior Profile. Subjects had unlimited time to finish the personality instruments and received intermittent monitoring to assure they remained on task. They were instructed not to put their names on the ACOA Behavior Profile. Subjects understood they were free to leave the private office at any time during the testing or after completing test items. They were not penalized for failing to complete testing or leaving before all test items were answered.

Results of Test Standardization

Demographics The distribution sample revealed characteristics invariably influencing test outcome scores (see Table 7–1). Gender was nearly equal (male, 49%; female, 51%), whereas racial dissimilarities were dramatic (white, 78%; black, 22%). Most subjects earned lower income salaries (39%) but worked in full-time positions ranging from 35 to 45 hours weekly (56%). High school graduates (42%) matched the number of subjects never completing high school or earning GEDs (41%). Ironically, the age of subjects was clustered from 21 to 40 years old (e.g., 21 to 30, 29%; 31 to 40, 27%) compared to the plethora of high-risk, medium-risk, or low-risk subject referrals above age 61 (4%). Reasons for referral largely centered on substance abuse issues (23%), custody disputes (20%), or stemmed from Protective Services investigation for child abuse (16%) or neglect (15%).

Analysis of reliability. There are several ways of assessing the reliability of psychological test scores. The most fundamental are estimates of internal consistency and split-half correlational analysis (McNemar, 1969). Tests of internal consistency employed the (Kuder-Richardson Reliability (KR21) formula (Kuder & Richardson, 1937). Like Cronbach's alpha (Cronbach, 1951), KR21 conventionally calculates reliability for instruments such as the ACOA Behavior Profile in which items are responded to in one of two ways: true/false, or yes/no. Alpha scores range from 0 to 1 and typically indicate internal consistency at the .60 level.

TABLE 7–1 Demographic Characteristics of Subjects in the Normative Sample

(n = 300)

Characteristic	Sample Size	% of Sample
GENDER		
Male	146	49
Female	154	51
RACE		
White	233	78
Black	67	22
SOCIOECONOMIC STATUS		
Gov't Subsidy	106	35
Lower income	117	39
Middle income	52	17
Upper income	25	08
EDUCATION		
Less than High School	124	41
High School or Equiv.	127	42
More than High School	49	16
EMPLOYMENT		
Full-time job	168	56
Part-time job	69	23
Unemployed	63	21
AGE		
15 to 20	37	12
21 to 30	88	29
31 to 40	81	27
41 to 50	56	19
51 to 60	27	09
> 61	11	04
REFERRAL REASON		
Domestic abuse	3	01
Child abuse	48	16
Child neglect	45	15
Substance abuse	68	23
CSC	8	03
Drug dealing	16	05
Custody dispute	59	20
Economic crimes	9	03
Other	44	15

TABLE 7–2 Internal Consistency Reliability Estimated by Kuder-Richardson across Subtests

Subtests	Number of Items	Mean	Variance	Alpha
Feelings	12	9.9	11.263	0.211
Relaxed	4	3.418	4.535	0.579
Loyal	6	5.24	3.901	0.655
Control	10	8.95	7.684	0.053
Relations	8	7.575	8.492	0.133
Drug/Alcohol	10	6.323	8.629	0.378
Fear	4	4	4.352	0.398
Parents	13	10.282	31.49	0.76

Distribution of alpha coefficients appears across subtests in Table 7–2. Noteworthy significance occurred in subtests on Loyalty (a = .65) and Parents (a = .76). These variables may predict correlations between parental influence during childhood and loyal obedience in adulthood. Surprisingly, low internal consistency repeatedly surfaced for the subtest on Drug and Alcohol; subjects from alcoholic families either answered divergently on addiction-related questions, underestimated their polydrug abuse, or misperceived their current drug use and family history as normal, not aberrant.

Table 7–3 presents alpha scores for all three standardization groups. Subtests on Loyalty (Groups 1 and 2, respectively: a = .70, a = .71) and Parents (Groups 1 and 2, respectively: a = .72, a = 71) again generated alphas across high-risk and moderate-risk groups, while the Parents subtest additionally earned high consistency in the low-risk group (a = .71). Subtests on Control and Drug/Alcohol, however, produced inferior findings, suggesting low interrelationship between regular drinkers and subjects who perceive themselves as vulnerable or "emotionally out of control."

A second estimate of reliability was computed using split-half reliability; these results appear in Table 7–4. Test items across all three groups were divided in half by odd and even items, and scores on the two half-tests were correlated. Computed correla-

TABLE 7–3 Internal Consistency Reliability Estimated by Kuder-Richardson across All Three Groups

	Group 1			Group 2			Group 3		
Subtests	Mean	Variance	Alpha	Mean	Variance	Alpha	Mean	Variance	Alpha
Feelings	5.676	8.385	.414	2.444	2.149	.050	1.787	2.676	.426
Relaxed	2.030	2.253	.423	.806	1.273	.690	.545	.836	.675
Loyal	3.777	1.982	.70	1.868	.97	.717	1.626	1.389	.033
Control	4.899	3.864	.151	2.454	3.04	.295	1.596	2.285	.415
Relations	4.071	2.667	.39	2.575	2.006	.133	1.808	.836	.485
Drug/Alcohol	3.346	5.013	.450	1.808	1.98	.202	1.222	1.224	.114
Fear	2.744	2.461	.221	.838	.89	.400	.5152	.899	.766
Parents	5.122	14.232	.721	3.141	8.531	.717	1.929	5.456	.718

tions then underwent correction using the Spearman–Brown formula (Nunnally, 1978, p. 212). Findings showed significant correlations obtained in subtests on Relaxed (r = .866, p < .01) and Parents (r = .599, p < .01). Low coefficient estimates for subtests on Control (r = .395, p < .01) and Loyal (r = .091, p < .01) sur-

TABLE 7–4 Split-Half Reliability Coefficient

	First half		Second half		
	Odd		Even		Correlation
Subtests	M	SD	M	SD	r
Feelings	1.02	.979	1.500	.839	0.087
Relaxed	.500	.580	2.000	.404	0.866
Loyal	1.56	.786	.420	.641	0.091
Control	1.14	.969	.920	.829	0.395
Relations	.920	.876	1.66	.894	0.474
Drug/Alcohol	.960	1.00	.560	.704	0.413
Fear	.520	.762	.380	.602	0.336
Parents	1.22	1.55	1.56	1.60	0.599

prisingly deviated from their higher, more significant scores when these groups were assessed separately. Intratest comparisons suggested a more conservative measure in predicting dominance and self-sacrificing behaviors.

Analysis of Validity This section discusses validity of the ACOA Behavior Profile. Clearly distinguishing each type of validity frequently is difficult, since research evidence bearing on one type of validity is often relevant to another type, as well. For example, the results of factor analyses directly have implications for both construct and predictive validity.

Construct Validity An instrument's construct validity is the extent to which it measures the trait it is intended to measure. For the ACOA Behavior Profile, the central construct validity is whether the domain of respondents' attitudes and values was specific enough to measure, and whether the measurements are relevant to ACOA characteristics.

One important index of construct validity is that an instrument's subtests exhibit a pattern of moderate intercorrelation (see Table 7–5). If the subtests are uncorrelated, they will not measure a coherent domain. If subtests are highly correlated, suggesting they are redundant, it means they measured the same underlying dimension under different names.

Table 7–5 exhibits a pattern of moderate intercorrelation consistent with the validity of the ACOA Behavior Profile as a whole, and consistent with the validity of subtests as they were labeled. Lower Relaxed correlations between and Control (r = 0.178, p < .01), for example, are consistent with the competing meaning of these constructs; that is, relaxed, unassertive, flexible people are unlikely to be rigid, aggressive and controlling. Likewise, low correlations between Loyal and Drug and Alcohol (r = .068, p < .01) suggested that drug users are atypically efficient, benevolent and loyal.

TABLE 7–5 Intercorrelation of ACOA Behavior Profile Subtests

(n = 300)

Subtests	Feelings	Relaxed	Loyal	Control	Relations	Drug/Alc	Fear	Parents
Feelings		0.136	.212*	.321**	.329**	.330**	.369**	.263**
Relaxed			.199*	0.178	0.181	0.111	.223*	0.16
Loyal				.318**	.293**	0.068	.205*	0.039
Control					0.196	0.09	.289**	.215*
Relations						0.069	.288**	0.096
Drug/Alc							.213*	.314*
Fear								.260**

* Correlation is significant at the .05 level (two-tailed).

** Correlation is significant at the .01 level (two-tailed).

A third measure of construct validity involved computing subjects scoring greater or equal to 50% on each subtest of the ACOA Behavior Profile across all three groups (see Table 7–6). High item-rated subtests suggest that the items relevantly sampled the underlying personality variables that the subtests are intended to measure. Subjects in Group 1 (high risk) rated considerably higher on Loyal (82%), Fear (76%), and Relations (63%) than did Groups 2 (medium risk) and 3 (low risk). The subtest on Loyalty, however, ranked consistently high across all three groups (Group 2, 25%; Group 3, 18%).

A fourth measure of construct validity employed a confirmatory factor analysis across the eight subtests, later rotated by a varimax method (see Table 7–7). A confirmatory analyses test selected boundaries of scores and measured meaningfulness of traits (e.g., Keith & Witta, 1997; Thompson & Daniel, 1996). The three identified factors appear to reflect the expected dimensions of anxiety (i.e., Factor 1: Feelings, Relaxed, Control, Fear); caretaking (i.e., Factor 2: Loyal, Relations); and family addiction (i.e., Factor 3: Drug/Alcohol, Parents).

TABLE 7–6 Subjects Scoring 50% or Greater in Each Subtest across All Three Groups

	Groups		
Subtests	1. High Risk n = 100	2. Medium Risk n = 100	3. Low Risk n = 100
Feelings	47%	2%	4%
Relaxed	53%	16%	15%
Loyal	82%	25%	18%
Control	57%	7%	6%
Relations	63%	24%	12%
Drug/Alcohol	25%	12%	0%
Fear	76%	27%	13%
Parents	37%	13%	6%

Computed correlations across Factors 2 and 3 showed significant support for the construct of Loyal. Altruistic and approval-seeking acts, in other words, may categorically belong to caretakers raised in polydrug-abusing families. Substantially higher were constructs of Feeling in Factor 3 ($r = 0.964$, $p < .01$) and Parents in Factor 1 ($r = 0.995$, $p < .01$). However, these same constructs revealed inferior results when correlated with caretaking (Factor 2), suggesting that elevated anxiety and dysfunctional parents may only correspond with but not cause enabling or codependent interpersonal relationships.

A final measure of construct validity involved designation of a Lie Scale. The Lie Scale was designed to identify a defensive response set manifested by a tendency to ascribe the most virtuous behaviors or to deny minor, commonly occurring behavior problems. The 12 items representing the scale appear in Table 7–8. Selected items appear under their respective subtests. Lie Scale scores further show how a respondent's "attitude" toward his or her problem, or toward life in general, may influence the way respondents answer the questions, thus affecting test outcome.

TABLE 7–7 Maximum Likelihood-Varimax Rotation Factor Loadings of the ACOA Behavior Profile Subtests across All Three Groups

Subtests	Rotated Factor 1	Rotated Factor 2	Rotated Factor 3
Feeling	0.202	0.17	0.964
Relaxed	0.132	0.386	0.397
Loyal	0.496	0.716	0.738
Control	0.155	0.461	0.214
Relations	0.174	0.418	0.346
Drug/Alcohol	0.373	0.144	0.206
Fear	0.277	0.391	0.216
Parents	0.995	0.008	0.275

Lie Scale scores fall into one of three ranges (high, neutral and law) based on criteria employed by the Taylor–Johnson Temperament Analysis (Taylor & Morrison, 1980. The high range includes scores 10, 11, and 12, the neutral range includes scores 7, 8, 9, and the low range includes scores 6 and below.

High Scores (10, 11, 12). High scores suggest a defensive test-taking attitude. Defensiveness may reflect a need to be seen in a positive light or overconcern about being perceived as "competent." Elevated scores also represent a rigidly moralistic outlook possibly contradicting the respondent's actual underlying psychopatholgy.

Neutral Scores (7, 8, 9). Neutral scores suggest little test-taking bias and that disclosures are frank, honest, open, and straightforward. Balance exists between self-protection and comfort at exposing personal faults.

Low Scores (6 and below). Low scores indicate self-deprecatory and over-negative answers. Respondents may be accentuating minor problems or worrisome symptoms either to exaggerate their degree of disturbance or for sympathy. Very low Lie Scale scores overall reflect poor adjustment and externalize a need for therapy.

Correlations between the Lie Scale and other ACOA Behavior Profile subtests are presented in Table 7–9. The Lie Scale reflected

TABLE 7–8 Lie Scale Item Content

ITEMS
F. (Feelings)
3. Do you believe your ideas are stupid or people will hate them? (T)
F. (Feelings)
7. Do you get angry if you get criticized? (T)
R. (Relax)
3. Does doing nothing make you feel guilty? (T)
L (Loyal)
2. Are you afraid to say "No"? (T)
C. (Control)
1. Do you feel nobody can do things better than you can? (T)
C. (Control)
8. Do you hate criticism? (T)
RE. (Relations)
1. Do you have to have an intimate relationship? (T)
RE. (Relations)
7. Is it hard to end relationships when you know you should end them? (T)
DA. (Drug/Alcohol)
3. When you're in a social situation, do you always have to drink or smoke something? (T)
FE. (Fear)
3. Are you afraid you might look stupid? (T)
P. (Parent)
1. When your parent(s) got angry, did it happen all the time? (T)
P. (Parent)
5. Did your parent(s) fight all the time? (T)

the absence of or denial of severe problems, especially for those classified as dysfunctional; it also reflected the absence of or denial of family problems and psychological discomfort. Elevated Lie Scale scores might suggest incredibility or malingering of self-ratings, as well as the subjects' motivation to protect themselves from exposing negative traits.

TABLE 7–9 Correlations between Lie Scale and Other ACOA Behavior Profile Subtests Estimated by ANOVA

Subtests	Group 1	Group 2	Group 3
Feelings	–0.248	0.053	0.103
Relaxed	–0.379	–0.131	0.384
Loyal	–0.152	0.141	0.444*
Control	–0.324	0.207	0.236
Relations	–0.248	0.169	.575**
Drug/Alcohol	–0.041	–0.04	.438*
Fear	–0.175	0.348	0.345
Parents	0.063	0.273	0.394

* Correlation is significant at the .05 level (two-tailed)
** Correlation is significant at the .01 level (two-tailed)

Conversely, low Lie Scale scores imply accuracy of subject ratings and a propensity for honesty. Table 7–9 showed predominantly lower correlations across all three groups. Exceptions include higher coefficients in Group 3 (low risk) on Loyal ($r = .444$, $p < .05$) and Drug and Alcohol ($r = .575$, $p < .01$) subtests.

Predictive Validity The term *predictive validity* refers to a test's ability to predict performance on other relevant measures. In general, moderate correlations with related measures are considered evidence of good predictive validity. Low correlations would fail to anchor the new test within the network of existing measures, and high correlations suggest that the new test is consistent with those already in existence.

Attempts at predictive validity employed a preliminary, small sample of MMPI–2 tests correlated with ACOA Behavior Profile scores. In this pilot study, subtests on the ACOA Behavior Profile were compared with specific MMPI–2 scores from 10 subjects randomly selected from Group 1 (high risk).

Table 7–10 presents the means, standard deviations, and correlations between the following MMPI–2 variables: Ma (hypomania); Si (social introversion); Anx (anxiety); Frs (fears); Lse (low self-esteem); Sod (social discomfort); Fam (family); A (anxiety); R (repression); MacR (MacAndrew Alcoholism Schedule); Aps (addiction potential); S1 (shyness, self-consciousness); S2 (social avoidance); and S3 (alienation, self and others). Selected MMPI–2 variables denote behavioral features similar to the eight subtests in the ACOA Behavior Profile.

Although the MMPI–2 was designed to measure abnormalities in personality, its scales also reflect clusters of behaviors overlapping with ACOA profiles. Significant correlations between variables on the ACOA Behavior Profile and the MMPI–2 were evident. Particularly noteworthy was that subtest on Relations (caretaker, enabler) strongly correlated with MMPI–2 scales of social introversion ($r = .66$ $p < .05$), low self-esteem ($r = .69$, $p < .05$), alienation of self and others ($r = .74$, $p < .05$), and anxiety on both basic ($r = .70$ $p < .05$), and content scales ($r = .78$, $p < .05$). Variables comprising Alcohol/Drugs also accurately matched the MacAndrews (MacR) scale ($r = .69$, $p < .05$), a subtest designed to measure alcohol recidivism.

The MMPI–2 scale of addiction potential (Aps) scored surprisingly poorly against the Drug/Alcohol subtest ($r = .11$, $p < .05$). Failure to predict relapse of nonalcohol drugs, however, may reflect that the MMPI–2 has a different focus in its questions: items measure past history of addiction rather than current polydrug abuses, whereas on the ACOA Behavior Profile items elicit progress on current abuses and recovery.

In general, salient differences appeared between Groups 1 (high risk), 2 (moderate risk), and 3 (low risk) on all items across the eight subtests. Elevated mean and percentage scores in Group 1 showed high relevancy of items for subjects abusing substances and directly predisposed to addicted parents. Measures of internal consistency further supported high alpha ratios for subtests on Parenting, Loyalty, Relaxed, and Fear. Assessment of construct and predictive validity additionally showed significant subtest intercorrelations with Lie Scale, MMPI–2

TABLE 7–10 Correlations between ACOA Behavior Profile Subtests and Selected MMPI–2 Variables

ACOA subtests	ACOA Mean	SD	MMPI–2 Ma	Si	Anx	Frs	Lse	Sod	Fam	A	R	MacR	Aps	S1	S2	S3
Feelings	6.4	2.3	0.24	0.45	0.61	0.03	0.47	0.3	0.38	0.6	0.05	0.42	−0.2	0.3	0.28	0.62
Relaxed	2.3	2.3	−0.06	0.33	0.38	0.13	0.49	0.23	0.56	0.5	−0.2	−0.29	−0.3	0.1	−0.3	0.37
Loyal	3.9	1.2	−0.25	0.08	−0.16	0.12	0.15	0.4	0.27	0	0.35	−0.06	−0.3	0.3	0.45	−0.17
Control	5.1	2	0.52	0.57	0.5	0.31	0.15	0.29	0.14	0.5	0.26	.71*	−0.5	0.2	−0.2	0.6
Relations	5	2.1	0.01	.66*	.70*	0.61	.69*	0.48	.67*	.78*	0	0.25	−0.3	0.3	0.11	.74*
Drug/Alc	5.5	1.7	0.36	0.08	0.35	−0.2	0.08	−0.1	−0.1	0.1	0.25	.69*	0.11	0	0.12	0.22
Fear	2.8	1.4	0.25	0.38	0.41	0.4	0.56	0.16	0.06	0.5	−0.3	−0.27	−0.1	0.3	−0.3	−0.14
Parents	6.8	3.8	−0.33	0.11	0.08	0.04	0.18	0.2	0.53	−0.1	0.48	0.19	−0.2	0	0	−0.14
Mean			65.1	56.5	69.1	56.3	64.6	56.5	67.8	68	46	62	56.5	56	58	65
SD			13.5	12.2	13	11.6	13.9	13.1	10.6	14	8	9.4	11.1	10	8.9	12

* Correlation is significant at the .05 level (two-tailed)

** Correlation is significant at the .01 level (two-tailed)

scores, and when factors were weighted using a confirmatory analysis.

Benefits for Diagnosis and Treatment

Recent research findings have correspond to many clinical case studies and psychometric assessments of ACOAs. Baker and Stephenson's (1995) psychopathic profiles of ACOAs resembled the categorical split between aggressive and passive caretakers. Respondents scoring high in caretaking proportionally generated high scores in loyalty and control. Both aggressive and passive caretakers shared common denominators insofar as (a) selfless dedication to other people, (b) self-esteem derived from altruistic and self-sacrificing action, and (c) attraction to and enabling of individuals with palpable personality disorders, especially in substance abuse.

In terms of probabilities, significant intercorrelations between subtests on Loyal and Control ($r = .318$, $p < .01$) further suggested caretakers needed decisive boundaries and implicit reassurance from other people for their efforts.

Comparative group outcomes have shown that low-risk subjects who were asymptomatic produced negligible scores on the ACOA Behavior Profile. This contrasted to high-risk and medium-risk subjects, who obtained significant scores. Consequently, offspring from addicted families not only face high risk of ACOA patterns but may also display polymorbid mental illness.

Longitudinal studies on intergenerational effects of family addiction (Chang & Krantz, 1996; Dupont & McGovern, 1991) have endorsed similar conclusions: that dual diagnosis of polydrug addiction and emotional disorders (anxiety, depression) are typical in children from alcoholic families. Kazdin (1995) further hypothesized a trajectory of behavioral dysfunctions suffered by emotionally embattled children through adolescence and adulthood.

Dysfunctions evolving from childhood were not surprising, they appeared for different reasons than typically reported in the literature. In the standardization study examined previously in this chapter, Group 2 (moderate risk) did not have polydrug-abusing parents; however, their parents appeared adversarial in other ways that manifested the ACOA pattern in the subjects—namely, through arbitrary and volatile tempers. Randomly explosive outbursts not only could account for high scores on the Parent subtest but also for equally elevated scores in the Relaxed and Fear subtests. The Relaxed subtest was an index of the need for constant motion and intolerance of idleness and boredom.

High scores on Relaxed suggest that subjects feel anxiety when they have "down time" and therefore are afraid of leisure and "doing nothing." Fears associated with inactivity may correspond to anticipatory fears of subjects being reprimanded for laziness, unproductivity and inefficiency. Anxiety symptoms replicated the patterns reported in children's spurious, ritualistic, obsessive, and fearful behaviors induced by superstitious conditioning (Wager & Morris, 1987; Zeiler, 1972).

The latest research has overcome the caveat of Schuckit, Klein & Twitchell (1995) that previous unreliable measures of the ACOA syndrome attributed to undifferentiated symptoms. The current data, by contrast, statistically quantifies distinctions between ACOA characteristics (subtests) and further shows correlational significance between specific features and specific groups of subjects.

Furthermore, ACOA test findings have solved the shortcomings of the Children of Alcoholics Screening Test (Pilat & Jones 1984–1985). CAST's clinical limitations of poorly sampling diverse groups and insufficient coverage of parental alcoholism were replaced by the ACOA Behavior Profile's three normative groups for standardization, and an entire subtest devoted to parental influence. Improvements over Claydon's (1987) pioneering research of college students not only expands the diversity of subject demographics but also methodologically expands the use of an ACOA instrument as part of a battery of psychological tests. Incorporating the ACOA Behavior Profile into protocol alcohol and drug assessment offers many advantages, ranging from precision of early diagnosis to concise treatment planning.

CONCLUSIONS

Several conclusions reached by these studies relate largely to clinical application and social implications of the ACOA Behavior Profile. First, quantifiable statistical analyses provided strong support for the content, construct, and predictive validity of the eight subtests, with six of the subtests—Parenting, Loyal, Relaxed, Fear, Relations, Alcohol/Drug Abuse—ranking exceptionally high. Elevated coefficient scores indicated that the ACOA Behavior Profile can estimate residual symptoms of dysfunctional childhood problems attributable to family addiction.

Children exposed to drinking or drug-abusing parents apparently suffered pervasive traumatic effects represented by the eight subtests. It is interesting that the highest correlational data (reliability and validity) was for the subtest on Loyal, implying that the worst psychopathologic ACOA side-effect is caretaking

In addition, clinically, ACOAs displaying polymorbid symptoms may suffer the most from caretaking. Concurrent diagnostic tools such as MMPI–2 and the Taylor–Johnson Temperament Analysis, among others, may produce high scores on compassion, hypersensitivity, and even submissiveness. But the inattentive clinician may overlook that these patterns comprise chronic caretaking insofar as the client diligently acts in an altruistic manner purely to secure approval from others. As Kazdin (1985) perceptively observed, behaviors targeted in prebaseline or assessment phases may be noncorresponsive or irrelevant to the treatment interventions. Consequently, clients treated for hypersensitivity with desensitization, or for submissiveness with interpersonal assertiveness skills, may never eliminate the underlying or more destructive behavior of caretaking (e.g., rescuing, appeasing, self-sacrifice, etc.).

Alternatively, results of the standardization study confirmed the clinical exigency to examine not only client-reported symptoms, but also the concurrent and sequential responses interrelated with client reported symptoms. Delprato's (1986, Delprato & McGlynn, 1988) reformulated methodology for a larger sample of behavioral analysis complements the current findings that caretaking, and, for that matter, the entire ACOA syndrome, is multicausal. Caretaking, for example, depends on subjects' behaviors in response to past, current, and future contingencies over against events occurring at the moment. Unlike Skinnerian or radical behaviorism, focused largely on confining moment-by-moment events, the revised field analysis might describe caretaking as evolving through multiple stimulus-response events that progressively conditions the caretaker to reinforce other people.

Application of the ACOA Behavior Profile is but one example of substantiating the empirical evidence of the ACOA syndrome. But these data are overdue. Dupont & McGovern's (1991) commentary on the ACOA advocacy movement lamented the absence of scientific data. It echoed Brown's (1991) sentiment that offspring of alcoholics represent an overlooked population of epidemic proportions. Victims of family addiction increasingly appear as defendants in Protective Services investigations, drunk driving convictions, and related alcohol and drug abuse criminal offenses. Unresolved interpersonal problems further account for staggering numbers of ACOAs convicted of domestic violence. In this respect, the criminal justice system is ripe for heuristic predictors of ACOA at-risk behaviors in order to assist probation and parole officers in prepare presentencing reports.

Recommendations

Analyses of all three risk groups strongly favored the clinical application of the ACOA Behavior Profile in diagnostic decision making. Drug-abusing as well as nondrug-abusing clients who completed the questionnaire reported personal histories predictive of behavior excesses and deficits. This makes targetable excesses and deficits directly amenable to treatment intervention. Unlike other alcoholism tests or the few ACOA tests available, the ACOA Behavior Profile offers a classificatory scheme explicitly designed for offspring of addiction and aggressive families. Combined with conventional uses of MMPI–2, CAST, and varying projectives, the ACOA Behavior Profile becomes an invaluable tool for forensic psychological examination.

Interpreting the data in this study is best done in the context of several ACOA assessment issues. First, like any self-report questionnaire, data reflected subjective responses generated from a pool of items. Poorly constructed items may evoke weak, unreliable, or irrelevant answers, whereas better constructed items produce replies consistent with authentic experiences. The Lie Scale attempted to compensate for bogus or malingering replies but may itself fall prey to low reliability and irrelevant responses.

Another drawback of the ACOA Behavior Profile was the low number of questions per subtest. Despite high internal consistency, subtests ranged from 4 to 13 items, averaging at 8 questions per subtest. Considering that the MMPI–2 contains 567 items covering more than 50 subtests, with each subtest averaging 11 questions, breadth of coverage potentially is greater on the MMPI–2. Fewer questions on the ACOA Behavior Profile, moreover, increased the chance of omitting critical information or gathering generalities over concrete examples of dysfunctional behavior.

Still another pitfall of the standardization research was lack of exclusivity and causality. Isolating variables that are purportedly correlated with ACOA characteristics necessitated many assumptions. For example, were subtests on Loyal and Parenting exclusively predictive of children from addicted families? As pointed out earlier, children predisposed to random schedules of aggressive punishment may develop symptoms analogous to children traumatized by polydrug-abusing families. The unicausal, or one-way causal, link between these variables is thus empirically inferior.

In defense of the subtests, multicausal or field-integrated links offer a more viable scientific explanation for using the ACOA Behavior Profile. In a field-integrated analysis, for example, personality is measured by covariance of behaviors in the context of many environmental stimuli. The ACOA Behavior Profile attempted to capture multiple contexts (fields) from the subjects' past and current experiences and measure covarying behaviors within those fields.

In short, much work lies ahead in the assessment of behaviors associated with ACOA. It appears that specific and microanalytic assessments may more accurately measure personal behaviors than do traditional measures and assessment procedures (Johnston & Pennypacker, 1980). However, assumptions about ACOA behaviors need to be tested more empirically, given the complexity and covariation among these behaviors.

To this conclusion, however, it may be added with some confidence, that measurable categories of the ACOA syndrome now can inform clients of why they struggle emotionally in life and how immediate interventions may reverse trajectories of future problems.

PART II

Treatment Methodology for Adult Children of Alcoholics

CHAPTER 8

Basic Components of Short-Term Treatment

Innovative treatment approaches for ACOAs enjoy wide dissemination among the mass media and in professional practice circles (e.g., Ackerman, 1983). Upwards of 100 books currently circulate in the human service field, focused on guiding troubled offspring with identification of symptoms and self-healing cures ranging from Judeo-Christian and humanistic pastoral versions to psychoanalytically strategies. In all, symptom-elimination methods underscore the posture that ACOAs face a long uphill journey to repair childhood emotional wounds and transform themselves into healthy adults. Estimates for recovery time may be optimistic but are guardedly cautious: advancing too quickly may overstep important stages of self-improvement that involve cleansing the past of shameful feelings and undertaking responsibilities. These transcendental stages inspire hope and clinical promise of personal growth in much the same manner as the twelve steps of Alcoholics Anonymous endow faith in self-pacing the attainment of sobriety.

The downside of transcendentally based stages of therapy is that their progress cannot be measured. Clinical practitioners who prescribe self-recovery methods through bibliotherapy (i.e., Glasgow & Rosen, 1978; Ruben, 1989a) or who employ conceptually abstract family systems theories are unable to empirically judge post-baseline improvements in specific behaviors that correlate with ACOA symptoms. In other words, actual behavior changes that clients report as significant, remain obscure and untraceable to specific methods. While self-reported improvements may be personally meaningful to the client and imply efficacy of treatment, reasons for symptom elimination will remain a mystery and pose risks of spontaneous generation of new symptoms. Moving therapeutically foreword without knowing the variables that cause problems not only risks relapse, it also risks interventions being unreliable and invalid. Therapies that are effective either undergo rigorous research replication on humans or are derived from both experimental and applied studies supporting generality to an ACOA population.

A Structured, Scientific Approach to Therapy

Interventions discussed for the ACOA emanate from structured, behavioral approaches guided by principles of science. Methods represent extrapolations from relapse prevention techniques (Gorski & Miller, 1986; Marlott & Gordon, 1985; Ruben, 1999b; Wilson, 1992), and from conventional cognitive-behavioral interventions (Bellack & Hersen, 1985; Macciomei & Ruben, 1979). The protocol for implementation is identical; the provider plans out the goals and objectives for client approval and proceeds in each session to work through exercises, strategies, or emotional obstacles along the path of these goals and objectives.

Diversions from the goals and objectives are normal and usually deal with personal reflections on why the goals are difficult, events happening that day or recently, or new reactions of other people. Naturally, attention is paid to client concerns, but the discussion should return to the goals or techniques in process, keeping the structure balanced throughout the session. Structure further establishes a milieu for teaching and learning and allows clients to predict exactly how the session will go, with minor variations. For clients with control issues, predictability provides a strong foundation for trust. Consider the following strategies that enter into a structured behavioral systems regimen:

Changing Beliefs

Altering irrational beliefs or impure inferences begins with identifying the inaccurate rules or meta rules governing the ACOAs' behavior. Beliefs most dangerous are self-critical, condemnatory, or those that compare the the ACOA with other people perceived as superior. Efforts made to dispute these beliefs include a three steps consisting of (a) interrupting the beliefs, (b) asking questions of the person from whom inferences are drawn, and (c) replacing self-criticism with self-complimentary and realistic statements. Self-complimentary or realistic statements are accurate rules liberating the person from false expectations and the need for perfectionism. Statements such as "it's no big deal," or "it's okay for mistakes to happen" seem superficial but help combat "negative tapes" mentally replayed by the ACOA under stress situations.

Correcting misperceptions by asking questions also involves a three-step process. First, teach the client to look only at what another person actually is saying or doing, not "why" behaviors occur. Discourage analytical-deductive thinking by focus purely on concrete verbal and nonverbal behaviors observed in other people. Second, instruct the client to dismiss culpability for unknown facts. Metaphorically, the expression used is "No facts, no fault," implying that absent facts about other people's behavior means the ACOA is not responsible for that person's behavior. Refusing ownership of fault, the ACOA immediately begins the third step: directly asking questions about the reason behind the person's intimidating or offensive behavior. Questions phrased naturally include, "Why did you do that? or Why did you say that?"

Politely questioning people about their behavior unfortunately can backfire. Instruct clients in a series of roadblock-detouring methods to avoid frivolous conflicts and remain objective and shame-free. There are two phrases recommended to interrupt rude rejoinders from disputants displeased by being queried. The first statement following aggressive remarks is, "I was just wondering." If badgering continues, follow with another defusal reply which terminates the conversation, "I'm sorry you feel that way."

Underlying the effectiveness of the belief-altering procedure are three important conditioning processes. First, asking questions at the instant of feeling offended *competes with rule-governed behaviors or thinking.* Physiologically, execution of the vocal musculature occurs for verbal behavior, whether verbal behavior is public or private. Public speech is magnified at audible levels mediated by the listener's reinforcement or punishment. Private speech production occurs at a lower magnitude than public speech and thus changes density, frequency, and duration, but not necessarily topography. Words emitted loudly, in other words, may be similar to words emitted silently, except at a lower magnitude. Since vocal muscular contractions can only occur either for public or private speech at any given moment, simultaneous emission of thought and speech is impossible; they are incompatible. Consequently, asking questions at the onset of adversity *competes,* if only for seconds, with self-defeating thoughts.

A second functional result is desensitization. Audible questions that occur under fear-provoking stimuli (i.e., the angry disputant) condition the ACOA to be less afraid. Repetition of questions builds stronger tolerance to fearful stimuli until anxiety dissipates, thereby enabling coping behaviors.

A third operational effect is rapid acquisition of skill prerequisites for assertiveness. Asking questions prepares the ACOA with rudimentary skills in facing the offender, looking at the offender, remaining in place when exposed to fear (versus avoidance and escape behaviors), and responding sequentially using defusal statements without escalating to anger.

Basic Assertiveness

Modifying rule-governed behaviors opens the doorway to basic assertiveness. Basic assertions represent several behaviors. First, they are questions asked of another person about words or actions possibly misunderstood by observation alone. Questions such as "Why did you do that?" require a brief answer that clarifies motives and reasons, and obviates the ACOA's inference that offensive or uncertain action must be attributed to something I did.

Basic assertiveness also includes three parts of directive confrontation, exposing the ACOA to elevated hierarchies of anxiety. These include: disagreements, opinions. and criticism. Disagreements commit the ACOA to make refusals or give opinions on objectionable remarks expressed by significant others on many different and relevant topics. Disagreements, however, threaten reprisals and frequently discourage risky attempts that result in conflict. But tactics on how to stay on the topic, to resist roadblocks, and remain focused prevent digression onto irrelevant issues and making personal defensive remarks.

Opinions are unprompted statements regarding a spontaneous idea that contributes to the ongoing discussion. Such statements also initiate discussion about some object, person, or event. Initiating opinions at first challenges the deeply rooted belief that personal ideas impose upon other people who did not *ask for the opinion and thus will regard it as intrusive*. Opinions that decry an object, event, or person are *criticisms*. Unprompted or prompted statements describing why the ACOA dislikes something are appropriate around significant others.

Initiation of assertive replies with people unaccustomed to the ACOA "speaking up" may backfire. Rather than produce reinforcing outcomes, punishing consequences occur in fierce retaliation for ACOAs deviating from their normal (dysfunctional) behavior. Frightened ACOAs may forget new techniques learned and revert to defusal tactics aimed at relieving or terminating anticipated criticism, conflict, or rejection. Defusal tactics vary depending on individual history but generally take five forms. Awareness of these mistakes represents the first step in self-monitoring effective assertions. These defusal mistakes include: (a) apologies, (b) discrediting, disqualifying statements, (c) defensiveness, (d) self-criticism, and (e) compensating.

Apologies Immediately after asserting an opinion, the ACOA may sense dissent from the listener and anticipate impending conflict. Apologies accept blame for perceived discomfort imposed on the listener and thus terminate the listener from acting negatively in retaliation for the discomfort. Of course, many assumptions play into this ACOA response that usually are inconsistent with the listener's real events.

Discrediting, Disqualifying Statements Rule-governed behaviors (inferences) again lead the person to false conclusions about self-culpability. Perceived discomfort in the listener may trigger ACOAs to dismiss, discredit, or disqualify opinions they just made by admitting they are wrong or that little validity supports their statements. Or, they may defer judgment to the listener's alleged expertise. For example, criticism about a modern painting may upset the listener and prompt the ACOA to rescind the statement and say instead, "I don't know much about art anyway, certainly not like you do."

Defensiveness Personal assaults signal ACOAs to protect their vulnerability by fighting back with disruptive statements or rationalizations that explicate their actions. Retaliatory comments argue the reasons, facts, and other "persuasive" evidence that satisfy the attacker's curiosity and support the validity of an idea. Defensiveness also rebuilds the ACOA's crumbling confidence against intrusive thoughts of "feeling like an impostor" or "looking stupid."

Self-criticism Self-criticism is believed to relieve imminent conflict. ACOAs who expect interpersonal trouble shift to their personal faults, and deflect comments away from faults of the listener. Self-denigration further restores control to the intimidating listener at the expense of the ACOA feeling inferior.

Compensating Opinions that have a negative impact on listeners evoke ACOAs into thinking that conflict is inevitable and that they have severely hurt the listener emotionally. Feeling ashamed of this, nonverbal apologies occur that compensate for or rectify emotional damage. ACOAs generously accommodate the listener, either by loyally handling their responsibilities or by providing them with a service or resource guaranteed to win love and friendship. Restitutional efforts also inadvertently produce reciprocal reinforcement. For ACOAs, conflict–avoidance ratios increase as do continuous social reinforcement schedules. For the listener, criticism and other verbally intimidating remarks gain enormous strength from ACOAs who provide caretaking behaviors on a CRF schedule. The response interdependence that results becomes cyclically volatile.

All five defusal tactics seriously endanger the psychological benefits of basic assertions in hostile situations. Efforts at teaching opinions, assertiveness and resistance to roadblocks must involve specific steps that block these tactics, despite rising anxiety levels and the ACOA's strong self-perception of guilt.

Reversal of Victimization

Rule-governed beliefs of victimization obsessively engulf many ACOAs who, since childhood, repeatedly suffered tragedies, emotional or financial setbacks, or recurrent relationship failures. Victimizational thinking went beyond externalizing locus of control to outside forces and helplessly surrendering to personal defeat. The result of victimizer symptoms was incapacitation of existing routine social behaviors and low motivation for new routines. Reduction of routines occurs because ACOAs poorly control and predict their schedules of reinforcement and punishment. Excessive variability among their consequences since childhood precluded congruent and synchronized behavior; instead, they developed impulsive and superstitious behaviors responsive to the arbitrary and capricious (i.e., variable ratio/interval) effects of past conditioning. Similarly, suppression of routines discouraged trying new routines, since the ACOAs entire response class of organized, self-control behaviors was deficient.

Reversing these suppressive patterns models after the reconditioning paradigm in learning helplessness. Forced opportunities for reinforcement can rebuild response strength if the response occurs and reinforcement is continuous. Steps that duplicate this experimental process include risking, faking, and confronting. Risking involves systematic efforts worked out ahead of time by therapist and client to restore small amounts of routines. The "risk" is fearing that impulsive behaviors may sabotage the process. Schedules of sleep, mealtime, work, and recreation all attempt to follow consistent time slots during the day, allowing the ACOA to gain prediction and control over simple life patterns.

Faking refers to the uncomfortable, robot-like and unnatural sensations experienced when restoring old routines. The person complains of feeling phony, theatrical, and out of character during emission of target behavior; discomfort even triggers misperceptions that "treatment is not working," or "that they have to pretend to be somebody they are not." Instead, therapists coach the distrusting client through intentional simulations of behavior-faking while simultaneously arranging for two concurrent conditions. First is repetition of the routine, first under clinical conditions and then in environmentally naturalistic settings. Practice of routines in the session using reenactment or role-play analogies is one approach. Opportunities occur in the natural environment to employ confederates or "safe people" (e.g., close friends or trusted spouses), or use feedback devices such as audiotapes and videotapes. With successive practice and as desensitized effects relax artificial efforts into new routines, therapists begin to encourage direct didactic trails with people around whom vulnerability arises.

For example, a 36-year-old woman married four times suffered recurrent beliefs about "being a loser" and was deathly afraid of being controlled. Since childhood, victimizational rule-governed behaviors gained reinforcement from many bad experiences: she was molested, harshly teased for her weight gain, relegated to special education classes, and in early adulthood gravitated toward physically abusive male partners. Converting her self-defeating rule-governed statements into healthy rule-governed behaviors required experience with healthy operant contingencies. She undertook a hierarchical series of anxiety-producing steps involving new routines and assertiveness around two people designated as making her feel vulnerable: her boss and boyfriend. First in front of the mirror, with rehearsals viewed by her mother, and, second, around her boss and boyfriend, this client mastered the routines of self-expression and giving opinions without self-suppression. Consequently, she constructed a new rule-governed statement that "I can say and do what I want and not feel stupid."

Calibrated Vulnerability

Calibrated vulnerability may appear to be somewhat of an oxymoron. How can one be methodical and seriously focused when one feels vulnerable? The answer lies with self-managing contingencies expected to produce favorable consequences. The "calibration" involves systematic use of humble, self-deprecatory remarks engineered to evoke empathy and response from a listener. ACOAs who deliberately identify self-faults or admit their shortcomings nearly always produce reinforcers. At first, clients complain this technique undermines confidence and subjects them to debasement; after all, they used to apologize and admit mistakes all the time and felt shameful for doing it. However, calibrated vulnerability is different from shame-induced humility and accomplishes two goals. First, it disinhibits fears of appearing incompetent, imperfect, or stupid. Second, self-exposure of negative traits draws compassion from the listener, reversing caretaking behaviors on the part of the ACOA—who was unilaterally altruistic to other people. Sadly, benevolent behaviors probably existed in people significant to the ACOA but were suppressed or shaped differentially by the ACOA, who always "enabled" the relationship.

Self-disclosive statements, in other words, serve the purpose of restoring reinforcing control over uncomfortable situations. Calibrated vulnerability verbally signifies that the ACOA is fallible, flexible, and willing to share personal secrets without self-incrimination or paralyzing anticipation of punishment.

Fred risked incredible humiliation when he braved an exercise in calibrated vulnerability. Socially passive and bordering on agoraphobic, Fred's chronic fears impaired his consulting skills as a computer analyst and took a toll on a score of bad relationships. He rarely voiced opinions about the significant partner but rather manufactured criticism about himself to guarantee social approval. Fred then tried a different approach. He learned to identify realistic, not fabricated, imperfections and rehearsed explanations of the faults without apologies or exaggerations. Analogue rehearsals within the sessions followed a stepwise transfer of the verbal exercise around his significant partner. Fred divulged his fears of looking irresponsible and intellectually insubordinate to his peers. When he did so, his significant partner passionately gave him feedback on how she, too, suffered embarrassing feelings of incompetence. To Fred's surprise, release of personal vulnerability received warmly intense reinforcement.

Self-regulating Mood Swings

Mood imbalances recently diagnosed as "bipolar affective disorder" refer to uncontrollable fluctuations in behavior from elative to depressive states. Elated patterns manifest hypermanic, overconfident, overactive, and aggressive behaviors—inducing sensory stimulation or the "adrenaline-rush" effects. ACOAs operating in these excitable states have a grandiose view of their abilities and strive for goals far surpassing realistic expectations. Hyperbolic thinking typically produces obsessive, stubbornly deterministic responses impervious to the resulting setbacks or adverse consequences that occur. On the swing side, high-frequency responses shift to a debilitating state of helplessness marked by lethargy, anhedonia, and social withdrawal. Cyclical episodes recur daily or weekly and invariably confuse both the mood-disordered ACOA as well as concerned observers in the ACOAs' lives.

Conventional treatment for bipolar disorder calls for medication, although nonmedication and behavioral interventions show strong promise (Fisher, Adelinis, Thompson, Worsdell & Zarcone, 1998; Wilson, Scott, Abou-Saleh, Burns, & Copeland, 1995). Integrative uses of response exposure plus prevention, behavioral family management, and habit-reversal methods all comprise innovative amelioration techniques. Among these, habit reversal involving self-awareness, rehearsal, and guidance may figure most prominently because of its generality to diverse behavioral maladaptations (Miltenberg, Fuqua & Woods, 1998). For example, the author's multicomponent use of habit reversal in eliminating self-injurious, skin-picking behaviors (Ruben, 1989b) found that in addition to deceleration effects, sensory stimuli (itching) evoking scratching became as reciprocally reinforcing as self-stimulation of scab irritation. Consequently, biophysical sensations act as powerful antecedents tantamount to external behaviors in prompting ritualistic habit behaviors.

Similarly, bipolar disorder may be functionally understood as ritualistic behavioral sequences comprised of concurrent and sequential response patterns involving "mood swings" (i.e., exhibited behaviors) and sensory differentiation from euphoria to labile states. Both states represent unpleasant extremes typically producing adverse interpersonal effects. Short or long cycles combine biochemical and behavioral factors that gain reinforcement when the moods shift. Cessation of exuberant, thrill-seeking states negatively reinforces these behaviors, just as rebounding from depressive states negatively reinforces future occurrences of depression. Habit reversal employed in self-regulating moods thus appears a logical extension from its protocol uses to control nail biting, hair pulling, stuttering, and muscular tics (Azrin & Nunn, 1977). Procedurally, steps begin with awareness and proceed to alteration and assistance. Terminology may differ, but the method remains essentially the same.

Awareness involves therapist-guided identification and recognition of elative and depressive symptoms. Rehearsed analogues involve deliberate inductions of "highs" and "lows" through a myriad of evocative sources ranging from audiotaped and videotaped antecedents (e.g., husband yelling at wife) to reenactments with live partners, and visual imagery. Once these simulations are complete, the therapist leads the client through a series of questions alerting the ACOA to sensory (private) and overt behavioral signs to discriminate relevant from irrelevant repine properties.

In alteration, the therapist asks the ACOA to reverse the existing sensory and behavioral modality to an opposite (competing) pattern, but moderates the reversed pattern so it does not become excessive. For example, hypermania reverses to verbal silence and sedentary behaviors. ACOAs experiencing sudden oscillations typically report being overcome with sadness and feelings of laziness, stupidity and shame. Slightly decelerated states, in their perspective, generate sensory changes mislabeled as "weak, helpless, and depressed." In truth, however, sensory and behavioral shifts may be minims when ACOAs complain of these unwanted sensations. A second component in alteration is duration of change. Therapists coach clients to maintain shifted behaviors by invoking reinforcers such as the opportunity to eat, sleep, or engage in pleasurable activities. By increasing duration, balance is established between both mood extremes, discriminately conditioning awareness of new sensory stimuli that can replace euphoric or depressive stimuli.

In the final step, *assistance,* the ACOA recruits the help of significant others, who observe and can positively support self-regulatory behaviors.

Marge was a 24-year-old married female Hispanic under investigation by protective services for using excessive corporal punishment on her 5-year-old daughter. Her daughter subsequently was moved into a foster home. Court-ordered interventions coerced Marge into attend parenting classes, visiting her daughter weekly in a neutral setting, and receiving therapy for mood swings that were blamed for her poor impulse control and over-reactive hostility. However, Marge resisted these programs and threatened the case worker with retaliation, using vulgar language. She became hypermanic and aggressive whenever talking to the caseworker; these states were followed by protracted periods of subdued isolation. Historically, Marge suffered rapidly cyclical mood swings while being raised in a chaotic, physically abusive household of drinkers. As she faced termination of parental rights, Marge figured therapy might be worth a shot. She met for six consecutive sessions, learning the three-step components of mood self-regulation and allowing her husband to monitor her. Evocative stimuli consisted of visual imagery and eventually direct contact with the nemesis case worker, around whom she maintained composure on several occasions. Most important, she mastered mood control with relative success without psychotropic medications.

Resisting Rejection

Toughest of all interventions is preparing the ACOA for rejection. Rejection underlies the emotional pathology evolved over years of avoidance and escape, where fear of rejection becomes habitual and elimination of it appears impossible. Modifying rejection thus entails a delicate process of short, socially assertive steps to avoid serious backsliding. Overzealous leaps of conditioning may re-suppress behaviors and sabotage trust in therapy. Steps follow a structured series of actions that commence only when ACOAs have mastered confrontation skills:

1. Delay responding for 3–5 minutes. Resist engaging in defusal tactics.
2. Assertively state what the person said and voice your emotional disapproval.
3. Walk away and ignore subsequent roadblocks or attacking remarks from listeners.
4. Make self-statements that it is okay for people to be upset with you.

This last rule is crucial but contradicts the very core of caretaking behaviors. Accepting that people get angry and that rejection is normal, and that it is even healthy for people to hate the ACOA violates every rule inculcated since childhood. Naturally, then, conversion to these new rule-governed behaviors takes time and may be resisted or doubted as techniques for recovery. But applying the rules generates three benefits immediately visible to the risker. First, it eliminates defusal tactics that undermine the ACOA's integrity and leave him or her angry for being subversive. Instead, confidence remains strong and gains momentum through self-restraint. Second, letting others be upset at the ACOA forces those other people to *adjust to new behaviors in the ACOA*. Third, walking away teaches the ACOA not to depend on approval for self-esteem. Confidence depends, instead, on individualized risks directly challenging the norms, morals, or values of childhood belief systems.

Building Trust

Development of trust forces the question, "Why should I trust anybody when I know I'll be hurt?" Distrust runs deep in the chronic history of abuse suffered by most ACOAs either from sexual, physical, verbal, or emotional damage. Slowly abandoning this "comfort zone" of distrust by sharing control or inviting others to control the ACOA faces immediate barriers of fear. First is the fear that trust will engender repetition of abuse. A second fear is that losing control will expose embarrassing imperfections and cause rejection. A third fear derives from literally not knowing how to share control. For example, ACOAs who as young children assumed parental responsibilities in caring for their siblings and drug-using parents received accelerated independence and achieved individuality. They habitually learned to cultivate their own recreation, solve their own problems, and be self-nurturing, never expecting compassion from adult caregivers. Without benefactors, they had no concept of being a beneficiary of love and protection. Consequently, in the classroom or on the playground, parental-style behaviors emerge that are bossy, domineering, controlling, and intolerant of boredom. Surrogate parents also never learn pleasures in cooperative behaviors; instead, they view "sharing" as anathema. Fear arises in abandoning contingency control to another person who may reverse the control and manipulate them.

Taken in context, control fears can impede progress toward building trust unless the fears are identified, explored, and replaced by functional alternatives that allow a stepwise strategy for sharing control. This generally involve four steps:

1. Divulge personal, embarrassing, or humiliating situations to a significant other. Resist using defusal tactics when telling the stories.
2. Ask significant others for favors. Ask them to do jobs you usually do or believe nobody else can do. Accept the product of their efforts regardless of errors or the inconsistency between their efforts and your own efforts.
3. Ask the significant other to interrupt your rigid schedule by planning, organizing, or directing social or business events that typically are left up to you.
4. Permit another person to make decisions or initiate efforts you typically handled yourself without your interference, even if the person recruits your assistance.

Vernon doubted this procedure would work. He had a long history of adult-accelerated experiences tracing to 11 years old, when caring for his baby-sister while his mother lay drunk on the couch. Her inebriation resulted in unpredictable yelling episodes, where Vernon was physically whipped for ignoring his mother and disobeying household rules. In truth, no matter what Vernon did right, his mother constantly blamed him for laziness, incompetence, and ignorance. By adulthood, polymorbid problems paralyzed his psychosocial skills and accounted for three failed marriages. In each marriage he bullied, bossed, and ordered around his passive wives, insisting they were lazy slobs who evaded responsibilities. Verbal reprimands were acidic, sarcastic, and bluntly abrasive, without any compensatory remorse. Ironically, being hypersensitive, Vernon pined for a balanced, passionate relationship relieving him of controlling duties.

Two months into therapy, Vernon learned the procedure for undertaking risk exposure to rebuild trust. He began asking girlfriends and male friends for favors and deliberately assumed a follower role in community volunteer organizations. He even let friends interrupt his tightly ritualistic weekend schedule without erupting in anger or refusing their initiatives. Vernon discovered that by giving people permission to be his caretaker, several changes rapidly materialized. Reductions occurred in anxiety, perfectionism, anger, impulsivity, and in determining the contingency control. He felt relieved other people came to his rescue and became the parent to his child.

Breaking the Impostor Syndrome

Low self-efficacy, we now understand, continues as long as ACOAs constantly avert exposure of faults. Fear of this exposure historically can be linked to assaults of random and arbitrary punishment for both appropriate and inappropriate child behaviors. Anticipating impending criticism or conflict, ACOAs remain on guard at their behavioral posts by hiding mistakes and reducing vulnerability. The *impostor syndrome* describes this phobia and protective habitual avoidant response. Distorted self-perceptions include the image of being imminently "discovered as fake, phony, or impersonator of skills, unmasking their real identity." Actor Leslie Nielson recently described this feeling best in reflecting on his career of doubting his acting talents, when he lamented, "I always feel like the Acting Police will arrest me at any time for not really being a good actor and just faking it." Obsessive fears of defamation derive from rule-governed beliefs that "Nobody will believe me," and "Who do I think I am, anyway?" An impostor self-concept not only disintegrates personal efforts, it also prevents aspirations from undertaking challenges in educational, vocational, or relational opportunities because of expectations of inevitable failures and identity assassination.

Removing the syndrome becomes a systematic process of balancing risk with panic through three steps. The first step prepares the person for desensitization—that is, of making verbal statements or displaying physical actions prone to errors while in a relaxed muscular state. Desensitization requires repeated use of progressive muscular relaxation, using in vivo visual imagery and followed by the client actually responding in the situations previously imagined. Visual imagery with relaxation, for example, involves the ACOA picturing himself telling a stupid joke and forgetting parts of it. Once stress is lower under imagery, analogues are constructed in the clinical setting and then applied in the real world until the client reports consistent degrees of comfort.

The second treatment step involves the ACOA remaining for increasing time periods in *the unpleasant, adverse, or frightening situation*. A less structured but equally effective desensitization is forcing the client to interact verbally or nonverbally around people, events, or objects feared as destructive to vulnerability. For example, the ACOA executive stays seated at a conference table throughout the entire meeting, forces input on topics, and verbally accepts constructive criticisms given to him so that fears about looking stupid and feeling like an impostor vanish as the ACOA sustains confidence. A final step is soliciting objective feedback from observers about exhibited behaviors. Instruct the ACOA to ask specific questions such as, "Did I speak clearly?," "Did I sound professional?," or "Did I make sense," which defuses skeptical thoughts and generates social reinforcers for appropriate "debriefing" behaviors.

ACOAs undergoing impostor desensitization further achieve two goals. One is spontaneous recovery from situational setbacks, which previously immobilized their efforts and caused unbearable humiliation. A second goal is risk initiation in situations previously perceived as fearful, unapproachable, or unattainable. For example, now ACOAs confidently believe they can advance in school, accept a job promotion, or embark on activities elevating their public exposure to criticism (e.g., election to school board or to a political office).

Risk-taking Effort

In addition to removal of the impostor syndrome, the ACOA needs to make methodically planned efforts to risk spontaneous behaviors regarded as foolish, childish, and posing further hazards to vulnerability. Procedurally, three steps follow in sequential order. ACOAs first construct a list of social, sexual, or playful activities they envy in other people or wish they could do themselves. Lists should contain realistic behaviors matching the ACOA's current skill repertoire or interbehavioral potentials after disinhibition of suppressed behaviors A second step is to assess how many of these responses immediately appear in the person's repertoire, despite the infrequency, inaccuracy, or overall consequences produced by them (i.e., approval, disapproval). Responses showing immediate strength are selected first for intervention by changing the rules governing them, and if necessary, involving the significant others directly affected by the behaviors. The third step is rehearsal of risk initiation under safe or highly reinforcing situations limiting setbacks, punitive reprisals, or feelings of impostorism. In the final step, analogue practice in the natural setting occurs by interacting with people or places targeted as phobic, and subsequently establishing response generalization.

For example, a 45-year-old, anorexic-looking woman ACOA suffered self-esteem damage from repeated childhood criticism about her weight from her alcoholic parents. For years, she overdressed during summer months to reduce exposure of legs and arms, and never accessorized her outfits. Her ultraconservative, Victorian attire included blouses buttoned up to her neck and unflattering slacks and blazers masking and masculinizing her figure. She envied people who could put on a bathing suit regardless of their weight and enjoy the swimming pool. Despite her current slender fitness, this client's modesty interfered with pursuing the risk. She knew how to swim, and was a member of a club having an indoor pool. As the first steps, she dressed in the bathing suit around the house for one week until feeling relaxed and unthreathened by social disapproval (desensitization process). The second step involved her wearing the bathing suit to the pool, then swimming, and gradually spending longer intervals in the pool around larger crowds of onlookers. Comfort in one setting opened the doors for successive fields. She altered her formidable attire to loose-fitting, neck-exposed shirts and baggy pants, with jewelry accessories, and even received a manicure weekly. The cosmetic overhaul revamped her appearance and generated a host of compliments from male and female peers, greatly enhancing her decision for more "deviant" fashion risks.

Disabling Enabling

As with eliminating distrust, eliminating the habit of caretaking provokes severe emotional resistance. ACOAs expect and automatically accept this dutiful obligation of caretaking without reservation, and depend on doing for others as a bloodline to self-preservation. However, repercussions of enabling are emotionally devastating and worth prompting reconsideration of this lifelong habit. Toward this end, systematic elimination of caretaking may be denoted operationally as disabling enabling. The process requires the ACOA to resist rescuing, resist pleasing, and demand reciprocity.

Resist Rescuing ACOAs have a remarkable talent for being acutely aware of people in distress who must be saved. Rescue efforts launched to relieve the emotional grief, burdens, and responsibilities of the perceived victim earn respect, gratitude, and approval from the rescuer. When told to refuse temptations to rescue, thereby allowing victims to suffer, the ACOA must also resist vicariously suffering this emotional grief, and consequently feel guilt associated with ignoring people. Concurrently, ACOAs revise rule-governed beliefs that people must suffer inconvenience to make changes for themselves. Interrupting rescue efforts involves deliberately withholding or refusing benevolent, stress-relief behaviors under compulsive situations driven by two factors: (a) the establishing operation of anxiety watching another person suffer, and (b) the CRF schedule of (negative and positive) reinforcement for self-intervention. Self-restraint mechanisms resemble phases of exposure plus response prevention, used frequently for treating bulimia (Rosen & Leitenberg, 1984). Within the session, distress cues signaling compulsive altruistic behaviors are rehearsed and competing non-rescuing behaviors are taught. Elevated anxiety arising from cessation of compulsive behaviors is combatted with muscular relaxation exercises. As duration of cue exposure increases, desensitized fears conditioned simultaneously with self-distractive (incompatible) behaviors allows the ACOA to resist needs imposed upon them.

Resist Pleasing Just as rescuing relieves grief observed in others, so *pleasing* relieves conflict, criticism, or impending rejection. ACOAs make concessions to avoid or escape arguments while gaining secondary benefits from seeing others happy. Giving gifts, surprises, parties, or other appeasements guaranteed to maintain peace and happiness in a family or friendship all are pleasing gestures. When instructed to resist pleasing, acute anxiety bordering on panic attacks surfaces because the ACOA feels egregiously selfish. Personal gratification shifts the pendulum from being the benefactor to becoming a beneficiary of others' efforts. Refusals also evoke distress from ACOAs perceiving abandonment from significant people who receive caretaking. Partner relationships may abound with hostility, criticism, and threats of terminating the relationship. This is why refusal exercises never occur until the client already demonstrates mastery of basic assertiveness and overcoming roadblocks.

Demand Reciprocity Disabling enabling further requires the demand for an exchange system. Reciprocity between the client and significant others ensures that for every personal sacrifice or concession made, there is a dividend earned. Resources returned by other people can vary and need not parallel the quality, quantity, or frequency of resources supplied by the caretaker, as long as timing of the reciprocal resource is proximal. Resources must be received after the caretaker gives a resource. While this sounds logical, ACOAs struggle with asking for rewards from people fearing that it looks rude, conceited, and selfish. Rewards may also feel fake and undeserved, despite the ACOA intellectually understanding the ubiquity and normalcy of self-gratification (Ruben, 1987b). This is based on distorted rule-governed beliefs that solicited or contrived rewards are inauthentic, whereas rewards or resources given on another person's own accord are genuine. Consequently, ACOAs fight internal messages that their actions are wrong and immoral as they modestly ask for something in return for their efforts.

Mary Sue grew frustrated with her cannabis-abusing husband who demanded her utmost obedience in housekeeping and satisfying his sexual needs. For 15 years, she unconditionally abided his authoritarian orders under the guise of marital love and thinking her husband eventually might respect her devotion. His incessant demands escalated as his cannabis smoking intensified and made her realize she was enabling both his addiction and controlling behaviors. On her mothers' advice, she sought therapy initially to resolve her husband's dissatisfaction with her, assuming she was culpable for marital problems. Her insight rapidly shifted from self-as-fault to viewing both partners as reciprocally conditioning caretaking behaviors; he set the occasion by threats, and Mary Sue conceded to avoid confrontation.

Treatment commenced whereby she refused the routine caretaking chores, not only for her husband but for co-workers and female friends whom she now perceived as manipulators. She also braved the task of asking friends, family members, and especially her husband for favors in return for her initiatives, and vigilantly monitored their compliance. Mary Sue did not tolerate unfulfilled promises and repeatedly insisted they follow through or she would withhold resources they automatically expected from her (e.g., making dinner, telephone conversations, etc.). Within two months, amid other tasks such as reconstructing rule-governed behaviors and assertiveness, she modified her partner's behaviors so that he no longer was smoking cannabis, partook equally in household chores, and politely asked Mary Sue for help instead of barking the orders.

Constructing Emotions

Anger, fear, anxiety, and depression comprise the emotional constellation of ACOAs. Emotions beyond these extremes are unusual and command a response that is severely deficient. Feelings such as love, passion, and intimacy may resemble the compassion ACOAs show in their caretaking gestures, but the responses are significantly different. Love, passion, and intimacy develop from a trusting and vulnerable relationship between two independent people whose needs are mutually satisfied and whose ambitions are largely compatible. By contrast, co-dependent, unilateral love shown by ACOAs is not love but rather benevolent caretaking. In sorting out the difference, ACOAs are shocked at mistaking love for pleasing, and then realizing they have no idea what love is.

Construction of emotions thus begins in a threefold process. First is the step, described above, of trusting another person and relinquishing control. Second is learning basic touching, from simple hand-holding or extended hand gestures to simple kissing (with a spouse or intimate). Affection in private is broadened to public displays of touching, embracing, and even kissing. Physical forms of exchange accompany verbal compliments and self-affirmations of looking and feeling feminine or masculine and looking attractive to a partner.

Disinhibited touching moves to another step of sexual intimacy. Arousal first is attempted by self-stimulation and by letting a partner caress erogenous areas around upper and lower torso. Foreplay that is excitatory continues for longer intervals instead of being a boring prelude to coitus. After foreplay is satisfactory, strategies are described for building up plateaus (for women) and stability of erection (for men) prior to and during intromission. Sustaining arousal during intercourse involves mutually selfish and benevolent efforts, shifted with balance and without one partner feeling disgraced by the other partner. Last, timing and satisfaction of single and multiple climaxes involve both knowledge of the biological process (refractory period, types of excitatory stimuli, etc.) and restraint from criticisms following completion of intercourse.

Third, affection is developed and practiced around children and around persons perceived since childhood as uncaring and cold. Physical embracing, kissing, and verbal compliments toward children usually are easy and ACOAs welcome this exercise for two reasons. The first reason is that it releases tenderness with special people whom they desperately want to love. A second reason is that showing affection to children breaks the intergenerational lineage of repressed or limited displays of emotion, in that the ACOA's offspring can perceive and understand touching as wonderful (not abusive, fearful, or wrong), and can freely exhibit it in their own adulthood.

Daniel's affinity for sex historically precluded healthy relationships. He focused so heavily on casual, recreational sex that he never bothered to build friendships with partners. He became bisexual, attaining orgasmic relief from any partner available.

Oversexed and underloved (Ruben, 2000b), Daniel's epiphany to seek therapy occurred only after being convicted for criminal sexual conduct with a teenaged boy with whom he had anal sex. Addictive drives for sexual relief superseded feelings of caring, love, and enjoying a reciprocal romance. Daniel began a systematic, structured approach to constructing appropriately affectionate behaviors without sexuality as the terminal reinforcer. First, he identified females as his preferred gender and listed a series of conservative meeting places and venues for new relationships (classified ads, glee club, workplace, coffee shop, Taekwondo class, etc.). With each encounter, conversations focused on both superficial and self-disclosure topics ranging from news headlines to personal interests.

He also allowed the prospective partner to divulge personal information without constant interruption, over-reinforcing the person with seductive remarks, and anger over feeling rejected when the person ended the conversation. Within a month, he became "friends" with two females, with whom he exchanged personal stories and partook in athletic activities but never approached sexually. One lady, in particular, transitioned from a platonic friend to an intimate companion as the couple spent short get-away weekends together and enjoyed passionate kisses and hugs. Two months after they "officially" began dating, Daniel reported having sex with her and realizing the eroticism meant nothing compared to their closeness.

Overcoming Avoidance and Escape

Underlying the pathology of ACOA behavior is avoidance and escape behavior. Actions averting criticism, conflict, and rejection constantly occupy the ACOA's mind and keep him or her hypervigilant to interpersonal social situations. Because this pattern is habitual, much like caretaking, cessation of the behavior must start with awareness. Clients learn self-monitoring methods to physically or "mentally" record instances of avoidance and escape and the consequences (types of relief) generated from these patterns. Interruption of the pattern is a twofold process, modeled after many of the desensitization procedures already discussed.

First, clients deliberately enter into apprehensive or high anxiety-prone situations and remain stationary until the situation runs its course and naturally ends. For instance, visiting friends who the ACOA believes hate him entails staying at the house for a couple of hours or until there is a natural lull to leave. Confronting the awful feeling that this person hates me desensitizes the ACOA's fears and inhibits functional social behavior. Second, ACOAs do what intuitively they regard as impossible. They create conflict situations through criticism or disagreements. Intentionally invoked confrontations elevate anxiety and compel escape responses. However, rehearsals both within and outside the clinical setting control for response abatement by using relaxation exercises and teaching problem-solving skills to resolve the conflict before it backfires. In this way, response duration increases under adverse situations because ACOAs learn self-inoculation methods of handling conflict, anger, and fear.

Accepting Compliments

Highly modest, shameful, and intimidated ACOAs resist drawing attention to themselves partly because of impostorism and partly because of risks of conflict, criticism, and rejection. Reasons are manifold for avoiding self-solicited compliments. Efforts to combat this phobia follow a structured approach consisting of three different types of compliments: *conversions, shifting the conversation,* and *solicitations.*

Conversions are when ACOAs first listen to what somebody else is talking about, then takes their last statement or phrase and transforms it into a compliment or strength about himself. The statement describes an ability, accomplishment, or success related to the last phrase. Melanie says, "That snow outside is so ugly I just can't stand it." The ACOA interjects with, "I don't know, I kind of like the snow. I love skiing and getting outside with the kids." Another example: Bruce observes, "Can't get any secretarial help around here and typing your own work is tedious." The ACOA replies, "Not for everybody. I type pretty fast, thank God, and can do it myself when the clerical staff is busy." Self-compliments, functionally, are intraverbal tacts and mands enjoining both the speaker and listener reciprocally to reinforce the speaker's verbalizations. Since "self-positive" remarks typify normal social dialogue, liability for punishment is minuscule.

Next is shifting the conversation. Shifting topics entails control, on the one hand, and tooting the client's horn, on the other. Moments into the dialogue or at a natural juncture, ACOAs use transitional statements to end one topic and shift to another topic of personal interest. For instance, while conversing about budgetary cuts, the ACOA waits for a pause and adds, "You know, I can see your point about shrinking budgets. Hey, incidentally, did I tell you my son is having a bar mitzvah?" By shifting gears, ACOAs draw attention to issues or values important to themselves without sounding pompous.

The third method of *solicitation* is more direct. Subtlety is wonderful for beginners. But by now the ACOA tries soliciting a compliment about some physical feature or activity he or she recently completed. "What do you think of this new dress?" Or, "Don't you think I got them to listen to me at that meeting?" Pointed questions regarding the ACOA's appearance risk approval or disapproval answers. Egos inflate rapidly from friendly praise and approval that others typically give. But even if feedback is negative, two benefits accrue from the solicitation efforts. One benefit is automatic reinforcement mediated by the autoclitic tacts and mands generated from asking the questions; ACOAs may think to themselves, "Hey, that didn't sound arrogant, and I think I do look good in this outfit even if the person doesn't agree." Another benefit that also supports pride is desensitization of residual anxiety from feelings of impostorsim and imposition on the listener.

The practice of soliciting compliments without slipping into old habits is tricky and can lead to common traps, such as when the client disqualifies the compliment ("I'm good at that—well not really."); is self-critical after the compliment, ("I'm good at that, and that's all I'm good at."); returns a compliment right away, (I'm good at that, but so are you); and laughs at himself, ("I'm good at that—isn't that a scream?"). Control over these setbacks begins under simulated conditions within the clinical setting and is generalizable across different people in the natural environment.

Diversifying Activities

Pathologically pervasive among ACOAs is *inflexibility*. Fear of adapting to new situations derives from inescapable and unavoidable punishment for autonomous behaviors. As children, independent explorations of toys, household objects, and supplies, and new furniture to climb on received a calamity of oppressive reprimands. Operant and respondent-trained adverse consequences for curious behaviors not only reduced mild-risk behaviors but negatively reinforced highly obedient, conservative, and "safe" tasks, or tasks about which the child felt competent to anticipate and exert damage-control for surprise punishment contingencies. From this cumulative history evolved the rule-governed behavior that "it is wrong to try or do some activity unless you know everything about it," which prevents trying new things. Fear-inhibiting rules paralyze attempts to alter existing plans or diversify the repertoire to include uncharted destinations involving adaptation of skills entirely unfamiliar to the ACOA. Consequently, methods to expand heterogeneity of activities are essential weapons in the treatment arsenal.

Diversity of activities refers to a systematic task analysis of identifying and then implementing small units of social and recreational behaviors. ACOAs follow three carefully monitored steps. First, they assemble a list of ideal but nearby travel locations, site-seeing destinations, or activities opposite to their habitual choices. For example, if, the client prefers athletic-oriented activities, opposite activities might include buying tickets for stage plays or visiting a planetarium. For ACOAs teased for their academic acumen and discouraged from college, habitual activities might be voraciously reading self-help books and volunteering for church fund-raisers. Antithetically, diversity might include taking college courses or spending time in college libraries.

Second, selected activities undergo a "reality-check," by matching the skills required for the activity with the ACOA's behavior repertoire. Activities involving skills outside the repertoire and delayed because of the need for extensive pre-learning are deleted. For example, scuba diving for aquaphobic ACOAs is impractical since it entails relaxation and facility with swimming. Where skills overlap, even marginally activities are rated by time schedule, locality, and by collateral behaviors, such as asking other people to join the excursion. Third, activity implementation involves fulfillment of all the tasks sequentially linked in producing reinforcement. Plans to sunbathe at the beach, for example, may entail contacting friends, arranging for time off work, delegating preparatory tasks among all beach-goers (lunches, vehicular cleaning, etc.), driving to the destination, and staying there during anxiety elevations that historically prompted escape behavior.

Burt considered diversifying his activities after discovering his life was circular. Every year in March he took the family up north for a snowmobile fun weekend filled with alcohol drinking, big meals, and late-night parties. He always made reservations at the same hotel for the same weekend, and ate at the same restaurants. Friends and his spouse urged interest in new resorts and even offered to surprise him for his birthday, but Burt adamantly refused their offers. Routines felt comfortable and minimized his fear of looking incompetent. However, on his last junket, Burt got arrested for operating a snowmobile under the influence of alcohol, which immediately ended the annual northern trips and placed him in the depressing predicament of forfeiting the family vacation.

Burt began a series of activity diversity by first listing his least favorite and even intimidating activities, which included tap dancing and attending musical plays. Fascination with these tasks ceased years ago when his alcoholic father aggressively emasculated him for being a "sissy" for dancing and desiring to audition for the school plays. Preferring outdoor sports, his father inculcated him in snowmobiles, hunting, and skiing. Burt learned to defuse and replace instinctive rules about him appearing "effeminate and weak." He attended plays and subsequently bought tickets to see *Annie Get Your Gun* and *Phantom of the Opera.* Diversity also generalized to selecting new family restaurants, new weekend destination spots, and allowing other people to surprise him with different plans.

New Criteria for Selecting Healthy Relationships

Above all, intimacy represents an elusive and dangerous territory for ACOAs. Forming new relationships or preventing repetition of bad relationships poses major obstacles because of inexperience with intimacy, and fear of failure. Inexperience literally means lacking the prerequisite knowledge concerning how to date, what to look for in a partner, how to engage in small talk, and remaining focused. Fear abounds over what the "date" thinks of the ACOA and whether the ACOA will fail the date's test. Fear of failure implies a history of dating and superficial intimacy, with a track record of negative relationships. One dysfunctional relationship after the other repeats the cycle until the ACOA gets discouraged that all potential partners present problems. Likewise, attempts at breaking the vicious cycle are ineffective, especially during early dating or honeymoon periods, when first impressions signal a green light for the ACOA to pursue the relationship, only to discover irreconcilable problems later.

Repeated failures create distrust, feelings of futility, and disrespect for parternships (see Gorski, 1984). ACOAs develop cynical and stereotypical attitudes about inherent defects of the opposite gender: for example, "all men can't be trusted," or "all women are ditsy." Machismo, feminism, and other liberal extremes egocentrically boasting superiority of a person's gender simply disguise underlying inabilities to form a genuinely caring relationship. Disguises fade away when the ACOA realizes that the world is a lonely place and when the need for a companion becomes desperate. Impulsive date searching by surfing the internet, participating in AOL chat sessions, or taking every class on Tai Chi approaches irresponsible over-reactions to not having companionship. ACOAs who poorly resist dating temptations, have recently left a bad relationship, or historically attract abusers, require a methodical revision of criteria used to select healthy partners.

Behavior patterns predictive of functional versus dysfunctional prospects appear in Table 8–1. Typologies of person A, Person B, and Person C contain pervasive personality traits along the continuum of addictive, codependent behaviors, from Person A (no addiction, well-adjusted) to Persons B & C (severely maladjusted, highly prone to addiction). In addition to applying these criteria, clients must undergo another rule change. The rule of "I'll know a partner is right when it feels right" competes with appropriate contingencies because instinctive feelings are unreliable and usually lead to repetitive dysfunctional relationships. The new rule replacing untrusted instincts goes something like: If you meet somebody and instantly feel you've known him all your life or you can't believe how comfortable you are around him, that's a warning sign. It means you're doing things that are too familiar, because you did them before in a bad relationship. Instead, if you

TABLE 8–1 Criteria for Healthy Relationships

PERSON A	PERSON B	PERSON C
Assertive	Aggressive	Passive
Expresses opinions	Criticizes only you	Is a "good listener"
Criticizes self and you	Boasts	Likes all that you do
Can be vulnerable	Not a listener	Discloses nothing
Admits mistakes	Makes demands	Edits remarks
Compliments self	Angry	Always sorry
Compliments you	Very serious	Afraid to say things
Listens and talks		
Flexible	**Rigid**	**Overflexible**
Easy-going	Can't break schedules	Gives in to pressure
Handles mean/nice people	Perfectionistic	Always agrees
Good with all age groups	Compulsive	Afraid of rejection
Offers to compromise	"My way or highway"	Afraid of criticism
Looks for reciprocity	Blames you	Eager to please
Adjusts to new situations	Never admits fault	
Asks for your help		
Consistent	**Impulsive**	**Inconsistent**
Does what he says	Lots of energy	Follows through for you
Words match actions	Never follows through	Procrastinates for self
Always follows through	Appears lazy	History of drug abuse
Admits he forgot	Blames you for forgetting	Impulsive
Typically is drug free	History of drug abuse	Loves sex and affection
Conservative, routine	Physically attractive	Physically attractive
Moderate sex and affection	Loves sex and affection	
Modestly attractive		

feel nervous, intimidated, or even inferior around somebody, thinking he's so much better than you, you probably are on to a good relationship. He's not any better than you are. But his actions are making you do new things you are not familiar with and should learn for a healthy relationship.

Consider these typologies across the categories of assertive (versus aggressive and passive), flexible (versus rigid and over-flexible), and consistent (versus impulsive and inconsistent). The "A" type can communicate openly and honestly with opinions that are critical or complimentary both toward the ACOA and toward himself or herself. An "A" effectively can adapt, adjust and reciprocally balance the dating contingency, and is self-sufficient but moderately altruistic towards the ACOA. Best of all, an "A" is persnickety about self-discipline. Execution of daily schedules is consistent, demonstrating efficient time-management skills. Follow-through on tasks is predictable. The "A" fulfills self-obligations, and reliably meets obligations set for other people, particularly for ACOAs. For example, if an "A" says she plans to pick up the ACOA for dinner at 6:00 PM, plan on a punctual arrival.

Type "B" persons typically attract ACOAs, who can also manifest these behavior patterns. They are inflexible, opinionated, egocentric, arrogant, accostic, sarcastic, and demand compliance from passive ACOAs. The "B" displays uncanny persuasion in two ways. One way is through aggression. Physical or verbal abuse coerces partner submission and creates the illusion for passive ACOAs of feeling wanted and loved. The "B" looks for people to blame and make a habit of breaking promises. Alternatively, a charismatic "B" is savvy about achieving compliance without force but through persistent persuasion. The "B" may inflate self-worth or exaggerate reasons for a decision that intuitively sound logical and even agreeable but rarely incorporate the ACOA's opinions. Demanding and excessively dependent, the "B" thrusts ACOAs into caretaking roles. Subordinative contrasts to the "B"s' authority figure facade maintains disequilibrium among the dating couple.

And then there is the "C" type. Affectionately called "the trap," a "C" evinces passionately warm and empathic behaviors that lure ACOAs, particularly those rebounding from dogmatically violent relationships. The "C" is laid back, easy-going, empathetically supportive, deeply benevolent, and noncommunicative. This type serves as effective an sounding board for hyperverbal ACOAs who unload decades worth of miseries and can receive unconditional loving. Reverberators and lovers, the "C" rarely ventures opinions or self-discloses vulnerability, fearing the repercussions would result in impostorism and termination of the relationship. Outwardly the masquerade hides inner dysfunctional behaviors equivalent to type "B," except the "C" person offers fewer clues of social impediments.

Therapists using these criteria may find ACOAs pleasantly surprised by the accuracy of correlations with their past partners. To this extent, high social validity of personality types piques the client's curiosity and excites their hunger for more information about wrong partners. Focus is less on defective partners (types "B" and "C") and more on the reasons that ACOAs avoid selecting the "A" type. Intellectually, ACOAs fully understand the advantages of dating an "A" and subsequently advocate this healthy choice when offering advice to friends or family members. In this case, however, instructional knowledge poorly corresponds to future discriminative responses since the informed ACOA still persists with unhealthy personal choices.

There are five reasons why the "A"-type person is undesirable to ACOAs. First, on the matter of communication, ACOAs misperceive assertive opinions as critically abrasive and suppressive. Despite praise and compliments also offered, sprinkles of criticism dig deeply through the wounded emotional surface and entirely obliterate the flattering gestures. Second, self-efficacy statements are viewed as arrogant, selfish, and rude. Proud "A" types who modestly boast about their positive traits leave a feeling of distrust and anxiety in ACOAs, who fear that they either are too competent and may not value the ACOA's caretaking, or that ACOAs will lose control to a more controlling person. A third reason deals with flexibility. An adaptive "A" poses toxic fears of making the ACOA do new things. Diversity of past experiences and the "A" excitement for career or educational advancement far exceeds the ACOA's boundary of comfortable limits or willingness to make changes.

Fourth, reciprocity of resources ensures that an "A" does as much for ACOAs as ACOAs do for the "A." And, to say the least, that phenomenon is very foreign. ACOAs literally lack a behavioral repertoire to understand or respond to being treated fairly. Victimizational thoughts and instigating chaos in neutral situations are more comfortable than accepting love without paying an emotional price. Fifth, while consistency offers the epitome of a trusting and predictable relationship, ACOAs perceive an organized partner as pathetically boring, robotic, unimaginative, and lacking diversification. Ironically, attraction to "B" types for their glowing energy and impulsivity is temporary and largely a placebo for ACOAs to feel adventurous, glamorous, or risk-taking outside of their normal behaviors.

Clarifying criteria for relationships and benefits of an "A"-type guarantees neither a perfect partner selection nor lifelong compatibility even when companions are healthy. What these typologies do offer are safe guidelines for reentry into the scary dating world that many ACOAs have all but obliterated. As the risks begin and the optimism for new relationships is stronger, ACOAs will discover that there really is a light at the end of the tunnel.

In short, behavioral methods prove strongly effective in eliminating categorically distinct ACOA symptoms. Interventions specify practical and measurable techniques already proven among different populations and for similar clinical disorders (phobias, affective disorders, anxiety disorders, etc.). Desensitization procedures figure prominently in this respect. Response exposure plus prevention, habit reversal, differential reinforcement, and task analyses are other easily applied strategies for clinicians to use. Admittedly, rivals of family systems may regard cognitive-behavioral approaches as superficial and ephemeral. Systems theory apostles may doubt ACOA symptoms are singularly treatable because causal variables include transgenerational family effects. Treating the person, in other words, requires treating the entire system. And, they are right to assume this. Although the ACOA syndrome is a family problem, treatment begins by isolating dysfunctional response patterns in one family member, whose self-modifications covary with broad and specific changes on other family members.

ACOA recovery also depends on the family members or therapist–coach being sensitive to the fragility and reactivity of clients during treatment. The next chapter focuses on how simple intratherapy mistakes and an unprepared family can sabotage client motivation.

CHAPTER 9

Side Effects of Healthy Recovery

One major bone of contention among practitioners is treatment failure. Behavioral advocates are particularly sensitive to treatment limitations caused by uncontrolled or "confounding" variables undermining client progress. Foa & Emmelkamp (1983) seminally reported pervasive inconsistencies and pitfalls plaguing behavioral interventions attributed to a wide variety of therapist and client reasons, with client refusals, dropouts, and relapses topping the list. Therapist obstacles, representing another serious downfall, accounted for poor attitudes, procedural weaknesses, and untrained interpersonal skills obstructing an effective therapist–client relationship.

This chapter follows a similar course of confession, outlining the common traps of ACOA treatment delivery systems—ranging from client and therapist mistakes to the inevitable problem of a client's recovery being undermined by unsupportive families.

CLIENT FAILURES

Progressively degenerative effects on therapy appear in numerous ways. Despite their multiple origins, symptoms can spontaneously resurface after a period of remission or client motivation can decay as mandates of the real world supersede the importance placed on therapy. Failures also arise during predictable transition from the first session to the last therapy session. At the outset, when confronted with diagnosis and expectations of goals and objectives, elevated eagerness for behavior change conflicts with overwhelming skepticism about fulfillment of treatment goals. Clients who learn their symptoms are ubiquitous, classifiable, predictable, and hence treatable are relieved that there is hope and instantly build trust in the therapeutic process. Educating clients about the etiology of their problems, however, has its downside of demystifying the incarnation of self-reported lifelong trauma and mistakenly trivializing the client's problems.

Advantages of knowledge can backslide when clients misperceive ready cures as superficial Band-Aids for underlying, deeply-rooted mental illness. Diagnostic knowledge poses a second problem for ACOAs feeling impostor symptoms. Therapists who astutely and accurately reveal a class of defective responses in graphically vivid terms are perceived differently from physicians uncovering organic defects. Sudden exposure to horribly sordid imperfections may trigger feelings of stupidity and incompetence, and the ACOA may withdraw, fearing the therapist knows too much about him. Impersonalizing therapy goals from diagnosis through stages of treatment invariably impacts factors of trust and can discourage client efforts.

Because transitional steps are inevitable, therapists alert to variables within each step that risk treatment obstruction can act more efficiently in taking preventive measures. The following review of the sequential course of these stages is followed by a closer examination of common client obstacles.

PREDICTABLE TRANSITIONAL STAGES

Stage 1: Denial

ACOAs report an initial sense of fear and uncertainty, of lacking confidence to overcome chronic symptoms. Denial of this confusion helps them cope with apprehension, anxiety, and stress, and minimizes facing self-criticism. Types of denial reactions frequently observed at the outset of therapy include compulsive self-change and attempts to impose recovery guidelines on others; defensiveness when talking about personal problems or recovery; and overconfidence

Compulsive Self-change and Attempts to Impose Recovery Guidelines on Others Recovering ACOAs pass through similar self-help discovery phases as their polydrug-using counterparts (Ruben, 1993c, 1993d). Inflated expectancies launched from motivating therapists who optimistically promise symptom eradication in three to six months can generate compulsive behaviors. ACOAs who regard this positive timeline as a challenge may vigorously exert efforts on self-improvement while disseminating their lively enthusiasm on significant others. Intensified, bursts of energy include excessively engaging in one or many concurrent health activities such as exercise. Vigorous exercise, including aerobics, may hold countless cardiovascular benefits such as collateral vascularization and improved efficiency of peripheral blood distribution. But clients may overexercise when they pack their entire day with such physical fitness activities and allow themselves no relaxation and no other interests. Instead, all waking hours must be scheduled for dieting or exercising, Such clients develop obsessive–compulsive regimens to regain control over helplessness and to stimulate excitatory reinforcing effects of exercise.

Another common indulgence is religion. Spirituality plays a surprisingly critical role in behavioral interventions. While secular and scientific methods may contradict theological reasons for recovery, faith empowers clients with motivation and frequently urges a covenant with moral and ethical behaviors. For actively polygamous ACOAs, for example, regular attendance at church or synagogue discourages promiscuity with multiple partners and restores self-integrity out of respect for rule-governed beliefs upheld by the institution. Prevailing rules such as "one ought to be responsible and principled" exert more control over otherwise weak moral responses when the client enters the sanctuary. This is why, for example, drug dealers in treatment recovery are advised to undergo "religious conversion" by regularly participating in church services as a means to develop pro-moralistic and victim impact sensitivity (see Ruben, 2000c).

Enhancement of moralistic values draws ACOAs back to religion and may eventually facilitate their reentry into feuding families. However, the downside of strong religious convictions is overspiritualizing. Clients who fall into the trap of zealous religious activity claim an existential reason for their sudden explosion of effort. They claim "renewal of faith," or "absolution of sins revitalizing their purpose in life," or simply state being "born again" under the guise of Judeo-Christian doctrines. Clients entering nontraditional religions bordering on cults may assume evangelical behaviors, quote explicit references to the Bible, frequently attend Bible study or fellowship meetings, and invest incredible dollars in purchasing audiotapes, videotapes, books, and other paraphernalia reinforcing their response immersion.

Compulsive diversions in exercise, religion, or any other activity artificially restoring internal locus of control are obstacles alone when only the client is involved. As fervor for compulsive behaviors intensifies, contingencies for social reinforcement are cultivated by clients who impose their misguided excitement on significant others. ACOA parents may voluntarily or involuntarily recruit their children into all-consuming tasks, projects, belief systems, or activities and justify the inculcation under the banner of "family recovery." Spiritually enlightened spouses may implore their partners to similarly partake in weekend retreats, or vicariously experience passion for a particular pastoral leader. One father, for instance, insisted that his children attend daily church meetings to hear gospels he considered inspirational and thus invaluable to the children's psychological growth. Proselytizing beliefs, he thought, would secure his own treatment recovery and help his family understand misdirections he took during his lifetime. The children, like any helplessly influenced family members, simply went along with their father's instructions, thinking the spontaneous preoccupation with church was normal.

Apart from effects on family, the major hazard of compulsive activity is its distraction from logically and sequentially structured treatment regimens. ACOAs who cling to dogmatic religions, rigid exercise schedules, or even inflexible workouts for competitive sports lose interest in therapy since they believe in another resource promising self-efficacy. The object of compulsion replaces organized goals of therapy by its CRF effects of conditioning immediate behaviors resembling or approximating self-control. By the second or third therapy session clients may talk of a rejuvenation since, for example, joining the local choir and spending every night in voice training. Contingency control exerted over one behavior in their lives, that of singing, apparently creates the illusion of competence and obviates efforts to correct the more malignant variables controlling their dysfunctional behaviors.

Defensiveness when talking about personal problems or recovery. One documented reason that therapy can fail is client resistance (Ellis, 1985; Wachtel, 1992). Resistance among ACOAs comes about when defensive statements disguise, mitigate, or misrepresent severity of psychopatholgy. Elevated malingering scales on MMPI–2 protocols may signal under reporting of negative traits, but reliable observable data typically include clients (a) blaming current problems of therapy setbacks on the therapist, (b) cursing and protesting behavior change suggestions, (c) exhibiting excessive levity and joking around, (d) evading disclosure of details and showing distraction from reporting progress on homework assignments, (e) crying and trembling upon inquiry of recovery, and (f) rescheduling appointments frequently. Avoidance of therapy dynamics emanates from several variables within and outside of treatment. These include an underdeveloped therapist–client rapport lacking sensitivity and compassion. Equally stifling are professionals whose demeanor resembles the ACOAs adversarial parent or significant other. In addition, family or employer resistance to the client's recovery efforts can sabotage motivation and serve as an excuse for not performing appropriate behaviors. Furthermore, inadequate reinforcement contingencies can be engineered for naturalistic practice of skills. Therapists may erroneously assume self-referred clients motivated for emotional wellness reside in enriched environments supportive of new changes, when instead the environments are punitive and destabilizing.

Another reason for defensiveness is polymorbidity. Resistant clients differentially diagnosed with multiple physical or psychopathological conditions are prone to distraction, disincentive, and intrusion by variables untreated within the scope of therapy. The elderly are a good example. ACOA patients 65 years and older suffering acute memory loss, physical coordination deficits, and recent cardiovascular accidents (CVAs) are unable to respond as efficiently as their younger, healthier counterparts. Medicated elderly particularly represent an unrecognized problem; their response inconsistency, frequent ratio strains, and disruptions in therapy may be due to overuse, underuse, or erratic self-administrations of medicine (Petersen, Whittington, & Payne, 1979; Ruben, 1986b). Other physically or dually disabled clients losing capabilities in independent daily living skills view therapy as a nuisance or further impediment to self-control; poorambulation, obstructed speech, diminished physical endurance, among other limitations, may preclude cooperation in attainment of treatment goals.

Overconfidence Clients' certainty about maintaining healthy recovery early on in therapy reflects an exaggerated confidence in their strengths. Chronic ACOAs emotionally feel much better–more energetic, optimistic, ambitious–as well as more accepted by their families for undergoing treatment. They regard mental health improvements as an over-eager sign of reformation and rebound from depression or anxiety with propulsive force. Recovering ACOAs who are overconfident assertively and decisively speak about their plans for life changes, including new directions in careers, education, religion, or family. Overconfidence, in one respect, is a measure of post-baseline improvement. Self-monitored awareness of behavior problems can itself enable modifications without much therapist intervention. But hyperbolic self-reporting misrepresents contingency management and deludes the clients into feelings of invulnerability.

ACOAs may disregard precautionary advice against engaging in risky behaviors. Risky behaviors include those for which ACOA symptoms are naturally prolific. They encompass places, people, or activities manifested for avoidance and escape behaviors, thereby restoring old habits to relieve aversive fears of failing therapy expectations. High-risk behaviors also include diametrically opposite reactions prompted by in-session training but extrapolated with inductive leaps. Aggressive behaviors rank high in this category. For example, ACOAs given preliminary tools for assertive self-expression may overuse these tools by boldly infringing on every family member's behavior rather than only that of offensive family members. Reversal assertive effects are not uncommon, and frequently appear in oppressed employees given the opportunity to voice concerns to their superiors (Ruben & Ruben, 1989). Such audacity results from acquisition of new skills generating some, but not all, of the relevant reinforcing variables to strengthen and maintain the new behaviors. In the workplace, assertively trained employees acquire diplomatic phrases to offset employer–employee conflict and suddenly feel their opinions are impervious to employer retribution. The aftermath of "speaking their mind" is twofold: on the one hand, personal anxiety is reduced (negative reinforcement); on the other, they receive a written reprimand for insubordination, thereby decreasing future assertiveness attempts (positive punishment).

Stage 2: Defocusing from self and driving other people away

Commitment to treatment recovery turns to depression across three phases. The first is *adamant conviction of self-improvement.* This is where clients convince themselves and significant others they will never be symptomatic again. Urgency to make this promise, however, diminishes motivation to pursue a recovery program. Magnified efforts at proving sincerity of treatment involve excessive purchase of self-help books, phoning neighbors, relatives, and friends to report self-revivalism, and duplicating the therapist's advice with less emotionally fortunate individuals. Misapplication of self-control results in boasting of miraculous improvements supposedly in progress or projected to occur. As ACOAs become the therapist, just as they vicariously impersonated behaviors and emotions of other people in the past, attendance at sessions falls of and they feel cured.

A second phase is *progressive loss of daily structure.* Daily routines become haphazard. Regular hours of sleep and wakefulness disappear, characterized by missed appointments and diminished social planning. Clients report feeling rushed, facing large blocks of idle time, and improperly coping with feelings of tension and frustration. The result is disintegration of contingencies for two reasons. First, elevated expectancies of therapy may exceed their current skills or interbehavioral potentials. Undetected skill deficits impeding stepwise learning may stop clients midway through therapy because they feel like failures. Second, rehearsed attempts at new behavior produced viscously suppressive effects that reconditioned inhibition and caused covariation effects on similar responses. Self-complimenting, for example, may have received a nasty criticism from the client's mother about, "Don't you go tooting your horn, now; nobody will like you." Recantation of the compliment was followed by excessive apologies and caused collateral behavioral damage. The client immediately resigned from two community volunteer boards fearing others will perceive her as arrogant.

The third phase is *periods of deep depression and deflection of others.* Cyclical mood swings become frequent, longer in duration, and more severely disruptive. Upward swings of happiness, elation, and productivity yield to self-victimization and isolationism. Depression occurs during unstructured time, around enabling family members, and in reaction to minor failures or peer rejection. Clients afraid to look vulnerable and distrustful withdraw from socialization. After initially gaining sympathy from benevolent sources, those caring people grow frustrated with the ACOA's stubborn persistence to continue maladaptive behaviors. Friends stop calling, family members disenfranchise, and the ACOA decompensates into a helpless state to the point of justifying the contingencies sustaining depression.

A 46-year-old female postal worker accosted on the job by another employee bumping her with a mail cart was devastated and received a stress leave. She returned unharmed and emotionally recovered until, a week later, her postmaster overexaggerated rumors that the same assaultive employee made death threats on the client. Given the client's ACOA history, she immediately took the day off and went on medical disability leave. Two years later, depression had become part of her life, despite her resiliency at overcoming the initial trauma. Still on medical leave, she grew behaviorally complacent with chronic inactivity, and twice attempted suicide. She blames her lability on the unfair and antagonistic postal system; whereas, behaviorally, her prolonged depression is from habituation with nonreinforicng contingencies and seclusion from people or places who might threaten to change those contingencies.

Progressive episodes of depression cause confusion over treatment goals and lead clients to doubt their capacity to recover. Loss of control over thoughts, judgments, and behaviors advances a state of helplessness, causing the following common symptoms:

1. Irritation with friends and family members.
2. Irregular eating and sleeping habits.
3. Listlessness and procrastination.
4. Irregular attendance at ACOA or other self-help group meetings.
5. Development of an "I don't care" attitude
6. Dissatisfaction with life.
7. Self-pity.
8. Thoughts of social drinking.
9. Conscious lying.
10. Complete loss of self-confidence.

Stage 3: Return to ACOA Pathology or Substance Abuse

Deterioration of self-control skills gradually returns to familiar behavior patterns. The client feels severe anger at the world in general and toward his inability to function. ACOAs discontinue outpatient therapy and attendance at self-help groups. Overwhelmed by failure, they report feeling totally afraid of and unable to rebuild motivation. As motivation erodes, habits resume insofar as avoidance and escape patterns or imbibing in alcohol or drugs. Intoxication restores social courage and relieve anxiety, with both behaviors regenerating defective contingencies which deviate from the course of self-betterment. ACOAs who relapse into old patterns also superstitiously develop "negative attitudes" about therapy and may resist seeking treatment in the future unless coerced by respected authorities (e.g., minister, rabbi, probation officer, etc.).

Therapist Failures

Another resonating sore spot for behavioral practitioners in the last three decades and blamed for therapy failures is therapist insensitivity. Frankly stated, "Is compassion part of behavioral clinical training?" Until a decade ago, operantly trained clinicians received a scientist–practitioner orientation inclusive of methodology and research, and exclusive of humanistic issues of empathy, transference, and rapport-building mechanisms (Halleck, 1971; Hersen, 1989; Ruben, 1986c). Knowledge of experimental and applied methods outweighed sensitivity to client feelings, thoughts, and anecdotal behaviors such as conversation, humor and levity, and responsivity to multicultural variables controlling the client's life. On a personal note, this author distinctly recalls conducting joint therapy as a neophyte graduate student at clinic run by the psychology department. In one session, the obese client treated for weight reduction neglected to complete her assignment of calorie-counting on the agency-issued food diary forms. She already was embarrassed. The lead therapist reprimanded her for noncompliance and insisted she would never lose weight acting so delinquently. The author knew something was wrong with this picture, but at the time did not know what.

Course curricula prepared behavioral clinicians to rigidly engineer and manage contingencies as the vertex to control and predict behavior changes. Successful contingency control meant outcomes proved effective; poor contingency control meant outcomes were ineffective. The philosophy was that rigid. But the author's experiences are not unique and several introspective behavioral practitioners have offered remedies for this training oversight (Iwata, Wong, Riordon, Dorsey & Lau, 1982; Miltenberger & Fuqua, 1985; Wachtel, 1979). Collectively, therapist mistakes result partly from emotional voids and partly from skill readiness and familiarity with idiosyncracies endemic to the ACOA population. Reviewed here are the most prominent problems encountered.

No training in substance abuse, ACOA symptoms, or family disorders. Failures frequently occur when therapists treat problems about which they know very little. Practitioners trained in one competency but deficient in other competencies may overstep the boundaries of professionalism by accepting clients beyond their expertise. With ACOA clients, graduate or post-graduate training is essential in alcohol and drug abuse, family systems theory and disorders, and behaviors indigenous to ACOAs. Certification programs in substance abuse are offered in most universities, focused on a curricular of etiology and diagnosis, treatment, legal and ethical ramifications, different populations affected, and multicultural diversity. Untrained professionals even can acquire minimum competence through manuals and then take licensing tests to earn recognized state credentials (e.g., Arneson, Ruben & Husain, 1984). Education in family systems also is available through scholarly resources and by enrolling in departmental courses on human and family ecology. For example, the author took post-graduate courses at a local university specializing in (nonbehavioral) developmental and family studies for additional insight on integrated field systems analysis.

Elevated awareness accomplishes the obvious goal of sensitivity and assessment of problems in the transgenerational role of ACOAs across alcoholic families. Absent this training, therapists may assume ACOA behavior patterns are adventitious (purely superstitious or accidental), entirely volitional (under simple self-contingencies), or correctable through concoctions of self-recording methods, which impose incredible data collection responsibilities on the client. As for etiology, behavior patterns do demonstrate superstitious conditioning. However, chronic avoidance and escape responses are both byproducts of punishment and imitative of the biological parents' disorders, which have been the norm for family generations.

A young man raised in a beer-drinking rural ethnic setting best illustrates this point. An ACOA, he approached therapy for binge drinking and presented a history of nearly every living relative being a social drinker or alcoholic, including tales of family gatherings revolving around beer tents. His consumptive habits went beyond physical ethanol tolerance or even uninhibited behaviors while inebriated. The repertoire consisted of cumulative reinforcement opportunities for imitating his elders and as a consequence, he believed that drinking met social criteria within the cultural ecosystem.

Self-contingency changes refer to the presumption that clients are aware of variables controlling their behavior and therefore can collect data on these variables. ACOAs live within an unrealistic vacuum tightly sealed by people who reinforce their dysfunctional behaviors. Insight into other people's problems may be exceptional, but they are clueless about dynamics underlying avoidance and escape behaviors and their many untoward manifestations. ACOAs need direction, not assumptions, in showing why their behaviors pose emotional hazards and the methods preventing these hazards. Because self-awareness is poor, enlisting ACOAs as self-monitors of behavior risks a backlash. ACOAs traditionally have been caretakers others, and rarely paid attention to themselves. Auto-recording devices presuppose that hardware users are accustomed to reinforcing personal needs and are nonchalant with their imperfections. For instance, as they record the frequency of apologies made, awareness sharpens about how apologetic and compensatory they are. Sadly, self-discoveries may be more anti-therapeutic than therapeutic. Data recording amplifies response deficits and lights up the imperfections with a neon sign. This panics ACOAs into submission from gross humiliation, feelings of impostorism, and especially the fear of being rejected by the therapist.

Moving too quickly or making too many demands. A common fault of zealous behavioral and nonbehavioral clinicians is moving too quickly through therapy goals. Admittedly, exigencies for briefer therapies under managed care systems place enormous stress on practitioners to design treatment both effectively and economically. The tendency is to overlook signs of backsliding and impose two to three concrete goals for closure on a case. Even employee assistance programs and other gatekeepers instruct therapists to limit goals only to immediately attainable skills, and complete treatment within three to 10 sessions. Restriction of sessions mobilizes therapy quickly and perhaps too prematurely, with unrealistic expectations overshadowing the sensitive therapist–client relationship.

Two results are common from this impetuous speed of intervention. First, clients resent this imposition for rapid recovery and view the therapist not as magnanimous but as aggressively demanding, cold, callus, and unforgiving reminiscent of their abusive parents. Second, high drop-out rates are inevitable from clients who show initial motivation but lose incentive the moment self-changes confront the unpleasant reality of family chaos. As one client so aptly put it, "After I left the session, I clicked my heels twice and returned to Kansas; I wasn't in Oz anymore."

Insensitivity to Client's Emotional Fragility The preponderance of errors emanate from underestimating the ACOA's emotional backbone. Therapist misperceptions may cast categorically wrong impressions of clients based on their behaviors. ACOAs who are aggressive caretakers, for example, present themselves as confident, organized, level-headed, and socially gregarious, and they are these things, for other people. Caretakers severely lack confidence and only exert administrative and social savvy when performing altruistic functions for the emotionally disadvantaged, never for themselves. Falsely stereotyping caretakers as emotionally stable overlooks the central function underlying treatment with ACOAs—therapy is both nurturing and constructive. Therapist attention is especially important in providing constant reinforcing feedback for any successive approximations of behavior improvement, accepting setbacks as normal (not disruptive) and using them as steppingstones for ameliorating target behavior, and allowing the client to experience a catharsis.

A what? Behaviorists did not learn this word in their technical vocabulary. Catharsis represents the critical pivotal point in therapy where ACOAs reflect on thoughts and emotions directly measuring complications with their old habits or newly formed behaviors. Expressed emotions are deeply intense and risk exposure of vulnerability, a side of themselves that ACOAs they rarely reveal.

Catharsis divulges information on responses that (a) are too difficult to emit, (b) cause serious adverse consequences, (c) prompt reversion to old behaviors, and (d) indicate motivation for continuation of therapy. Openly embracing these statements as predictors of progress is a very different approach than dismissing catharsis as symptomatic of histrionic behavior. ACOAs permitted to freely ventilate fears about recovery not only remain active behavior modifiers, they also label the therapist as credible for teaching them new skills.

Insensitivity to Cultural Diversity Landmark harassment settlements in the workplace have stemmed from employers being insensitive to the culturally diverse needs of employees. Sensitivity to cultural variables has quickly spread beyond the office to all human service delivery systems, and particularly within clinical settings where therapists uncover private lives of ACOAs from multifarious socioeconomic as well as cultural groups (see Friedman, 1997). Knowledge of cultural orientation provides a platform for proper assessment decisions, specific interventions, and anecdotal elements essential in the facilitation of therapy. For example, self-report instruments may contain experiences identifiable for Caucasian but not Asian clients, or request exposure of behaviors violating the cultural norm. Assessment of non-Caucasian-based contingencies further requires an expanded understanding of appropriate versus inappropriate behaviors, and why maladaptive behaviors in one country may be the norm in another country.

For example, a Nigerian couple seen for marital discord presented the wife as chronically passive, caretaking, and subservient to her husband. Her husband was aggressively controlling and domestically violent. Counterintuitively, the wife was less angry over her husband's physical abuse or her subordination, and more disturbed by his parenting excesses. When sequestered, she further admitted her particular cultural heritage condoned the authoritarian role of husbands and submission of wives. She saw nothing wrong with her behavior and presumed all faithful wives reconciled to secondary status under the male figure.

Modifying treatments designed for crosscultural groups also creates flexibility and appreciation of specialized client needs. Methods may have inherent flaws warranting a slight variation. Cognitive–behavioral approaches, for example, contain visual-imagery components instructing clients to close their eyes and imagine relaxing scenarios. The visual-induction exercise may violate customs of closing eyes in front of people or it may imply transfer of power away from client to therapist and be misinterpreted as insultive. Procedurally, construction of images may be irrelevant to the client's reactional biography and thus interrupt concentration for the exercise. Asking questions ahead of time about experiential differences among cultures and unique reinforcers for that client can save time, energy, and, yes, even humiliation for the therapist.

A final concern about cultural diversity regards propriety of behavior. An Asian student intern raised a highly insightful point during one of the author's recent inservices. On the topic of Asians seeking professions in engineering, medicine, and technical fields, she asked, "Does that mean that all Asians must have suffered punishment during childhood to grow up as perfectionists and seek exact science careers?" Clearly her question begged a larger question fundamentally relating the ACOA syndrome to culturalization: Do cultures endorsing punishment over reinforcement produce dysfunctional offspring? The answer, naturally, is complex. It requires knowledge of environmental contingencies endemic to the culture under question and whether there are intergenerational cases of mental illness resembling the behavior patterns discussed in this book. Not to obfuscate the point, but clients raised in cultures condoning punishment who show no maladaptive behaviors in their country of origin, but become emotionally unstable once they adapt to another country whose norms frown on punishment, do exhibit ACOA features and would be amenable to assessment and treatment interventions provided in this book.

For example, a Vietnamese father referred by Protective Services for overusing corporal punishment on his two American-born children met for court-ordered therapy. A very intelligent and sensitive individual, he understood the competing contingencies facing his ordeal. On the one hand, raised by verbal and physical punishment himself in Viet Nam, he used the same child discipline approach with his children that his country regarded as normal. He also never showed love and affection consistent with cultural norms. Corporal punishment, he learned, was not acceptable in the United States and even sparked complaints with governmental sources (Department of Social Services). Because of his abuse and violations, he lost his children temporarily in foster placements. On the other hand, his American-born children experienced in foster homes novel stimuli such as nurturance, affection, and reinforcing contingencies. Both of his children pleaded to stay at the foster home away from their "physically abusive father" because they did not want to resubmit under adverse cultural practices. To make matters worse, the inexperienced foster case manager followed agency protocol of trying to reunify the family, oblivious to the prounounced incompatibility of contingencies facing this family once they are back together. The decision, obviously, required more concerted review of the interbehavioral conditions surrounding the biological father and his Anglo Saxon-conditioned children.

Family Resistance

In any social system, for every action there is a reaction. The more intimately reciprocal the social system, the more each participant influences the system output. This simple but critical concept is central to understanding predictable problems generated in families who encounter a recovering ACOA. Patterns are insidious; they silently and unobtrusively evolve over months and typically are misinterpreted by ACOAs as sabotage. Clients facing resistant families are perplexed that their behavior changes disrupt family continuity and leave family members resentful, aggressive, and emotionally distant. ACOAs feel betrayed and may revert to pre-baseline symptoms purely to restore civility to their crumbling world.

This erosion of treatment progress occurs because the ACOA's family members live in an insulated, environmental bubble, conditioned to expect punishment and never forming reasons to protest it. Changes in that bubble upset the equilibrium; the integrative-field system suffers damage as new contingencies coerce complacent family members to radically adjust. Failure to adjust, metaphorically speaking, creates a system *hemorrhage*. Havoc is unleashed upon the family as members lose control over previous contingencies and lack the skills to access new contingencies. The aftermath of this Armageddon is either conformity with the changes or resistance.

Among the foreseeable obstacles of family resistance that ACOAs face are distrust, protectiveness, unrealistic expectations, newly surfaced resentment, and recovery as threat to family.

Distrust Distrust guards against repeated emotional and even physical injury in an unpredictable family environment. Partners or children uncertain when the next mood swing, aggressive outburst, or odd behavior might occur, are hypersensitive to all precipitatory events. Suspicion of relapse arises partly as self-defense from the abuser, and partly because of habituation; conditioned rituals compromise family contingencies perceived as normal and expectable. For this reason, it is virtually impossible for the family not to harbor distrust even after months or years of client recovery, depending on the severity of previous abuses. Distrust even endures when family members intentionally conspired to get help for the ACOA client. Collaborative family caring can work in two ways. First, families that encourage treatment and ask questions about progress are akin to *in vivo* changes consistent with the therapist's objectives. Resistance, therefore, is marginal. But families who say the ACOA is the only person who needs change may politely inquire about steps of improvement but remain uncommitted to change reciprocally.

Protectiveness Oddly, family cohesion can have reversal effects during recovery. While family members alienated themselves when abused, now that ACOAs accept their problems, seek treatment, and are legitimately making changes, family compassion tends to increase. Strong interest occurs in helping ACOAs reach recovery goals and become a productive contributor within the family. Intensity of effort, however, may increase to excess. Members who anticipate recidivism go overboard to protect the fragile client from emotional infractions. They spare ACOAs from major decision making, financial responsibilities, household chores, and compare the recovery period to a recuperation from post-operative surgery. Just as stitches might reopen, so it is that emotional stitches sewn together by a loose thread are perceived as delicate. The family caters to the ACOAs' needs and places the recovery process on a pedestal.

The flaw with this beneficence is that, unlike those in periods of medical recuperation, ACOAs are not immobilized. They must participate actively in altering family interactions using techniques that replace abusive, neglectful, or self-sacrificing behaviors. When families shower ACOAs with undemanding nurturance, techniques are wasted and ACOAs revert to old patterns. The client receives bootleg reinforcement for behaviors incompatible with clinically targeted behaviors rehearsed in the session. Failures to generalize behaviors occur when to families serve as caretakers, and clients mistake that caretaking for renewed family love.

Married couples are notorious for this. A passively dependent male ACOA sought treatment to build social assertiveness skills. His wife, a dominator, was favorable about therapy and pledged to support her husband's advancements. One month into the sessions, he effectively employed basic assertion methods and boasted in therapy about provoking conflict without running away to the neighbor's house or easing anxiety with a beer. His wife, he reported, was a big fan of his progress: "She's let me say and do whatever I want and doesn't force chores on me like she used to." On the surface, self-reports demonstrated that assertive strategies nicely balanced their communication and decreased his wife's aggressive behaviors. But closer inspection of household contingencies revealed another story. Choice of chores, recreational activities, and topics of communication were not a mutual decision. The client's wife told him what he could do and deliberately withheld conflict to protect him from recidivism of ACOA symptoms.

Unrealistic expectations. Damage from ACOAs already takes a heavy toll on family members. As families slowly recover from hurt and observe improvement in the client, they begin to believe that the disaster is over and now the family can be happy. Expectations falsely derive from how things should be or are with other families. Idealism deludes the picture of recovery with the image of a house with a white picket fence, and all painful memories of the past eradicated. Misperceptions of therapy include that it constitutes a definite cure and will resuscitate family values.

However, therapy cannot deliver a utopian package. Glorified treatment goals are disasters waiting to occur. As the charm of recovery subsides and ACOAs backslide into old habits, families feel betrayed, devastated, and retaliate in self-defense. They regard relapse as inexcusable and resend generous schedules of reinforcement. Outrage persists against the therapist, whom they view as a traitor and a shaman who led them down a rosy path of deception. Anger rages against toward the client and inwardly throughout the family system, where spouses and children grow distrustful, discohesive, and dissociate themselves from mainstream family activities. ACOAs now face a bumpy, uphill battle either to restore tranquillity among feuding members or permit the family dissension as a noncaretaker. Either choice impedes therapy

Newly surfaced resentment. Anger kept repressed during years of the ACOA's torment finally surfaces when the client is receptive to criticism. Family members can express longstanding resentment for being victims of emotional and physical abuse, neglect and abandonment, and for losing precious childhood or adult experiences under the ACOA's reign. Anger flows like a river through an exploding floodgate; children and spouses rotate rounds of abrasive criticism, peppering the ACOA with hateful bullets of shame. Antipathy can last for a period a weeks and months and causes ACOAs great consternation, since they cannot understand why their family ganged up on them. Effects of this group assault are threefold. First, ACOAs accuse the family of sabotaging recovery and never really wanting them to get better. Second, alienation from abundant criticism causes ACOAs to revert to reactionary behaviors from aggression to caretaking to avoidance, all serving to avert family acrimony. Third, criticism both positively punishes recovery efforts as well as feeble attempts at old ACOA symptoms; conditioned suppressive effects incapacitates the client who lapses into depression.

Observing this downward spiral to depression, family members radically shift behaviors from being defiantly antagonistic to passionately forgiving and worried about the emotional safety of the ACOA. Resentment vanishes as the partner and children reaffirm support for recovery goals and internalize their angry behaviors. Within days, superficially depressed ACOAs "magically" rebound and energetically pledge to resume their commitment to behavior change. Recession of family anger therefore spared ACOAs from adapting to adversity and likewise discouraged the family from healthy confrontation.

Recovery as Threat to Family Naturally, recuperation involves ongoing adjustment. The reformed personality of ACOAs is foreign, odd, and even diametrical to past behavior patterns observed over years. Superficially, the family applauds this healthy personality and states that the ACOA deserves a new lease on life.

Inwardly, however, family members remain skeptical about recovery and seriously question the impact of recovery on their own lives. Mixed family messages systemically distort and unravel support and reinforcement contingencies. The result is peculiar family patterns indicated as resistance to change, overcompensating for change, and distance from change.

Resistance to Change Observed changes in the client's behavior signal a necessary family adjustment in ways that are uncomfortable and thus avoided. Partners are not accustomed to "communicating" with the ACOA, just as children rarely expect hugs, kisses, money, or gifts given unconditionally. Displays of affection and family interest frighten members away from the client and cause them to aggressively resent this improvement. Resistance arises when the family must engage in behaviors about which they are ignorant or have deficiencies.

Consider affection, for instance. Construction of emotions and appropriate uses of lovemaking may lend a female ACOA an insightfully new perspective on her marriage. But her husband may think differently. After years of sexual denials, emasculative teasing, and erectile inhibitions, he finds his wife making romantic sexual overtures and expecting him to immediately respond. History aside, the husband has also developed incompatible behaviors such as frequent masturbation, cybersex with chat-session partners, and flirtation at work. Consequently his ambivalence is obvious. Reception to his wife's romantic overtures requires spontaneous regeneration of suppressed behaviors based on temporary reinforcement contingencies. Or, he can avoid the overtures and engage in safe, auto-eroticism reinforced on CRF schedules. The choice, predicated on behavioral contrast laws, depends on reinforcement schedules for the competing behaviors and length of inter-response time.

Another factor confusing the dilemma is rule-governed behaviors. Beliefs about fidelity and forgiveness (e.g., "I ought to be loyal to my wife") arouse anxiety, the removal of which by sexually conforming, produces negative reinforcement. Concurrent and multiple contingencies thus exert control over decisions to resist his wife or reinforce her recovery behaviors.

Overcompensating for Change Families aware of their resistance may go overboard to make improvements. A wife who realizes she is aorgasmic and wants normal sexual relations with her ACOA husband may read literature on all the "right positions," dress in seductive lingerie, and possibly even attend inspirational conferences on healthy lovemaking. Laborious effort goes into crafting new skills, into polishing those skills until they reach perfection, and finally putting those skills to the test of spousal approval. Overcompensation thus resonates from approval-seeking and enabling behaviors of the victimized family members. Restored love, caring, and family unity are perceived as natural consequences of methodically engaging in excessive positive behaviors.

Distance from Change Resistance from new behaviors during adjustment produces a common outcome. Affected family members dissociate from the client to keep things the way they were. Maintaining the status quo consists entirely of avoidance and escape behaviors. As referenced earlier, choosing to have sex with a rehabilitated spouse after years of contrast effects feels hypocritical and anxious. By leaving the situation unchanged, spousal interactions slightly improve because there are no new surprises and psychological warfare has stopped. Intimacy never grows, and the husband essentially retains his incompatible behaviors of alternative sexual outlets. A neutral plateau emerges where neither spouse regresses nor advances but simply holds the romantic behaviors in abeyance. In a strange way, the couple's neutrality can be refreshing and significantly different from their history of reciprocal discordance.

Treatment failures represent a challenge for practitioners interested in helping ACOAs. Therapists trained in specialty skills on addiction, family systems, and eliminative and constructive techniques for ACOA symptoms have an edge over unskilled providers. Efficacy of treatment is more secure and less susceptible to confounding factors such as therapist insensitivity and unrealistic expectancy demands. Client failures, as well, can jeopardize treatment by unplanned stages of transition intruding on the therapist–client relationship and lowering motivation. Subterfuges of improvement such as overconfidence, compulsions, and denial, can also occur, masking unstable recovery skills. The stabilizing force—the family—hypothetically expected to propel client progress, can be the most debilitating factor in treatment. Resistance, resentment, overprotection, and distrust, among other disincentives, evolve from chronic suppressive effects on the family. Members suffer ambivalence over granting ACOAs another chance at family attachment or keeping the status quo. Keeping things as they are involves alienation and discompassion, but at least household contingencies remain constant and predictable.

Correcting these failures lies in future research endeavors charted within an interdisciplinary field. Behavioral systems analysis serves as a good starting point to navigate empirical directions for researchers. But a topic such as ACOAs that overlaps disciplines of sociology, psychology, counseling, and addictionology is broad in scope and requires investigation of principles in common. For now, practitioners have new tools to sculpt behaviors and inspire hope in wonderful people who are eager to rebuild their lives.

GENERAL REFERENCES

Abramowitz, A.J., & O'Leary. S. (1990). Effectiveness of delayed punishment in an applied setting. *Behavior Therapy, 21,* 231–239.

Ackerman, R.J. (1983). *Children of alcoholics: A guidebook for educators, therapists and parents.* Holmes Beach, FL: Learning Publications, Inc.

Ackerman, R.J. (Ed.). (1986). *Growing up in the shadow.* Pompano Beach, FL: Health Communications.

Ackerman, R.J. (1987). *Children of alcoholics.* New York: Simon & Schuster, Inc.

Allison, P.D., & Furstenberg, F.F. (1989). How marital dissolution affects children: Variations by age and sex. *Developmental Psychology, 25,* 540–549.

Ambert, A. (2000). *Parents, children, and adolescents: Interactive relationships and development in context.* New York: Haworth Press.

Arneson, A.H., Ruben. D.H., & Husain, S. (1984). Credentialing of substance abuse counselors: A field evaluation. *Journal of Drug Education, 14,* 297–306.

Axelrod, S., & Apsche, J. (1983). *The effects of punishment on human behavior.* Orlando, FL: Academic Press.

Azrin, N.H., & Nunn, G. (1977). *Habit control in a day.* New York: Simon & Schuster.

Azrin, N.H., & Holz, W.C. (1966). Punishment. In W.K. Honig (Ed.). *Operant behavior: Areas of research and application.* New York: Appleton-Century Crofts (pp. 380–447).

Azrin, N.H., Hutchinson, R.R., & Hake, D.F. (1967). Attack, avoidance and escape reactions to aversive shock. *Journal of the Experimental Analysis of Behavior, 10,* 131–148.

Azrin, N.H., Hutchinson, R.R., & Sallery, R.D. (1964). Pain aggression toward inanimate objects. *Journal of the Experimental Analysis of Behavior, 7,* 223–229.

Azrin, N.H. & Nunn, G. (1977). *Habit control in a day.* New York: Simon & Schuster.

Baker, D.E., & Stephenson, L.A. (1995). Personality characteristics of adult children of alcoholics. *Journal of Clinical Psychology, 51,* 694–702.

Balsam, P.D., & Bondy, A.S. (1983). The negative side effects of reward. *Journal of Applied Behavior Analysis, 16,* 283–296.

Banks, R.K. (1965). Effect of pairing a stimulus with presentations of the UCS on extinction of an avoidance response in humans. *Journal of Experimental Psychology, 70,* 294–299.

Barbour, K.A., Eckhardt, C.IO., Davison, G.C., & Kassinove, H. (1998). The experience and expression of anger in maritally violent and maritally discordant-nonviolent men. *Behavior Therapy, 29,* 173–191.

Bedau, H.A. (1978). Retribution and the theory of punishment. *Journal of Philosophy, 50,* 601–620.

Bellack, A.S., & Hersen, M. (Eds.). (1985). *Dictionary of behavior therapy techniques.* New York: Pergamon Press.

Bellieveau, J.M., & Stoppard, J.M. (1995). Parental alcohol abuse and gender as predictors of psychopathology in adult children of alcoholics. *Addictive Behaviors, 20,* 619–625.

Bennett, R.H., & Cherek, D.R. (1990). Punished and nonpunished responding in a multiple schedule in humans: A brief report. *Psychological Record, 40,* 187–196.

Bensley, L.S., Spieker, S.J., & McMahon, R.J. (1994). Parenting behavior of adolescent children of alcoholics. *Addiction, 89,* 1256–1276.

Bifulco, A.T., Brown, G.W., & Harris, T.O. (1987). Childhood loss of parent, lack of adequate parental care and adult depression: A replication. *Journal of Affective Disorders, 12,* 115–128.

Biglan, A., Glasgow, R.E., & Singer, G. (1990). The need for a science of larger social units: A contextual approach. *Behavior Therapy, 21,* 195–215.

Bijou, S. (1975). Moral development in the preschool years: A functional analysis. *Mexican Journal of Behavior Analysis, 1,* 11–29.

Bijou, S. (1976). *Child development: The basic stage of early childhood.* Englewood Cliffs, NJ: Prentice-Hall.

Bijou, S., & Baer, D. (1978). *Behavior analysis of child development.* Englewood Cliffs, NJ: Prentice-Hall.

Bijou, S., Umbreit, J., Ghezzi, P.M., & Chao, C.C. (1985). Research methodology for language studies: A Kantorian perspective. *Experimental Analysis of Human Behavior Bulletin, 3,* 1–4.

Bijou, S., Umbreit, J., Ghezzi, P.M., & Chao, C.C. (1986). Psychological linguistics: A natural science approach to the study of language interactions. *The Analysis of Verbal Behavior, 4,* 23–29.

Black, C. (1982). *It will never happen to me.* Denver, CO: Medical Administration Company.

Blanchard, E.B., and Schwarz, S.P. (1988). Two-year follow-up of behavioral treatment of irritable bowel syndrome. *Behavior Therapy*, *19*, 67–73.

Boe, E.E., & Church, R.M. (Eds.). (1968). *Punishment: Issues and experiments.* New York: Appleton-Century-Crofts.

Bolles, R.C. (1972). Reinforcement expectancy and learning. *Psychological Review, 79,* 394–409.

Boylan, R.J., & Boylan, L.K. (1994). *Close extraterrestrial encounters.* Tigard, OR: Wild Flower Press.

Brandt, R.B. (1976). The psychology of benevolence and its implications for philosophy. *The Journal of Philosophy, 63,* 424–453.

Brown, S. (1988). *Treating adult children of alcoholics.* New York: Wiley Press.

Brown, S. (1991). Adult children of alcoholics: The history of a social movement and its impact on clinical theory and practice. In M. Galanter, H. Begleiter, R. Deitrich, D. Gallant, D. Goodwin, E. Gottheil, A. Paredes, M. Rothschild, and D. Van Thiel (Eds.), *Recent developments in alcoholism, Vol. 9: Children of alcoholics* (pp. 267–285). New York: Plenum Press.

Brown, S., & Lewis, V. (1999). *The alcoholic family in recovery.* New York: Guilford Publications.

Browning, R.M., & Stover, D. (1971). *Behavior modification in child treatment.* Chicago: Aldine Publishing.

Campbell, D.T., & Stanley, J.C. (1966). *Experimental and quasi-experimental designs for research.* Chicago: Rand McNally.

Cautela, J.R. (1981). *Behavior analysis forms for clinical intervention (Vol. 2).* Champaign, IL: Research Press.

Chang, J.K., & Krantz, M. (1996). Personal and environmental factors in relation to adjustment of offpsring of alcoholics. *Substance Use and Misuse, 31,* 1401–1412.

Charlop, M.H., Burgio, L., Iawta, B.A., & Ivancic, M.T. (1988). Stimulus variation as a means of enhancing punishment effects. *Journal of Applied Behavior Analysis, 21,* 89–95.

Chassin, L., Pits, SC., DeLucia, C., & Todd, M. (1999). A longitudinal study of children of alcoholics: Predicting young adult substance use disorders, anxiety and depression. *Journal of Abnormal Psychology, 108,* 106–109.

Cherek, D.R., & Dougherty, D.M. (1997). The relationship between provocation frequency and human aggressive responding. *Psychological Record, 47,* 357–370.

Cherek, D.R., Spiga, R., Bennett, R.H., & Grabowski, J (1991). Human aggressive and escape responding: Effects of provocation frequency. *Psychological Record, 41,* 3–17.

Chomsky, N. (1957). *Syntactic structures.* The Hague: Mouton.

Chomsky, N. (1959). A review of B.F. Skinner's *Verbal Behavior. Language, 35,* 26–58.

Chorpita, B.F. (1997). Since the operant chamber: Are we still thinking in Skinner boxes? *Behavior Therapy, 28,* 577–583.

Christensen, A. (1988). Dysfunctional interaction patterns in couples. In P. Noller & M.A. Fitzpatrick (Eds.), *Perspectives on marital interaction.* Philadelphia, PA: Multilingual Matters Ltd. (pp. 31–52).

Claydon, P. (1987). Self-reported alcohol, drug and eating-disorder problems among male and female collegiate children of alcoholics. *Journal of American College Health, 36,* 111–116.

Conner, K.R., & Ackerly, G.D. (1994). Alcohol-related battering: Developing treatment strategies. *Journal of Family Violence, 9,* 143–155.

Cook, T.D., & Campbell, D.T. (1979). *Quasi-experimentation: Design and analysis issues for field settings.* Boston: Houghton Mifflin Co.

Cork, R.M. (1969). *The forgotten children.* Toronto: Paperjacks.

Crespi, T.D. (1995). Adult children of alcoholics: The family praxis. *Family therapy, 22,* 81–95.

Cronbach, L.J. (1951). Coefficient alpha and the internal structure of tests. *Psychometrika, 16,* 33–42.

Crosbie, J. (1998). Negative reinforcement and punishment. In K.A. Lattal & M. Perone (Eds.), *Handbook of human operant behavior research methods.* New York: Plenum.

Davey, G., & Cullen, C. (Eds.). (1988). *Human operant conditioning and behavior modification.* New York: John Wiley & Sons.

Davis, JL.J., de la Fuente, J.R., Morse, R.M., Landa, E., & O'Brien, P.C. (1989). Self-administered Alcoholism Screening Test: Comparison of classificatory accuracy in two cultures. *Alcoholism: Clinical and Experimental Research, 13,* 224–228.

Delprato, D.J. (1986). Response patterns. In H.W. Reese & L.J. Parrott (Eds.), *Behavior science: Philosophical, methodological, and empirical advances* (pp. 61–113). Hillsdale, NJ: Lawrence Erlbaum Associates.

Delprato, D.J., & McGlynn, F.D. (1988). Interactions of response patterns and their implications for behavior therapy. *Journal of Behavior Therapy and Experimental Psychiatry, 19,* 199–205.

Dembo, R., Pacheco, K., Schmeidler, J., Fisher, L., & Cooper, S. (1997). Drug use and delinquent behavior among high risk youths. *Journal of Child & Adolescent Substance Abuse, 6,* 1–25.

Denny, R. (Ed.). (1991). *Fear, avoidance, and phobias: A fundamental analysis.* Hillsdale, NJ: Lawrence Erlbaum Associates.

Deutsch, C. (1982). *Broken bottles, broken dreams: Understanding and helping the children of alcoholics.* New York: Teachers College Press.

Dixon, M.R., & Hayes, L.J. (1998). Effects of differing instructional histories on the resurgence of rule-following. *Psychological Record, 48,* 275–292.

Dollard, J., & Miller, N.W. (1950). *Personality and psychotherapy.* New York: McGraw-Hill.

Domjan, M.P. (1996). *The Essentials of Conditioning and Learning.* Pacific Grove, CA: Brooks/Cole Publishing.

Dupont, R., & McGovern, J.P. (1991). The growing impact of the children-of-alcoholics movement on medicine: A revolution in our midst. In T. Rivinus (Ed.), *Children of chemically dependent parents: Multiperspectives from the cutting edge* (pp. 313–329). New York: Brunner/Mazel.

Dutton, D.G. (1998). *The abusive personality.* New York: Guilford Press.

Dymond, S., & Barnes, D. (1997). Behavior-analytic approaches to self-awareness. *Psychological Record, 47,* 181–200.

Edgington, E.S. (1980). Random assignment and statistical tests for one-subject experiments. *Behavioral Assessment, 2,* 19–98.

Eifert, G.H., Forsyth, J.P, Zvolensky, M.J., & Lejuez, S.W. (1999). Moving from the laboratory to the real world and back again: Increasing the relevance of laboratory examinations of anxiety sensitivity. *Behavior Therapy, 30,* 273–283.

El-Guebaly, N., & Offord, D. (1977). The offspring of alcoholics: A critical review. *American Journal of Psychiatry, 134,* 357–365.

Elk, R., & Johnson, C.W. (1989). Police arrest in domestic violence. *Response, 12,* 7–13.

Ellis, A. (1985). *Overcoming resistance.* New York: Springer.

Emmendorfer, J.L., & Crosbie, J. (1999). Effects of punishment proportion and condition sequence on contrast and induction with humans. *Psychological Record, 49,* 261–271.

Eysenck, H.J. (1979). The conditioning model of neurosis. *The Behavioral and Brain Sciences, 2,* 155–166.

Fairbank, J.A., & Brown, T.A. (1987). Current behavioral approaches to the treatment of posttraumatic stress disorder. *The Behavior Therapist,* 3, 57–64.

Falls, W.A., & Davis, M. (1995). Behavioral and physiological analysis of fear inhibition: Extinction and conditioned inhibition. In M. J. Friedman, D.S. Charney, & A.Y. Deutch (Eds.), *Neurobiological and clinical consequences of stress: From normal adaptation to post-traumatic stress disorder* (pp. 177–202). Philadelphia, PA: Lippincott-Raven Publishers.

Ferster, C.B. (1973). Behavioral language. *International Journal of Psychiatry, 11,* 189–195.

Ferster, C.B. & Skinner, B.F. (1957). *Schedules of reinforcement.* Englewood Cliffs, NJ: Prentice-Hall.

Ferster, C.B., Culberston, S., & Boren, M.C.P. (1975). *Behavior principles.* Englewood Cliffs, NJ: Prentice-Hall.

Filstead, W.J., McElfresh, O., & Anderson, C. (1981). Comparing the family environments of alcoholic and "normal" famililes. *Journal of Alcohol and Drug Education, 26,* 24–31.

Firestone, P., & Douglas, V. (1975). The effects of reward and punishment on reaction times and autonomic activity in hyperactive and normal children. *Journal of Abnormal Child Psychology, 3,* 201–216.

Fischer, W.W., Adelinis, J.D., Thompson, R.H., Worsdell, A.S., & Zarcone, J.R. (1998). Functional analysis and treatment of destructive behavior maintained by termination of "don't" (and symmetical "do") requests. *Journal of Applied Behavior Analysis, 31,* 339–356.

Fishman, D.B. (1999). *The case for pragmatic psychology.* New York: New York Press.

Foa, E.B., & Emmelkamp, P.M.G. (Eds.). (1983). *Failures in behavior therapy.* New York: John Wiley & Sons.

Foa, E.B., Steketee, G., & Rothbaum, B.O. (1989). Behavioral/cognitive conceptualizations of post-traumatic stress disorder. *Behavior Therapy*, 20, 155–176.

Foa, E.G., & Foa, U.G. (1974). *Societal Structures of the Mind.* Springfield, IL: Charles Thomas.

Foa, E.G., & Foa, U.G. (1980). Resource theory: interpersonal behavior as exchange. In J. Gergen, L. Greenberg & A. Wilils (Eds.). *Social Exchange: Advances in theory and research* (pp. 35–60). NY: Plenum.

Follette, W.C. (1998). Expanding the domains of clinical behaviorism: A comment on Dougher. *Behavior Therapy, 29,* 593–601.

Friedman, S. (Ed.). (1997). *Cultural issues in the treatment of anxiety.* New York: Guilford.

Friel, J., & Friel, L. (1988). *Adult children: Secrets of dysfunctional families.* Pompano, FL: Health Communications.

Gelfand, D.M., & Hartmann, D.P. (1968). Behavior therapy with children: A review and evaluation of research metholdogy. *Psychological Bulletin, 69,* 204–215.

Gelfand, D.M., & Hartmann, D.P. (1984). *Child behavior analysis and therapy.* New York: Pergamon.

Glasgow, R.E., & Rosen, G.M. (1978). Behavioral bibliotherapy: A review of self-help behavior therapy manuals. *Psychological Bulletin, 85,* 1–23.

Goldfried, M.R. (1977). Behavioral assessment in perspective. In J.D. Cone & R.P. Hawkins (Eds.), *Behavioral assessment: New directions in clinical psychology* (pp. 3–22). New York: Bruner/Mazel.

Gorski T.T. (1984). *Intimacy and recovery—a workshop manual.* Hazel Crest, IL: CENAPS Corporation.

Gorski, T.T., & Miller, M. (1986). *Staying sober: A guide for relapse prevention.* Independence, MO: Herald House.

Gough, B., & Reavey P. (1997). Parental accounts regarding the physical punishment of children: Discourses of disempowerment. *Child Abuse and Neglect, 21,* 417–430.

Green, E.J., Sanders, R.M., & Squier, R.W. (1959). Schedules of reinforcement, and discrimination learning. *Journal of the Experimental Analysis of Behavior, 2,* 293–299.

Halleck, S. (1971). *The politics of therapy.* NY: Science House Inc.

Hamberger, L.K. (1997). Female offenders in domestic violence: A look at actions in their context. *Journal of Aggression, Maltreatment, and Trauma, 1,* 117–129.

Hans, S.L. (1999). Demographic and psychosocial characteristics of substance-abusing pregnant women. *Clinical Perinatology, 26,* 55–74.

Haskell, R.E. (1993). *Adult-child research and experience: Personal and professional legacies of a dysfunctional co-dependent family.* Norwood, NJ: Ablex Publishing Company.

Hawkins, C.A., & Hawkins, R.C. (1995). Development and validation of an adult children of alcoholics tool. *Research on Social Work Practice, 5,* 317–339.

Hawkins, R.P., & Forsyth, J.P. (1997). The behavior analytic perspective: Its nature, prospects, and limitations for behavior therapy. *Journal of Behavior Therapy and Experimental Psychiatry, 28,* 7–16.

Hay, W., Hay, L.R., Angle, H.V., & Nelson, R. (1979). The reliability of problem identification in the behavioral interview. *Behavioral Assessment, 1,* 107–118.

Hayes, L., & Chase, P.N. (Eds.). (1991). *Dialogues on verbal behavior.* Reno, NV: Context Press.

Hayes, S.C. (Ed.). (1987). *Rule-governed behavior: Cognition, contingencies, and instructional control.* New York: Plenum Press.

Hayes, L.J., Adams, M.A., & Dixon, M.R. (1996). Causal constructs and conceptual confusions. *Psychological Record, 46,* 97–112.

Heffner, M.P., Lejuez, C.W., & Freeman, K.A. (1999). A behavioral formulation of HIV-related anxiety: Etiology and treatment implications. *The Behavior Therapist, 22,* 125–129.

Herrnstein, R.J. (1966). Superstition: A corollary of the principles of operant conditioning. In W.K. Honig (Ed.), *Operant behavior: Areas of research and application* (pp. 33–51). New York: Appleton-Century-Crofts

Herting, J.R., Eggert, L.L., & Thompson, E.A. (1996). A multidimensional model of adolescent drug involvement. *Journal of Research on Adolescence, 6,* 325–361.

Hersen, M. (1989). Limitations and problems in the clinical application of behavioral techniques in psychiatric settings. *Behavior Therapy, 10,* 65–80.

Hills, S.Y., Lowers, L., Locke, J., Snidman, N., & Kagan, J. (1999). Behavioral inhibition in children from families at high risk for developing alcoholism. *Journal of American Academy of Child Adolescent Psychiatry, 38,* 410–417.

Hodgins, D.C., & Shimp, L. (1995). Identifying adult children of alcoholics: Methodological review and a comparison of the CAST-6 with other methods. *Addiction, 90,* 255–267.

Hodgins, D.C., Maticka-Tyndale, E., el-Guebaly, N., & West, M. (1995). Alternative cut-point scores for the CAST-6. *Addictive Behaviors, 20,* 267–270.

Hollis, J.H. (1973). "Superstition": The effects of independent and contingent events on free operant responses in retarded children. *American Journal of Mental Deficiency, 77,* 585–596.

Honig, W.K. (Ed.). (1966). *Operant behavior: Areas of research and application.* New York: Appleton-Century-Crofts.

Hotch, D.F., Sherin, K.M., Harding P.N., & Zitter, R.E. (1985). Use of the self-administered Michigan Alcoholism Screening Test in a family practice center. *Journal of Family Practice, 17,* 1021–1026.

Hough, P., & Kalman, M. (1997). *The truth about alien abductions.* New York: Sterling.

House, A.E., Manelis, L., & Kinscherf, B.M. (1983). Vigilance as a model of self-monitoring accuracy: emprical effects and a conceptual framework. *Behavioral Assessment, 5,* 83–96.

Huesmann, L.R., Eron, L., & Lefkowitz, M. (1984). Stability of aggression over time and generations. *Developmental Psychology, 20,* 1120–1134.

Huitema, B.E. (1980). *The analysis of covariance and alternatives.* New York: John Wiley & Sons.

Hunt, M.E. (1997). A comparison of family of origin factors between children of alcoholics and children of non-alcoholics in a longitudinal panel. *American Journal of Drug and Alcohol Abuse, 23,* 597–613.

Hutchinson, R.R. (1977). By-products of aversive control. In W.K. Honig & J.E.R. Staddon (Eds.). *Handbook of operant behavior.* Englewood Cliffs, NJ: Prentice-Hall (pp. 415–431).

Iwata, B.A., Wong, S.E., Riordon, M.M., Dorsey, M.F., & Lau, M.M. (1982). Assessment and training of clinical interviewing skills: Analogue analysis and field replication. *Journal of the Applied Behavior Analysis, 15,* 191–204.

Jacob, T., & Lessin, S. (1982). Inconsistent communication in family interaction. *Clinical Psychology Review, 2,* 295–309.

Jacobson, N., & Gottman, J. (1998). *When men batter women: New insights into ending abusive relationships.* New York: Simon & Schuster.

Jacobson, N., & Margolis, G. (1979). *Marital therapy: Strategies based on social learning and behavior exchange principles.* New York: Brunner/Mazel.

Jahn, M.F. (1995). Family secrets and family environment: Their relation to later adult functioning. *Alcoholism Treatment Quarterly, 13,* 71–80.

Jennison, K.M., & Johnson, K.A. (1998). Alcohol dependence in adult children of alcoholics: Longitudinal evidence of early risk. *Journal of Drug Education, 28,* 19–37.

Johnson, J.L., & Leff, M. (1999). Children of substance abusers: Overview of research findings. *Pediatrics, 103,* 1085–1099.

Johnston, J.M., & Pennypacker, H.S. (1980). *Strategies and tactics of human behavioral research.* Hillsdale, NJ: Lawrence Erlbaum Associates.

Kantor, J.R. (1959). *Interbehavioral Psychology.* Granville, OH: Principia Press.

Kantor, J.R. (1977). *Psychological linguistics.* Chicago, Principia Press.

Kantor, J.R. (1980). Manifesto of interbehavioral psychology. *Revista Mexicana de Analisis de la Conducta, 6,* 117–128.

Kazdin, A.E. (1994). Models of dysfunction in developmental psychopathology. *Clinical Psychology: Science and Practice, 1,* 35–52.

Kazdin, A.E. (1995). Child, parent and family dysfunction as predictors of outcome in cognitive-behavioral treatment of antisocial children. *Behaviour Research and Therapy, 33,* 271–283.

Kazdin, A.E., Kraemer, H.C., Kessler, R., Kupfer, D.J., & Offord, D.R. (1997). Contributions of risk-factor research to developmental psychopathology. *Clinical Psychology Review, 17,* 375–406.

Keane, T.M., Zimmerling, R.T., & Caddell, J.M. (1985). A behavioral formulation of post-traumatic stress disorder in Vietnam Veterans. *The Behavior Therapist,* 8, 9–12.

Kivlahan, D.R., Sher, K.J., & Donovan, D.M. (1989). The Alcohol Dependence Scale: A validation study among inpatient alcoholics. *Journal of Studies on Alcohol, 30,* 170–175.

Knapp, M. (1972). *Nonverbal communication in human interaction.* New York: Holt, Rinehart and Winston.

Kodera, T.L., & Rilling, M. (1976). Procedural antecedents of behavioral contrast: A re-examination of errorless learning. *Journal of the Experimental Analysis of Behavior, 25,* 27–42.

Keith, T.Z., and Witta, E.L. (1997). Hierarchical and cross-age confirmatory factor analysis of the WISC-III: What does it measure? *School Psychology Quarterly*, *12*, 89–107.

Kollins, S.H., Lane, S.D., & Shapiro, S.K. (1997). Experimental analysis of childhood psychopathology: A laboratory matching analysis of the behavior of children diagnosed with attention-deficit hyperactivity disorder (ADHD). *Psychological Record, 47,* 25–44.

Kritsberg, W. (1985). *Adult children of alcoholic syndrome.* New York: Bantam.

Kuder, G.F., and Richardson, M.W. (1937). The theory of the estimation of test reliability. *Psychometrika*, 2, 151–160.

Kunkel, J.H. (1996). What have behaviorists accomplished—and what more can they do? *Psychological Record, 46,* 21–37.

Kunkel, J.H. (1997). The analysis of rule-governed behavior in social psychology. *Psychological Record, 47,* 699–716.

Kuperman, S., Schlosser, S.S., Lidral, J., and Reich, W. (1999). Relationship of child psychopathology to parental alcoholism and antisocial personality disorder. *Journal of American Academy of Adolescent Psychiatry, 38,* 686–692.

L'Abate, L. (Ed.) (1998). *Family psychopathology: The relational roots of dysfunctional behavior.* New York: Guilford Press.

LaVigne, M. (1995). *The alien abduction survival guide.* Newberg, OR: Wild Flower Press.

Levy, S.J., & Rutter, E. (1999). *Children of drug abusers.* San Francisco, CA: Jossey-Bass.

Lipke, H. (1999). Comments on "Thirty Years of Behavior Therapy..." and the promise of the application of scientific principles. *The Behavior Therapist, 22,* 11–14.

Lyon, D.O. (1982). Concurrent behavior: Are the interpretations mutually exclusive? *Behavior Analyst, 5,* 175–187.

Lyon, M.A., & Seefeldt, R.W. (1995). Failure to validate personality characteristics of Adult Children of Alcoholics: A replication and extension. *Alcoholism Treatment Quarterly, 12,* 69–85.

Macciomei, N.R., & Ruben, D.H. (1979). *Homebound teaching: A handbook for educators.* Jefferson, NC: McFarland Publishing.

Macciomei, N.R., & Ruben, D.H. (Eds.) (1999). *Behavioral Management in the Public Schools: An Urban Approach.* Westport, CT: Praeger Press.

Maisto, S., Connors, G., Tucker, J., McCollan, J., & Adesso, V. (1980). Validation of Sensation Scale: A measure of subjective physiological responses to alcohol. *Behaviour Research and Therapy, 18,* 37–43.

Malloy, P., & Levis, D.J. (1988). A laboratory demonstration of persistent human avoidance. *Behavior Therapy, 19,* 229–241.

Malpique, C., Barrias, P., Morais, L., Salgado, M., Pinto da Costa, I., and Rodriques, M. (1998). Violence and alcoholism in the family: How are the children affected? *Alcohol, 33,* 42–46.

Mansdorf, I.J., Calapai, P., Caselli, L., & Burstein, Y. (1999). Reducing psychotropic medication usage in nursing home residents: The effects of behaviorally oriented psychotherapy. *The Behavior Therapist, 22,* 21–23:39.

Marlatt, G.A. (Ed.). (1998). *Harm reduction.* New York: Guilford Press.

Marlatt, G.A., & Gordon, J.R. (Eds.). (1985). *Relapse prevention: Maintenance strategies in the treatment of addictive behaviors.* New York: Guilford Press.

Marshall, W.K., Fernandez, Y.M., Hudson, S.M., & Ward, T. (Eds.). (1998). *Sourcebook of treatment programs for sexual offenders.* Hingham, MA: Kluwer Academic

Maser, J.D., & Seligman, M.P. (1977). *Psychopathology: Experimental models.* San Francisco: W.H. Freeman.

Masterson, J.F. (2000). *The personality disorders.* Phoenix, AZ: Zeig, Tucker & Co.

Matson, J.L., & DiLorenzo, T.M. (1984). *Punishment and its alternatives.* New York: Springer.

Mayor, J., & Ruben, D.H. (1991). *After War: Overcoming post-traumatic stress syndrome.* Okemos, MI: Best Impressions International, Inc.

Maxwell, W.A., Miller, F.D., & Meyer, P.A. (1971). The relationship between punishment and unavoidability in eliminating avoidance behavior in humans. *Psychonomic Science, 23,* 435–436.

McGrath, C.E., Watson, A.L., & Chassin, L. (1999). Academic achievement in adolescent children of alcoholics. *Journal of Studies on Alcohol, 60,* 18–26.

McNemar, Q. (1986). *Psychological statistics.* New York: Wiley and Sons.

Mechner, F., Hyten, C., Field, D.P., & Madden, G.J. (1997). Using revealed operants to study the structure and properties of human operant behavior. *Psychological Record, 47,* 45–68.

Meyer, K.A. (1999). Functional analysis and treatment of problem behavior exhibited by elementary school children. *Journal of Applied Behavior Analysis, 32,* 229–232.

Michael, J. (1982). Distinguishing between discriminative and motivational functions of stimuli. *Journal of the Experimental Analysis of Behavior, 37,* 149–155.

Michael, J. (1993a). Establishing operations. *Behavior Analyst, 16,* 191–206.

Michael, J. (1993b). Evocative and repertoire altering effects of an environmental event. *VB News, 2,* 21–23.

Midgely, B.D., & Morris, E.K. (1988). The integrated field: An alternative to the behavior-analytic conceptualization of behavioral units. *Psychological Record, 38,* 483–500.

Miltenberger, R.G., & Fuqua, R.W. (1985). Evaluation of a training manual for the acquisition of behavioral assessment interviewing skills. *Journal of Applied Behavior Analysis, 18,* 323–328.

Miltenberger, R.G., Fuqua, R.W., & Woods, D.W. (1998). Applying behavior analysis to clinical problems: Review and analysis of habit reversal. *Journal of Applied Behavior Analysis, 31,* 447–469.

Molina, B.S., Pelham, W.E., & Lang, A.R. (1997). Alcohol expectancies and drinking characteristics in parents of children with attention deficit hyperactivity disorder. *Alcohol Clinical and Experimental Research, 21,* 557–566.

Moore, J. (1982). Choice and segmented interreinforcement intervals. *Journal of the Experimental Analysis of Behavior, 38,* 125–132.

Morris, E.K. (1988). Contextualism: The world view of behavior analysis. *Journal of Experimental Child Psychology, 46,* 289–323.

Morris, E.K. (1997). Some reflections on contextualism, mechanism, and behavior analysis. *Psychological Record, 47,* 529–542.

Mowrer, O.H. (1950). *Learning theory and personality dynamics.* NY: Roland Press.

Myer, J.S. (1968). Associative and temporal determinants of facilitation and inhibition of attack by pain. *Journal of Comparative and Physiological Psychology, 66,* 17–21.

Neziroglu, F., & Yarjura-Tobias, J.A. (Eds.) (1999). *Over and over again: Understanding obsessive–compulsive disorder.* San Francisco, CA: Jossey-Bass.

Nezu, C.M., Nezu, A.M., & Dudek, J.A. (1998). A cognitive behavioral model of assessment and treatment for intellectually disabled sexual offenders. *Cognitive and Behavioral Practice, 5,* 25–64.

Nunnally, J. (1978). *Psychometric theory.* New York: McGraw Hill.

Nurco, D.N., Blatchley, R.J., Hanlon, T.E., & O'Grady, K.E. (1999). Early deviance and related risk factors in the children of narcotic addicts. *American Journal of Alcohol Abuse, 25,* 25–45.

O'Donahue, W., & Kitchener, R. (Eds.) (1998). *Handbook of behaviorism.* New York: Academic Press.

O'Leary, K.D. (1993). Through a psychological lens: Personality traits, personality disorders, and levels of violence. In R.J. Gelles & D.R. Loeseke (Eds.), *Current controversies on family violence* (pp. 7–30). Newbury Park, CA: Sage.

Ollendick, T.H. (1996). Violence in youth: Where do we go from here? Behavior Therapy's response. *Behavior Therapy, 27,* 485–514.

Pagelow, M.D. (1997). Battered women: A historical research review and some common myths. *Journal of Aggression, Maltreatment and Trauma, 1,* 97–116.

Patteson, G.R., & Hops, H. (1972). Coercion, a game for two: Intervention techniques for marital conflict. In R.E. Ulrich & P.T. Mountjoy (Eds.)., *The experimental analysis of social behavior.* (pp. 424–440). New York: Appleton-Century-Crofts.

Patterson, G.R., & Reid, J.B. (1970). Reciprocity and coercion: Two facets of social systems. In C. Neuringer & J. Michael (Eds.), *Behavior modification in clinical psychology.* (pp. 133–177). New York: Appleton-Century-Crofts.

Peterson, L., Gable, S., Doyle, C., & Ewigman, B. (1997). Beyond parenting skills: Battling barriers and building bonds to prevent child abuse and neglect. *Cogntive and Behavioral Practice, 4,* 53–74.

Perry, M.W., & Millimet, C.R. (1977). Child-rearing antecedents of low and high anxiety in eighth-grade children. In C.D. Spielberger & I.G. Sarason (Eds.), *Stress and anxiety, Vol. 4,* (pp. 189–204). New York: Wiley.

Petersen, D.M., Whittington, F.J., & Payne, B.P. (1979). *Drugs and the elderly: Social and pharmacological issues.* Springfield, IL: Charles C. Thomas.

Pilat, J.M., & Jones, J.W. (1984–1985). Identification of children of alcoholics: Two empirical studies. *Alcohol Health and Research World, Winter,* 27–36.

Pinelandia Biophysics Laboratory (1999), *private communication.*

Pisacreta, R. (1998). Supersititous behavior and response stereotypy prevent the emergence of efficient rule-governed behavior in humans. *Psychological Record, 48,* 251–274.

Plaud, J.J., & Eifert, G.H. (1998). *From behavior theory to behavior therapy.* Needham Heights, MA: Allyn & Bacon.

Pronko, N.H. (1980). *Psychology from the standpoint of an interbehaviorist.* New York: Wadsworth.

Rapee, R.M. (1997). Potential role of childrearing practices in the development of anxiety and depression. *Clinical Psychology Review, 17,* 47–67.

Ratner, S.C. (1958). Hypnotic reactions of rabbits. *Psychological Reports, 4,* 209–210.

Ratner, S.C., & Thompson, R.W. (1960). Immobility reactions (fear) of domestic fowl as a function of age and prior experience. *Animal Behaviour, 8,* 186–191.

Ray, R., & Delprato, D.J. (1989). Behavioral systems analysis: Methodological strategies and tactics. *Behavioral Science, 34,* 81–127.

Reese, H.W., & Parrott, L.J. (Eds.). (1986). *Behavioral science: Philosophical, methodological and empirical advances.* Hillsdale, NJ: Lawrence Erlbaum Associates.

Rehfeldt, R.A., & Hayes, L.J. (1998). The operant–respondent distinction revisted: Toward an understanding of stimulus equivalence. *Psychological Record, 48,* 187–210.

Reiss, S. (1987). Theoretical perspectives on the fear of anxiety. *Clinical Psychology Review, 7,* 585–596.

Rescorla, R. (1988). Pavlovian conditioning: It's not what you think. *American Psychologist, 43,* 151–160.

Robb, H. (2000). Adult children of humans. *The Behavior Therapist, 23,* 18.

Rosen, J.C., & Leitenberg, H. (1984). Exposure plus response prevention treatment of bulimia. In D.N. Garner & P.E. Garfinkel (Eds.), *A handbook of psychotherapy for anorexia nervosa and bulimia* (pp. 193–209). New York: Guilford Press.

Ruben, D.H. (1979). Are game behaviors self-rewarding: A behavior analysis. *Proceedings of the Heraclitean Society, 4,* 78–93.

Ruben, D.H. (1983a). The effects of praise and ignoring on relevant and irrelevant verbalization by preschool children within a classroom setting. In

P.T.Mountjoy & D.H. Ruben (Eds.), *Behavioral genesis: Readings in the science of child psychology* (169–181). Lexington, MA: Ginn Publishing.

Ruben, D.H. (1983b). Interbehavioral implications for behavior therapy: A clinical perspective. In N.W. Smith, P.T. Mountjoy, & D.H. Ruben (Eds.), *Reassessment in psychology: The interbehavioral alternative* (pp. 445–469). Washington, DC: University Press of America.

Ruben, D.H. (1984a). Major trends in interbehavioral psychology from articles published in *The Psychological Record (1937–1983), Psychological Record, 34,* 589–617.

Ruben, D.H. (1984b). *Drug abuse and the elderly: An annotated bibligraphy.* Metuchen, NJ: Scarecrow Press.

Ruben, D.H. (1985). Private events revisted: Does unobservable mean private? *Journal of Contemporary Psychotherapy, 18,* 16–27.

Ruben, D.H. (1986a). The management of role ambiguity in organizations. *Journal of Employment Counseling, 23,* 120–130.

Ruben, D.H. (1986b). The elderly alcoholic: Some current dimensions. *Advances in Alcohol & Substance Abuse, 5,* 59–70.

Ruben, D.H. (1986c). Alcoholism/drug abuse counselors in industry: Do they need interpersonal skills? *Employee Assistance Quarterly, 1,* 57–62.

Ruben, D.H. (1987a). Epilogue: Science, myth, and magic ... and then what? In Hagelthorn, J. & M.J. Ruben (Eds.), *I've never told anyone but ... exploring the hidden reality of natural events* (pp. 157–161). Lincoln, NE: Media Publishing.

Ruben, D.H. (1987b). On the origins of selfishness. *Behavioural Approaches with Children, 11,* 116–127.

Ruben, D.H. (1989a). Bibliotherapy: Practical considerations when writing for substance abuse readers. *Journal of Alcohol and Drug Education, 34,* 70–78.

Ruben, D.H. (1989b). Reducing interruptions in functional activity through control of self-medication and habit-reversal. *Corrective & Social Psychiatry and Journal of Behavior Technology, Methods and Therapy, 34,* 35–45.

Ruben, D.H. (1990). *The aging and drug effects: A planning manual for medication and alcohol abuse treatment of the elderly.* Jefferson, NC: McFarland & Company.

Ruben, D.H. (1992a). Interbehavioral analysis of adult children of alcoholics: Etiological predictors. *Alcoholism Treatment Quarterly, 9,* 1–21.

Ruben, D.H. (1992b). Behavioral systems approach. In C.E. Stout, J.L. Levitt, & D.H. Ruben (Eds.), *Handbook for assessing and treating addictive disorders* (pp. 3–39). Westport, CT: Greenwood Press.

Ruben, D.H. (1992c). *Bratbusters: Say Good-bye to Tantrums and Disobedience.* El Paso, TX: Skidmore-Roth Publishers.

Ruben, D.H. (1993a). A behavioral analysis of impulsive child behavior. In L.F. Koziol, C.E. Stout, & D.H. Ruben (Eds.), *Handbook of childhood impulse disorders and ADHD* (pp. 78–107). Springfield, IL: Charles Thomas.

Ruben, D.H. (1993b). *No more guilt: Ten steps to a shame-free life.* Bedford, MA: Mills & Sanderson.

Ruben, D.H. (1993c). Transition failures in alcohol and drug abuse treatment. In D.H. Ruben & C.E. Stout (Eds.), *Transitions: Handbook of managed care for inpatient to outpatient treatment* (pp. 115–146). Westport, CT: Praeger.

Ruben, D.H. (1993d). Alcohol and drug abuse. In Squire, M.B., Stout, C.E. & D.H. Ruben (Eds.). *Current advances in inpatient psychiatric care* (pp. 131–161). Westport, CT: Greenwood.

Ruben, D.H. (1999a). Why traditional behavior modification fails with urban children. In N.R. Macciomei & D.H. Ruben (Eds.), *Behavioral management in the public schools: An urban approach* (pp. 3–37). Westport, CT: Praeger.

Ruben, D.H. (1999b). Behavioral systems approach: case response. In E.T. Dowd, & T. Rugle (Eds.), *Comparative Treatments of Substance Abuse* (pp. 79–95). New York: Springer.

Ruben, D.H. (2000a). *Forever sober.* Bloomington, IN: Advanced Marketing.

Ruben, D.H. (2000b). *Oversexed and Underloved: A recovery guide for sex addiction.* New York: Writers Digest Press.

Ruben, D.H. (2000c). Sensitizing drug dealers to victim impact using mandatory psychoeducation. *Offender Program Report, January/February,* p. 68

Ruben, D.H., & Delprato, D.J. (1987). *New ideas in therapy: Introduction to an interdisciplinary approach.* Westport, CT: Greenwood Press.

Ruben, D.H., & Ruben, M.J. (1984). Interviewing skills: Implications for vocation counseling with alcoholic clients. *Alcoholism and Treatment Quarterly, 1,* 133–140.

Ruben, D.H., & Ruben, M.J. (1985a). Is applied behavior analysis ready for parapsychology? A return to natural events. *Psychology: A Quarterly Journal of Human Behavior, 22,* 1–11.

Ruben, D.H., & Ruben, M.J. (1985b). Behavioral implications of the postpartum "blues." *Birth Psychology Bulletin, 6,* 1–9.

Ruben, D.H., & Ruben, M.J. (1989). Why assertiveness training programs fail. *Small Group Behavior, 20,* 367–380.

Russell, M., Henderson, C., & Blue, S.B. (1984). *Children of Alcoholics: A review of the literature.* New York: Children of Alcoholics Foundation.

Rutter, M. (1980). The long-term effects of early experience. *Developmental Medicine and Child Neurology, 22,* 800–815.

Ryall, M., & Dietiker, K. (1979). Reliability and clinical validity of the Children's Fear Survey Schedule. *Journal of Behavior Therapy and Experimental Psychiatry, 10,* 303–310.

Salzinger, E., & Salzinger, K.S. (1967). *Research in verbal behavior and some neurophysiological implications.* New York: Academic Press.

Schlinger, H.D., & Poling, A. (1998). *Introduction to scientific psychology.* Norwell, MA: Kluwer Academic.

Segrin, C., & Menees, M.M. (1996). The impact of coping styles and family communication on the social skills of children of alcoholics. *Journal of Studies on Alcohol, 57,* 29–33.

Seligman, M.E.P. (1975). *Helplessness: On depression, development and death.* W.H. Freeman and Company.

Seligman, M.E.P., & Johnston, J.C. (1973). A cognitive theory of avoidance learning. In F.J. McGuigan and D.B. Lumsden (Eds.). *Contemporary approaches to learning and conditioning.* Washington, D.C.: Winston & Sons.

Seligman, M.E.P., Maier, S.F., & Geer, J. (1968). The alleviation of learned helplessness in the dog. *Journal of Abnormal and Social Psychology, 73,* 256–262.

Shemwell, H.G., Dickey, K., & Timothy, A. (1995). Adult children of alcoholics: Examination of the category. *Journal of Alcohol and Drug Education, 40,* 109–118.

Schuckit, M.A., Klein, J.L., & Twitchell, G.R. (1995). The misclassification of family history status in studies of children of alcoholics. *Journal of Studies on Alcohol, 56,* 47–50.

Sidman, M. (1962). Classical avoidance without a warning stimulus. *Journal of the Experimental Analysis of Behavior, 5,* 393–395.

Sikkema, K.J., & Kelly, J.A. (1996). Behavioral medicine interventions can improve the quality-of-life and health of persons with HIV disease. *Annals of Behavioral Medicine, 18,* 40.

Skinner, B.F. (1948). Superstition in the pigeon. *Journal of Experimental Psychology, 38,* 168–172.

Skinner, B.F. (1953). *Science and human behavior.* New York: Macmillan Inc.

Skinner, B.F. (1957). *Verbal behavior.* Englewood Cliffs, NJ: Prentice-Hall.

Skinner, B.F. (1974). *About behaviorism.* New York: Vintage.

Skinner, B.F. (1977). The force of coincidence. In B.C. Etzel, J.M. *Experiments in behavioral psychology: Theory, methods and applications* (pp. 3–6). Hillsdale, NJ: Lawrence Erlbaum.

Skinner, B.F. (1989). *Recent issues in the analysis of behavior.* Columbus, OH: Merrill Publishing Company.

Smith, N.W., & Smith, L.L. (1996). Field theory in science: Its role as a necessary and sufficient condition in psychology. *Psychological Record,* 46. 3–19.

Sobell, M.B., Sobell, L.C., Ersner-Hershfield, S., & Nirenberg, T.D. (1982). Alcohol and drug problems. In A.S. Bellack, M. Hersen, & A. Kazdin (Eds.). *International handbook of behavior modification and therapy* (501–533). New York: Plenum.

Solomon, R.W., & Wynne, L.C. (1954). Traumatic avoidance learning: The principle of anxiety conservation and partial irreversibility. *Psychological Review, 61,* 353–385.

Sonuga-Barke, E.J., & Lea, S.E. (1989). Childrens' choice: Sensitivity to changes in reinforcer density. *Journal of the Experimental Analysis of Behavior, 51,* 77–85.

Staats, A.W. (1994). Psychological behaviorism and behaviorizing. *Behavior Analyst, 17,* 93–114.

Staats, A.W. (1996). *Behavior and personality: Psychological behaviorism.* NY: Springer Publishing.

Stampfl, T.G., & Levis, D.J. (1967). The essentials of implosive therapy: A learning-theory-based psychodynamic behavioral therapy. *Journal of Abnormal Psychology, 72,* 496–503.

Stark, E., Flitcraft, A., Zuckerman, D., Grey, A., Robison, J., & Frazier, W. (1981). *Wife abuse in the medical setting: An introduction for health personnel.* Domestic violence Monograph Series. Washington DC: National Clearinghouse on Domestic Violence.

Steinhausen, H.C. (1995). Children of alcoholic parents: A review. *European Child and Adolescent Psychiatry, 4,* 143–152.

Stockwell, T., Hodgson, R., Edwards, G., Taylor, C., & Rankin, H. (1979). The development of a questionnaire to measure severity of alcohol dependence. *British Journal of Addiction, 74,* 79–87.

Stuart, R.B. (1969). Operant-interpersonal treatment for marital discord. *Journal of Consulting and Clinical Psychology, 33,* 675–682.

Sundberg, M.L. (1993). The application of establishing operations. *Behavior Analyst, 16,* 211–214.

Sundberg, M.L., & Partington, J.W. (1983). Skinner's *Verbal Behavior:* An update of the reference list. *Verbal Behavior News, 2,* 10–13.

Tarter, R.E., Arria, A., Moss. H., Edwards, N.J., & Van Theil, D.H. (Eds.). (1987). DSM-III criteria for alcohol abuse: Associations with alcohol consumption behavior. *Alcoholism: Clinical and Experimental Research, 11,* 541–543.

Terrance, H.S. (1966). Behavioral contrast and the peak shift: Effects of extended discrimination training. *Journal of the Experimental Analysis of Behavior, 9,* 613–617.

Tharp, R.G., & Wetzel, R.J. (1969). *Behavior modification in the natural environment.* NY: Academic Press.

Thomas, E.J., & Santa, C. (1982). Unilateral family therapy for alcohol abuse: A working conception. *The American Journal of Family Therapy, 10,* 49–58.

Thompson, B., and Daniel, L.G. (1996). Factor analytic evidence for the construct validity of scores: A historical overview and some guidelines. *Educational and Psychological Measurement, 56,* 197–208.

Thompson, T., & Lubinski, D. (1986). Units of analysis and kinetic structure of behavioral repertoires. *Journal of the Experimental Analysis of Behavior,* 46, 219–242.

Thorndike, E.L. (1969). *Selected writings from a connectionist's psychology.* NY: Greenwood Press.

Todd, J.T., & Morris, E.K. (Eds.). (1995). *Modern perspectives on B.F. Skinner and contemporary behaviorism.* Westport, CT: Greenwood Press.

Ullmann, L.P., & Kransner, L. (1975). *A psychological approach to abnormal behavior.* Englewood Cliffs, NJ: Prentice-Hall.

Ulrich, R. (1967). Interactions between reflexive fighting and cooperative escape. *Journal of the Experimental Analysis of Behavior, 10,* 311–317.

Ulrich, R.E., Holz, W.C., & Azrin, N.H. (1964). Stimulus control of avoidance behavior. *Journal of the Experimental Analysis of Behavior, 7,* 129–133.

Ulrich, R.E., Wolfe, M., & Dulaney, S. (1972). Punishment of shock-induced aggression. In R.E. Ulrich, & P.T. Mountjoy, (Eds), *The experimental analysis of social behavior* (pp. 232–242). New York: Appleton-Century-Crofts.

Uttal, W.R. (1998). *Toward a new behaviorism: The case against perpetual reductionism*. Hillsdale, NJ: Lawrence Erlbaum Associates.

Vargas, E.A. (1982). Intraverbal behavior. *VB News, 1,* 2–3.

Vogeltanz., N.D., & Drabman, R.S. (1995). A procedure for evaluating young children suspected of being sexually abused. *Behavior Therapy, 26,* 579–597.

Wachtel, P. (1979). Contingent and noncontingent therapist response. *Psychotherapy: Theory, Research and Practice, 16,* 30–35.

Wachtel, P. (Ed.). (1992). *Resistance*. New York: Plenum.

Wagner, G.A., & Morris, E.K. (1987). Superstitious behavior in children. *Psychological Record, 37,* 471–488.

Washton, A.M. (Ed.). (1996). *Psychotherapy and substance abuse*. New York: Guilford Press.

Watson, J.B. (1924). *Behaviorism*. Chicago: University of Chicago.

Wegscheider-Cruse, S. (1986). *Understanding me*. Pompano Beach, FL: Health Communications.

Weiner, H. (1969). Conditioning history and the control of human avoidance and escape responding. *Journal of the Experimental Analysis of Behavior, 27,* 515–528.

Wertheim, G.A. (1965). Behavioral contrast during multiple avoidance schedules. *Journal of the Experimental Analysis of Behavior, 5,* 269–278.

White, A.P., & Liu, W.Z. (1995). Superstitious learning and induction. *Artificial Intelligence Review, 9,* 3–18.

White, H.R., & Labouvie, E.W. (1989). Towards the assessment of adolescent problem drinking. *Journal of Studies on Alcohol, 50,* 30–37.

Willis, T.A., Weiss, R.L., & Patterson, G.R. (1974). A behavioral analysis of the determinants of marital satisfaction. *Journal of Consulting and Clinical Psychology, 42,* 802–811.

Wilson, K.C., Scott, M., Abou-Saleh, M., Burns, R., & Copeland, J.R. (1995). Long-term effects of cognitive-behavioural therapy and lithium therapy on depression the elderly. *British Journal of Psychiatry, 167,* 653–658.

Wilson, P. (Ed.) (1992). *Principles and practice of relapse prevention*. New York: Guilford Press

Winston, A.S., & Baker, J.E. (1985). Behavior analytic studies of creativity: A critical review. *The Behavior Analyst, 8,* 191–205.

Wisnieski, N.M., Glenwickj, D.S., & Graham, J.R. (1985). MacAndrew Scale and socio-demographic correlates of adolescent alcohol and drug use. *Addictive Behaviors, 10,* 55–67.

Woititz, J.G. (1985). *The struggle for intimacy*. Pompano Beach, FL: Health Communications.

Wolfe, J., Keane, T.M., Lyons, J.A., & Gerardi, R.J. (1987). Current trends in the assessment of combat-related posttraumatic stress disorder. *The Behavior Therapist*, 10, 27–32.

Wolpe, J. (1958). *Psychotherapy by reciprocal inhibition.* Stanford: Stanford University Press.

Yeatman, F.R., Bogart, C.J., Geer, F.A., & Sirridge, S.T. (1994). Children of Alcoholics Screening Test: Internal consistency, factor structure, and relationship to measures of family environment. *Journal of Clinical Psychology, 50,* 931–936.

Yuksel, S., Kora, K., Benzei-Ozkan, M., Karali, N., Gok, S., & Tunali, D. (1999). Group treatment for domestic violence in Turkish women. *The Behavior Therapist, 22,* 167–172:181.

Zeiler, M.D. (1972). Superstitious behavior in children: An experimental analysis. In H.W. Reese (Ed.), *Advances in child development and behavior* (pp. 1–29). New York: Academic Press.

Zettle, M.D. (1972). Superstitious behavior in children: An experimental analysis. In H.W. Reese (Ed.). *Advances in child development and behavior* (pp. 1–29). New York: Academic Press.

Zettle, R.D., & Hayes, S.C. (1982). Rule-governed behavior: A potential theoretical framework for cognitive-behavioral therapy. In P.C. Kendall (Ed.). *Advances in cognitive-behavioral research and therapy (Vol. 1).* (pp. 73–118). New York: Academic Press.

Zettle, R.D., & Young, M.J. (1987). Rule-following and human operant responding: Conceptual and methodological considerations. *The Analysis of Verbal Behavior, 5,* 33–39.

Zeiler, M., & Harzem, P. (Eds.). (1981). *Predictability, correlation, and contiguity.* New York: John Wiley & Sons.

Zimmerman, D.W. (1996). Is a final theory conceivable? *Psychological Record, 46,* 423–438.

Zung, B.J. (1984). Correlates of the Michigan Alcoholism Screening Test among DWI offenders. *Journal of Clinical Psychology, 40,* 607–612.

INDEX

S

T

U

V

Treating Adult Children of Alcoholics

A Behavioral Approach